Modal Integrative Psychotherapy

Aleksandar Fatic

Modal Integrative Psychotherapy

A Logical Integration of Psychotherapy

palgrave
macmillan

Aleksandar Fatic
Inst for Philosophy and Social Theory
University of Belgrade
Belgrade, Serbia

ISBN 978-3-031-91933-6 ISBN 978-3-031-91934-3 (eBook)
https://doi.org/10.1007/978-3-031-91934-3

This Palgrave Macmillan imprint is published by the registered company Springer Nature Switzerland AG.
The registered company address is: Gewerbestrasse 11, 6330 Cham, Switzerland

Competing Interests

The author has no competing interests to declare that are relevant to the content of this manuscript.

Contents

About the Author

Aleksandar Fatic is a philosopher working primarily in ethics, philosophy of psychology and psychiatry and social philosophy. He is Professor of Philosophy at the Institute for Philosophy and Social Theory at the University of Belgrade and director of the Institute for Practical Humanities, a training and research hub for philosophically informed psychotherapy. Aleksandar is the author of *Virtue as Identity: Emotions and the Moral Personality* (Rowman and Littlefield, 2016) and many other books and numerous articles dealing with a range of issues in philosophy, particularly as it relates to the community, issues of responsibility, belonging, individual recognition, dignity, and wellbeing.

List of Diagrams

CHAPTER 1

Introduction

Abstract The Introduction outlines the key differences between the traditional use of propositional logic in psychotherapy and modal logic as the logical foundation of Modal Integrative Psychotherapy. One of the main differences between the two is that, while the emphasis of traditional psychotherapy is on changing the client (thus the subjective experience of the world), modal logic (and, correspondingly, Modal Integrative Psychotherapy) ventures into seeking to change the modal worlds, or "possible worlds" as sets of circumstances outside the person that determine the person's experience of reality. This introduction points at the role of sociality as a normative foundation of our perceptions and self-perceptions and sets the stage for a fuller discussion of key elements of modality in the theory, interventions, and overall methodology of Modal Integrative Psychotherapy.

Keywords Propositional/modal logic • Modal/possible worlds • Sociality • Language • Psychoanalysis

Any conceptual structure fundamentally rests on logic, which allows the elements of that structure to connect to each other and to remain sustainable against adversity, whether of opposing argument or, as in the case of psychotherapy, of clinical practice and challenging human experience. There are two main types of logical thinking that are relevant for Modal

A. Fatic, *Modal Integrative Psychotherapy*,
https://doi.org/10.1007/978-3-031-91934-3_1

Integrative Psychotherapy, which is the paradigm discussed in this book. One is the so-called propositional logic. This is the logic that focuses on the conditions that make certain beliefs and statements ("propositions") true or false. For example, in a disturbed parental relationship that includes a child's estrangement from a parent, the belief that "my child will come back to me once he grows older", is a statement whose truth-conditions involve various circumstances and variables that the therapeutic process makes its themes. They include the person's understanding of the personality of the child, the nature of the parental relationship as it is, the relationship between the child and of the parent, the relevant third persons involved (the other parent, the peer group, the society, etc.). Whether or not this proposition is true will determine the wellbeing of the parent and of the child, and the elucidation and elaboration of the truth conditions themselves is seen as potentially liberating, emancipating and empowering for the client, in this case the parent. By understanding what conditions may make a belief true or false, especially when the belief, or proposition, is existentially important to our wellbeing, as is the case with this example, one gains greater leverage over one's life experience and, thus, a better quality of life. This happens not the least because one understands what truth conditions for particular, important propositions one can influence given the reality within which one's relationships with the important others unfold, and which truth conditions for a statement one cannot influence, as well as how to act to bring about the truth conditions that might make the belief, or desire, true or attainable. Thus, one might adjust one's attitudes and behavior towards the child in order to bring about the truth conditions that will validate the belief that the child will come back to the parent into a harmonious relationship that has been disturbed prior to therapy.

Propositional logic operates within the realm of possible truths. This means that one may seek to influence the truth conditions for propositions whose truthfulness is possible. Propositional logic does not venture into the conditions of possibility, or of making what is currently impossible possible; this is why standard psychotherapy often insists on a "realism" in the clients' perception and interpretation of the world. "Be realistic" is the often-heard suggestion. "Appraise the circumstances realistically". "Can you really change the facts of the situation as they are?" For this reason, the prospects of change envisaged by propositional logic-informed psychotherapy are limited, mainly to a change arising from one's perceptions, interpretations, and reactions to "facts". Conventional psychotherapy typically does not venture into the business of changing the "reality" of the "external facts" of one's general existential situation and one's experience.

In some situations, it is factually impossible to re-establish contact with an estranged child given the foundational facts of the situation, for example, in situations where there is a deep-seated conflict of basic values between the parent and the child and a simmering resentment arising from the mutual sense of betrayal or failed legitimate expectations. Many such cases appear in psychotherapy, and sometimes they are what psychotherapy knows as "impossible cases", where the "realistic" therapeutic goals are often to save the suffering family member from decompensation, to maintain their sense of dignity and identity, and to help them preserve an optimum quality of life in the unenviable and, fundamentally, incorrigible "objective" situation.

The other type of logic is modal logic. Its focus is not on the truth conditions for a proposition, or belief, but rather on the conditions of the possibility of certain propositions being true or false. Propositional logic, on a deeper logical level, is one of the various modal logics. As a modal logic, namely as a logic that works with the operators of possibility and necessity, rather than truth conditions, the propositional logical situation of the described example would be interpreted in the following way. In the example, modal logic would imply that the client and the therapist consider not whether or not the child will come back to the parent under certain conditions, but rather what makes certain situations in the parent's relationship with the child possible. The current situation is that the child does not want to spend time with the parent and this is hurtful to the parent. This is the reality of their relationship. A different reality ("modal world" or "possible world" in modal logic) would be for a child to be close to the parent and to maintain intimate family contact. The latter is currently not real; it is simply not the case. Logically speaking, the statement that the child does not want to communicate with the parent is true, because that is the current modal reality of the relationship. The statement that the child is close to the parent and maintains regular daily contact is false, because that is not the current reality. However, on a modal level, instead of asking whether a statement is true or not, one may ask whether the state of affairs described by a proposition is possible or necessary. In this case, is it *necessary* for the child to refuse contact with the parent? Or, contrariwise, is it *necessary* for the child to maintain regular contact with the parent? The answer to both questions is obviously negative. Is it, then, *possible* for the child to refuse contact? Obviously yes, as it is currently the case. Is it *possible* for the child to maintain close communication? Clearly, yes. What are the conditions for the statement that is not true, but possible, to be called into reality? This is the modal way of asking the same question as that about the truth conditions for the speculative proposition: "The child will come back to the parent". These are two levels of describing the same therapeutic situation: the former in terms of truth conditions, and the latter in terms of modality.

However, after all, propositional logic is only one of the various modal logics. What happens when the contact between the parent and child is impossible? When the child feels that it is *necessary* for him to cut contact with the parent? What happens when, without a major change in the entire "theatre" of "modal world" ("possible world") within which the relationship between the parent and the child unfolds, no alteration in the truth conditions would make the statement "The child will come back to the parent" true?

How do we make the "realistically" impossible possible in therapy? This is the primary task of deep modal logic. How do we venture into hard, hopeless situations where no ordinary variation in truth conditions, or interventions, can make an inroad?

In many situations, being "realistic" means resigning oneself to the "objective circumstances" that define the modality of our existence. Thus, many traditional schools of psychotherapy would experiment with the truth conditions for the various statements describing the parenting situation at hand and would encourage the parent to try the various changes in behavior that might alter the truth conditions of the statement: "The child does not want to communicate with the parent". Once these fail, the therapist would likely suggest to the client that resigning oneself to the "real" situation over which one no longer has any control is the healthiest and least damaging course of action "in the given circumstances".

Modal therapy does not experiment with truth conditions, but with possible worlds. It plays with the concepts of making the impossible possible by changing the conditions of possibility or necessity of the truthfulness of certain propositions. The modal therapist would likely steer the therapeutic process in the direction of the client's changing one's life and circumstances in fairly fundamental and comprehensive ways in order to shift to a different modality; a different modal world; a different identity for oneself and, indirectly, for the child. The modal therapist would look for a different emotional and more generally relational ecosystem of the parent's relations with the child. This might include shifting the parent's values; their place of living; career, life partners, manner of communication; their perspectives on various important issues in life, thus reformatting the very current modal world within which happy and satisfying relationships with one's child might, at present, be impossible.

Modal logic questions the very structure of the basic facts about our current existence as a prelude to addressing our otherwise insoluble relationships and problems from an entirely different existential position.

Modal Integrative Psychotherapy, and modal logic as its methodological foundation, militate against reality in the sense that the modal integrative therapist is against being "realistic" as a strategy of pursuing one's life. Modal therapy *undermines* the current modal worlds. It encourages major shifts in identity and thus also in epistemic and decision making perspectives in order to shake up the reality and *contract the impossibility.* In such a changed reality, or modal world, some things that might have been possible in the previous reality will become impossible; however, other things will become possible. Modal logic is a logic of challenging ourselves as identity projects and processes. Such deep challenges of identity are a strategy of attaining specific goals. This is not merely a logic of self-development, but rather of abandonment one world in favor of another, much like switching between dreams and awakening where they are difficult to mutually distinguish.

Modal logic, when applied to modal therapy, is much like a process of dreaming up a different reality and making it "real" in order to see what happens with our key issues. Some clients explain the process by comparing it to moving from the cloudy and rainy scenery of a European countryside to the scorching sunny and dry environment of the North African dunes along the sea. In such a shift, the perspective changes, the relationships change, often in ways that are incomprehensible to us, and our epistemic access to various models of decision-making and action changes. A part of the radical change is that the significant others' perceptions of us also change. In a nutshell, this book is about such use of modal logic in the various therapeutic contexts and about the philosophical underpinnings of modal thinking about key therapeutic themes such as suffering, change, the good life, or love.

Modal Integrative Psychotherapy (MIP) has arisen from philosophical practice. Thus, writing an introduction to what is fundamentally a blueprint to therapeutic philosophy requires both mentioning some of the key paradigms in philosophical practice and addressing some broader societal tendencies that play pivotal roles in the development of MIP as a philosophical integration of psychotherapy. In my vision, MIP is not merely philosophical practice, or the practical application of philosophy.

MIP is an integration of psychotherapy seen as an art of philosophical interpretation of psychic experiences. Most major psychotherapeutic theories are fundamentally philosophical. Consider only some of the most influential psychoanalytic schools, such as the Freudian, Lacanian, or Jungian psychoanalysis. All are based on philosophical assumptions about the forces that govern our lives that are beyond our conscious control. These schools develop specific theories of psychotherapeutic intervention and the concepts instrumental to such intervention based on the broad philosophical assumptions about human nature, the way the mind operates, and the normative content that is only partly consciously accessible to individuals in their everyday states of mind. The interpretation of dreams (since Freud), the analysis of subconscious symbolism (Jung's "analytic psychology"), or assumptions about the unconscious content of the mind as directly reflected in the organization of language (Lacan, following Wittgenstein and a whole tradition of analytic philosophy) are examples of broad philosophical views of the human psyche and its operation that have decisively contributed to the development of psychology as a discipline. Thus, psychology and philosophy go hand in hand in many respects, and the same applies to psychotherapy. The foundation of MIP is making a particular logical perspective in philosophy the foundation of a psychotherapeutic methodology.

One important aspect of how psychotherapy is positioned in society is as a way of understanding *sociality*. Our ability to understand our relationships is couched in the fundamental practices within our society, which Giorgio Agamben calls "special actions" that affirm our social intentionality, or the dominant ways of our "directedness" towards each other within a particular society's set of projected virtues and normative expectations (Agamben, 2013). Thus, the sort of individuals we can become is fundamentally determined by the normative nature of our societies. As the fate of any interpretative and helping discipline depends on the sort of individual we encounter in our practice, psychotherapy and its potentially optimal outcomes are predicated upon the sociability and sociality of the individuals we work with, and of us as counselors, or therapists (there is a normative difference between the two roles that is largely technical, and it is not relevant for the particular claim I am making here). The dominant types of individual pathology in most societies tend to correspond to the trends of social pathology, just as the most prominent types of social virtue correspond to the social projections of the most important moral qualities in individuals (Fatic, 2016). The prevalent types of individuals "on the couch" in psychotherapy are largely determined by the normative structure of modern society, in the same way in which the prevalent types of personalities in any walk of life in society depend on the sociality as it is articulated in that society. In its progression towards the attainment of modal outcomes, MIP sees the social context and its variations as key elements of switching between "modal worlds". Its themes and interventions intertwine the clinical themes of mental health with those of sociality. In this respect, MIP is a further logical development of the very connection between philosophical practice as a discipline of philosophy and the psych-professions as clinical fields.

MIP's use of philosophy in psychotherapy is a key aspect of its representing a type of philosophical integration of psychotherapy. While most traditional psychotherapeutic schools arise from various philosophies, and most explicitly acknowledge such a legacy (e.g. Cognitive Behavioral Psychotherapy draws from Stoicism, Transactional Analysis arises from phenomenology, so much so that its founder, Eric Bern, described himself as a "phenomenological philosopher", rather than psychotherapist, etc.). In this respect, the connections between philosophy, specifically practical and applied philosophy, and psychotherapy are well known, fairly obvious and uncontroversial. However, MIP goes a step further in integrating the methodology of interventions in psychotherapy through a particular area of philosophy, namely modal logic.

MIP uses the paradigm of shift of possible or modal worlds, which, in modal logic, designate various sets of circumstances that define our life experience at particular moments, to introduce philosophical concepts as the substance of psychotherapeutic interventions. One, perhaps interesting, such intervention is the use of philosophical pessimism as an unlikely psychotherapeutic intervention.

Much of psychotherapeutic methodology rests on the relatively uncritically accepted philosophical assumptions, of which two are particularly pervasive. The first, as I mentioned at the beginning of this Introduction, is the reliance on propositional logic, namely the logic that implies that beliefs and propositions are defined by their truthfulness or falsity, and that manipulating various beliefs is the process whereby one achieves a relationship to one's reality. Such a perspective implies that there is a reality, typically a social reality for the person, permeated with what Lacan calls "structure", namely with relevant social relationships, and that, within that reality, there is a person whose task is to somehow improve one's relationship to the reality and the significant others in their life. This is a perspective all traditional psychotherapeutic schools share, as do many of the humanities and social sciences. Modal logic, on the other hand suggests that beliefs and propositions are not primarily characterized by truth and falsity, or the conditions for particular beliefs to be true (truth-conditions), but by broad contextualizations that determine the necessity or possibility of certain beliefs being true or false. In other words, modal logic, subtly, removes a focus on the reality and the person's relationship to it and introduces an alternative vision of clusters of possible worlds, or possible contextual realities, one of which is "true" in the sense that it is actual, or current, while many others are "almost true", hanging out there within the person's reach and ready to be actualized with a refocusing of attention and action. Importantly, the alternative possible or modal worlds make possible what is (logically, within propositional logic, or factually, experientially) impossible within the current modal world. Conversely, they make impossible certain things that, in the current modal world, are possible. Much of this book is about this principle, and I will not delve deeper into it here, in the Introduction, where I only touch upon some of the topics that are more fully developed in the following chapters.

The second pervasive and uncritical assumption in the standard psychotherapeutic approaches is the assumption of the need for optimism. Typically, the conventional approaches to therapy rest on certain unquestioned goals: to instill hope in the client, to empower them and offer them support to "overcome" their predicament. In one of the most influential textbooks of psychotherapy today, Irvin Yalom singles out optimism and hope as a fundamental therapeutic factor in the process, and in this he repeats the tacit assumption of psychotherapy that without hope psychotherapy has a grim prospect with almost any client (Yalom & Leszcz, 2005, pp. 4–6). An influential school of psychotherapy in America is methodologically tied to hope and forgiveness, and its author is Everett Worthington (Worthington & Rypley, 2024). An entire tradition of "positive psychology" follows suit in a very pronounced way, denouncing "negative" emotions, views and interpretations that are not optimistic in nature (Seligman, 2000).

There are a number of issues that can be identified in these approaches and perhaps it is sufficient to mention only a few here. For example, the idea that there are "positive" and "negative" emotions and experiences—a distinction inherent to "positive" psychology is philosophically naïve and, strictly speaking, psychologically incorrect. Emotions cannot be positive or negative; they are rather pleasant, or unpleasant. There is a theory of emotions that suggests that emotions reflect our values in light of our experiences, and that the more important our value that is affirmed by a certain experience is, the more intense positive emotion will be experienced; conversely, the higher in our value hierarchy a particular value is that an experience militates against, the more intense unpleasant emotion we will experience (Milivojevic, 2014). This theory is only the simplest way known to me from literature to illustrate an otherwise philosophically more complex and very well developed tradition of arguing that emotions are as important for cognition as are our rational faculties and thus they can by no means be classified into "positive" and "negative", nor should "negative", that is, unpleasant, emotions be castigated in any way lest one is willing to risk superficiality and serious errors of judgement, both in one's personal orientation in life and in offering therapy to others. Thus, uncritical optimism, namely optimism taken in the way Yalom describes it, as a necessary, "Number One" therapeutic factor without which success in psychotherapy is virtually impossible, is highly problematic.

MIP often experiments with pessimism, as opposed to optimism. A shift of paradigms, or modal worlds, for a client may involve the consideration of a pessimistic alternative, rather than being consistently encouraged to seek optimistic outcomes. Once a person has exhausted most of one's resources to address a particular problem, the adoption of a pessimistic, even tragic view of life as a whole, and the concomitant interpretation of a particular situation one faces in light of that overall tragedy of life, might both liberate the client and relieve much suffering. Many times have I seen clients revived and functionally restored from a state of utter despair after adopting a tragic and pessimistic vista on their predicament. This seems paradoxical, but on closer scrutiny it is not. Allowing things and events to be seen as hopeless and abandoning them early on is in the spirit of Nitzscheanism in philosophy, whose application to psychotherapy should not be underestimated. Seeing life as a whole as a general tragedy that inevitably ends badly and courses through one's years mostly in the form of suffering, with brief periods of respite that we tend to call "joy" or "happiness", is in the spirit of Schopenhauer's philosophy, whose impact on psychotherapy may be immense, but has, for various reasons, so far been limited. The shift of modal worlds is curative even when it is a shift from uncritical optimism to pessimism, even to nihilism.

The above suggestions are frightening to many psychotherapists, because they have been trained on a more or less universal model of the particular paradigm that Yalom so clearly describes as the instilment of hope. However, difficult life situations can lead one to the conclusion reached by Varlaam Shalamov while he was an inmate in a Syberian gulag, where hope was the most deadly thing: if one had hope and was unable to resign oneself to the tragic circumstances of one's predicament, expecting to end one's life in the gulag, this created such internal torment that such a person had to go mad (Shalamov, 1980). A similar sentiment is expressed in the iconic movie *The Shawshank Redemption*, when Red, the old inmate, says to Andy, the main character who maintained hope and eventually found a new life far away: "Hope is a dangerous thing. Hope can drive a man insane".

Does the above mean that pessimism is superior to optimism as a psychotherapeutic paradigm? By no means. Viktor Frankl describes how, as a slave prisoner in Auschwitz, after he had lost his entire family and unborn child to the Nazis, he observed a regularity: people who had someone to come back to, who could articulate meaning and hope for the future, were systematically and significantly more likely to survive than those who had nothing to expect and had lost everyone (Frankl, 1978).

Neither optimism nor pessimism are the answer to every situation and every psychotherapeutic process: the assumption that a culture of "instilment of hope" is universally required for successful therapy and that optimism is a therapeutic factor that is a strong predictor of improvement is both logically and experientially naïve, as is the idea that psychology can be "positive" or "negative", where the former is effective and productive of good outcomes, while the latter is destructive, discouraging, or suboptimal. What matters and delivers major change is a shift of modalities, or possible worlds. MIP questions the very foundations of the situations and modal worlds where the clients' problems articulate themselves early on in the psychotherapeutic process. In this sense, MIP is more radical than traditional psychotherapy because it shakes the foundation of such modal worlds without prejudice, seeking to see if what is difficult or impossible in the current modal world might become possible in the next. That is the substance of this book and, most crudely speaking, the broad defining feature of MIP.

References

Agamben, G. (2013). *Opus Dei: An archaeology of duty*. Stanford University Press.

Fatic, A. (2016). *Virtue as identity: Emotions and the moral personality*. Rowman and Littlefield International.

Frankl, V. (1978). *The unheard cry for meaning*. Simon and Schuster.

Milivojevic, Z. (2014). *Emocije*. Psihopolis.

Seligman, M. (2000). Positive psychology: An introduction. *American Psychologist, 55*(1), 5–14. https://doi.org/10.1037/0003-066X.55.1.5

Shalamov, V. (1980). *Kolyma tales*. Norton.

Worthington, E., & Rypley, J. (2024). *Hope, forgiveness and positive psychology in couple therapy*. Routledge.

Yalom, I., & Leszcz, M. (2005). *Theory and practice of group psychotherapy*. Basic Books.

CHAPTER 2

Normalcy and Other Key Concepts

Abstract This chapter develops a perspective of how psychological normalcy is construed, both in a clinical context and philosophically, and how our perceptions and judgments of normalcy arise from the broader theoretical assumptions and worldviews. The chapter explores both the context-relevancy of the idea of normalcy and its functional aspects, casting normalcy as a modal concept that is articulated by an interplay of modalities in modal logical thinking and therapeutic interventions.

Keywords Social normativity • Behavioral philosophy • Philosophical counseling • Psychotherapy • Transcendence

One of the key normative concepts in psychotherapy is that of normalcy, as opposed to pathology. Normalcy is not an uncontroversial norm: it is an ideal, a social, and political construct as much as a clinical category, yet one that is indispensable for our understanding of the very meaning of the helping interventions in psychotherapy, including those within MIP. This chapter introduces the disciplinary and conceptual context of normalcy, both philosophical and psychological, as well as other key concepts for MIP, including those of behavioral philosophy, philosophical counseling, and the social normativity, value and spiritual aspects of normalcy, all of which play crucial roles in our understanding of the place that we seek to reach through our journey in MIP.

A. Fatic, *Modal Integrative Psychotherapy*,
https://doi.org/10.1007/978-3-031-91934-3_2

Key Concepts

In order to introduce a structured discussion of normalcy in the context of philosophical and psychotherapeutic depictions of normalcy, several key definitions at the outset appear to be in order. This, specifically, concerns the distinctions between philosophical counseling, psychotherapy, and behavioral philosophy as an over-arching philosophical perspective on both, as well as what is exactly meant by the "spiritual" dimension of the psychotherapeutic or counseling processes. I will thus focus on the conceptual issues and then move to developing the argument that posits normalcy at the very foundation of all self-improvement and at the same type of the therapeutic and corrective interventions within MIP, where normalcy as the methodological and conceptual focus is capable of factually replacing psychopathology as the focus of discussion.

One of the key discussions in the modern depiction of philosophical counseling as a complement, or even alternative, to traditional psychotherapy revolves around the roles of ***psychotherapy and philosophical counseling***. The most common assumption is that psychotherapy deals with mental pathology, or mental disorders (although this is not always the case), while philosophical counseling is concerned with values, quality of life, and self-development of "healthy" individuals seeking a critical perspective on their life experience (Frunza, 2018; Marinoff, 2002; Martin, 2001). An offshoot of this type of thinking about the distinction between the two is the idea that psychotherapy is concerned with "cerebral" dysfunctionalities, while philosophical counseling addresses thought patterns, logic, and values. Neither seems convincing enough.

Perhaps one of the best descriptions, and indirectly, definitions, of psychotherapy was offered by Otto Kernberg, one of the "fathers" of the modern theory and treatment methodology for personality disorders. According to Kernberg, psychotherapy is a relationship marked by two key elements: a care by the therapist for the client, to the extent that the therapist is prepared to undergo unpleasantness and, sometimes, even abuse by the client (when personality disorders are concerned), and a sincerity in the reactions the therapist offers to the client, which can in fact exert a corrective influence on the client (Kernberg et al., 2008). Kernberg describes, in a variety of sources and interviews, his own development toward the point in his life when he decided to become a psychiatrist and says that the key driver for him was his desire to change his own personality. This subsequently led him to explore ways in which psychotherapy could change the personalities of clients, and the psychological, existential, and cognitive investments psychotherapists had to make into the therapeutic relationship in order to help effect such change in the clients.

The above description is perhaps the most general depiction of psychotherapy that goes beyond the various sectorial approaches that focus on a particular "method". In fact it seems that the method is little more than a refuge for therapists with a crisis of intellectual identity, where neither the clients, nor the society at large are concerned with the particular method a therapist uses: what they are interested in is the therapist's skill and the effectiveness of therapeutic relationships. Various empirical surveys have found that the success of therapy crucially arises from the quality of the therapeutic relationship and does not depend almost at all on the particular "school" or ideological self-identification of the therapist (Lewis et al., 2000).

Assuming that psychotherapy in general is seen as a relationship, and not as a "grab bag of techniques" that are chosen based on a "deep understanding of the human condition" (the way it was recently described by the American psychodynamic therapist Jonathan Shedler on social networks), the next question to consider is what distinguishes the psychotherapeutic relationship from a philosophical counseling relationship, and whether in philosophical counseling the relationship itself has the same prevailing significance.

Philosophical counseling as a dimension of psychotherapy is an approach that is based on the examination of assumptions, beliefs, and values, and as such it has characterized philosophy from its very inception, at least in its western tradition (Hadot, 1995). In fact, there is reason to assume that modern psychotherapy has grown out of what ancients might have called philosophical counseling, if that the entire philosophy at the time was a kind of "philosophical counseling". The idea is expressed in Epicurus's proverbial statement that the philosophy that is not capable of curing human suffering is not worth the name of philosophy, and in the more recent advent of the movement of philosophical practice, which seeks to apply the philosophical ideas to the psychotherapeutic process and to organizational and individual consulting. It is doubtful whether this perspective can be separated from psychotherapy when it is seen, as it is by Kernberg, as a relationship whose aim is the improvement of one's personality and, concomitantly, the achievement of personal change.

Even the idea that psychotherapy deals primarily with "mental illness" (though it obviously does not, as most clients in psychotherapy are reasonably healthy individuals who seek a resolution to their problems) does not necessarily distinguish between psychotherapy and philosophical practice, in the sense that there is nothing to prevent an otherwise "mentally ill" person from seeking philosophical counseling. I had personally refrained, for quite some years, until a particular transformative experience, from engaging in counseling with psychotic persons, for a variety of reasons, including, as I had thought, the need for such persons to be focused on their medication and the psychiatric therapist who would have been familiar with the history of that medication and had the institutional prerequisites to hospitalize the patient, if necessary. This changed on an occasion when I was approached by the mother of a schizophrenic man who desperately tried to get an appointment for her son. I refused, for all the mentioned reasons, plus the fact that it was the mother, who appeared to be overwhelming, who sought the appointment, where the role of the mother would likely need to be explored prior to even starting work with her son. However, the next day I received a phone call from her son, who said to me: "I know that I am ill, and I know that this is the reason no psychotherapist would talk to me. You all assume that I am taken care of by my psychiatrist, but I am not. My psychiatrist does not want to talk to me, either. She just gives me drugs. Although I am ill, I am still a human being, and I should have the opportunity to talk to someone and discuss my difficulties". I realized, after this conversation, that the root of my refusal to work with psychotic patients was my fear, my own sense of insufficiency, and my misperception of what it was to be "psychotic". In most situations, psychotic patients are not psychotic all the time: most of the time they are what we would describe as normal, with occasional decompensations and psychotic episodes. One wonders whether such episodes are triggered by "cerebral illness" (a hotly debated topic in psychiatry and psychotherapy, for which there is nowhere near enough space to discuss it separately here), or by the impasses in everyday life that might, at least to an extent, be addressed by counseling, just like with any other client. I thus remain undecided on what position to take on the appropriateness of psychotherapy in general, and philosophical counseling in particular, for psychotic clients. Perhaps the most reasonable approach is to judge this on a case-to-case basis, until more principled conclusions on the matter are reached in the ongoing debate among psychiatrists, psychotherapists, and neuroscientists (Damasio, 1994; Moncrieff, 2018).

The controversies over the actual role of psychotherapy and philosophical counseling highlight, by my lights at least, an important conceptual conclusions, namely that the difference between psychotherapy and philosophical counseling is an illusion. There is no such thing as philosophical counseling that would be distinct from psychotherapy. Both practices occur in the same format, with the same types of expectations, limitations and are subject to the same types of controversy. For example, the controversy over whether psychotic subjects are proper interlocutors for psychotherapy/philosophical counseling stretches across the range of psychotherapy, where it is assumed that individuals who cannot express themselves coherently may not be appropriate clients in psychotherapy. The same type of argument applies to philosophical counseling. In fact, psychotherapy is as informed by philosophy and by value considerations as is philosophical counseling (Fatic & Zagorac, 2018). Thus, the difference between psychotherapy and philosophical counseling collapses when both are considered in light of the behavioral issues that reflect values, patterns of decision-making, and affective reactivity to the influence exerted by our micro-social environment, or what the Lacanians call our relevant "structure" (Verhaeghe, 2008). This blending together of psychotherapy and philosophical counseling that is based on the behavioral aspects of decision-making and a subjective sense of being "stuck" as the prerequisite for attending psychotherapy/philosophical counseling brings us to the overarching concept of behavioral philosophy.

Behavioral philosophy is a concept that unifies the traditional applications of psychotherapy and the recently revived practice of philosophical counseling with the other behavioral interpretations of values, cognitions, and affective responses on levels ranging from the individual to society-wide. It is based on the assumption that behavior is not merely a manifestation of our mental processes, but that the application of autonomous decision-making as it is exemplified in the disciplined and deliberate self-improvement exerts influence on cerebral processes. On a limited scale, this is the idea of Cognitive Behavioral Psychotherapy, which rests on the assumption that a change in behavior results in the breaking apart of old patterns and the corresponding neural pathways and in the creation of new ones. The principle is sometimes associated with the plasticity of the brain thesis, where a part of brain plasticity is taken to consist in the brain's ability to adapt its structure, morphology, and especially the size and electrical activity of its particular regions to changes in the person's behavior and experience. A consequence of this idea is the controversy over many psychiatric diagnoses, including that of "major depression", which is taken to set in after four weeks of what would otherwise be considered a "reactive (healthy) depression", where the four-week cut-off is associated with the observed changes in the morphology of the brain, where certain regions swell and others shrink. This has so far been taken to indicate the need for an aggressive use of antidepressants, because of the idea that once the brain has changed, recovery is much more difficult. In fact, a lot of the research on depression suggests that, unlike any other organ in the human body, the brain responds to experience and, if the experience changes sufficiently, then the changes observed on the brain will either revert to the previous condition or further develop (Radulescu et al., 2021).

If behavior has such a comprehensive effect on brain plasticity, this generates several major changes in the way neuroscience must think about the central nervous system (Damasio, 1994), including consequences for the philosophical concept of free will. While there is much to discuss philosophically about the very meaning of the new neurological findings that Damasio, Moncrieff, and others detail in their work, I will be content here with a relatively safe and uncontroversial preliminary conclusion, namely that the orientation to determining a person's or a community's values and general issues inculcates both the manifestations of the internal processes and assumptions in the person's or collective's behavior, and the actual ability of the person's or group's behavior to change such internal processes. What we deal with is behavior, and it is on the basis of behavior that, in any kind of counseling, we are able to speculate about the person's values and affective structures behind their decisions. The psychotherapeutic theories that start from behavior stipulate various structures behind behavior: for example, they may assume that a person's or group's behavior signals that certain decisions pay off to the person on some level despite the pain and harm to the agent or agents that they obviously cause (the psychological concept of secondary benefit, characteristic primarily of Transactional Analysis), that the neural processes are learning curves triggered by conscious decisions in practical life (Cognitive Behavioural Therapy), or that subconscious architectures of experience account for the suppressed dynamics of current behavior (psychoanalysis broadly conceived). All these theoretical constructs are aspects of behavioral philosophy. I thus use the concept of behavioral philosophy as that of a value-informed interpretation of behavior with a variety of practical emphases, including that of psychotherapy and philosophical counseling as overlapping, or coinciding, forms of therapeutic practice. The use of behavioral philosophy as an inclusive concept here relieves us of the burden of needing to distinguish precisely between the more and the less philosophical forms of counseling that should be appropriately labeled "philosophical practice" or "psychotherapy".

The Quest of "Normalcy" as a Social Normative Ideal

Normalcy as a therapeutic ideal is predicated upon a social structure of virtue that articulates particular aspects of what it means to be an ideal community member (Damasio, 1994). In other words, we construct what it is to be "normal" based on a construct of social desirability. Not everything that is not ideal is necessarily seen as pathological, but if it is sufficiently unacceptable, disturbing, or unusual, it is highly likely that it will be labeled "abnormal". Thus, the construction of normalcy is an aesthetic, as well as an ethical and generally social normative, category. For example, a person acting humorously, while apparently neglecting the reality of the situation and relationships in the particular social setting, will generally be accepted as amusing, perhaps odd, but most likely not "abnormal". Another person, with the same level of apparent departure from what would be a realistic appreciation of the social facts and relationships, in the same situation, who acts in a dislikeable way (not necessarily threatening, but causing others to feel confused or their mood to decline) is more likely to be seen as mentally ill. Our perception of what it is to be "normal" and "abnormal" is shaped aesthetically as much as it is determined through "objective" medical criteria (cognitive grasp of reality, ability to control affect, presence of emotional dissociation, etc.) (Musalek et al., 2022).

The aesthetic dimension of normalcy presupposes that the ability to be "normal" requires a degree of common aesthetic sensibility between the individual and society—a sensibility that is typically developed through socialization. If a person is caught in a structure of cognitive, affective, and behavioral patterns that others find aesthetically unacceptable, the person is likely to be treated as deviant, or as mentally disturbed. While not all types of mental disorders are perceived as a primarily aesthetic displeasure by the majority, generally the greater the divergence between an individual's sensibility and values and that of the society, the more likely it is that the person will be perceived as "abnormal". This point is debated at length in the current debates of mental illness in terms of "neurodivergence" as opposed to any type of clear-cut pathology (Legault et al., 2021).

One of the tasks of psychotherapy is to reconcile this need to bring the individual's sensibility and behavior more or less within the aesthetic and broader socially normative realm of general acceptability (in order to be considered "normal") and at the same time to perceive the individual, the client, in light of one's entitlement to a substantial degree of "neurodiversity". To do so, the psychotherapist must typically align with the client within a discursive process that places them in a position of common quest of change. The therapist does not demand change from the client; he allies with the client in a common expectation of change that they hope would arise from their therapeutic relationship. This relationship of the two co-wanderers and co-sufferers seems remarkably like the work of faith, where without a belief in light from above, in the possibility of a miracle of change occurring in the midst of a common quest, the therapeutic profession would indeed remain an ultimately "impossible profession" (Freud, 1964). To use the metaphor of Maria Zambrano, the therapist and the client wander around a wilderness of the client's divergent and socially dysfunctional mindscape, seeking a "clearing" as an inroad to change. Whether, how, and when a clearing will emerge is unknown either to the client or to the therapist (Johnson, 2005).

The motif of clearing, of expecting an opening or an opportunity for constructive change while cultivating a community of therapy, is what characterizes almost every successful therapeutic process. The closeness that develops between the therapist and the client grows into a therapeutic community, where the therapist is an ally, an example, and a powerful life resource for the client. By "having" therapy and the therapist, the client already changes important aspects of one's life. However, the meaning and mission of this community go beyond the mere healing relationship: they also include an expectation of the opportunity to do something together that will result in lasting positive change for the client. There is a sense of common expectation based on the virtue of togetherness and mutual dedication within the therapeutic relationship that resembles common prayer. In modal logic terms, the therapist and the client expect a change of the modal worlds of the client's (and, sometimes, the therapist's, as well) life experience that might occur simply by a different modal world being "called into reality" by the dedicated therapeutic relationships and process (Fatic, 2023a, 2024).

The exact way in which this change of modal worlds happens is usually unclear to both the client and the therapist. In strictly logical terms, a change that neither participant in the therapeutic relationship can exactly explain, understand, or predict may be described as an experiential "miracle" (Leal et al., 2002). Perhaps the best documented type of specific, concrete "miracles" in psychotherapy of this type are synchronicities, which are now generally accepted as phenomena for which we remain without a strictly rational explanation, yet ones that regularly occur in psychotherapy (Cambray, 2009).

The way in which modal worlds are called into actuality is by generating different psychological conditions. Typically, this requires the creation of a community that is powered by particular values or intentional psychological content (Searle, 1983). The latter might include various psychological dispositions, such as desires, fears, anticipations, anxieties, or intentions. A community that shares the same or similar intentional content is characterized by a particular "mentality", and within a different communal mentality, different kinds of social realities are possible. Such a changed community mentality is a different modal world that facilitates possibilities that were previously unforeseeable (Keany, 2018).

Sharing the same type of beliefs decreases the likelihood that some within the community will perceive themselves as intellectually superior to others, that they will engage in what the Lacanians call "master discourse", or hierarchical communication that is usually ineffective in psychotherapy (Verhaeghe, 2008). Being a part of the community of like-minded peers increases the likelihood of equality, solidarity, and collaboration as opposed to the strategies of verticality, domination, and control. The former are all attributes of the therapeutic community, while the latter are literally anti-therapeutic. Thus, the change in modal worlds that makes possible large leaps in personal change within psychotherapy may arise from as little as the cultivation of a therapeutic relationship itself, as a nuclear community of belief and mentality, consisting just of the client and the therapist.

A good example of therapeutic communities outside the therapy setting per se is that of close religious communities, where many members are there because otherwise they would be lonely and isolated. The relationships that they establish within the church community are with the like-minded individuals. When such relationships are intimate (such as marriages), they have much higher chances of long-term success, because there is a value resonance between the spouses which they have adopted from the value structure and sensibility of the community that they are a part of. The modal world of marriages in such communities is different from the modal world within which most other couples get together in the society at large; consequently, their prospects, and quality of life, tend to be more stable and better than in the broader society. Some of the modern physicians and physicists have grounded the scientific explanation for this type of resonance in modern energy-based physics. While I am not able to comment on physics authoritatively, there appears to exist a striking similarity between the social intuition of "resonance" within harmonious communities and the quantum physics theories of vibration and frequency that suggest potential ways in which individuals establish rapport that is neither verbal, behaviorally explicit, nor is it limited to the physical proximity of the other individuals (Chopra, 1993). The concept of normalcy within a religious community is somewhat different from that in the general society: many behaviors that are widespread in society are considered "abnormal" in more organic communities. In such communities, the structure of virtue and value define normalcy more strictly than in the society at large and thus narrow the room for individuals to be "stuck" in their ways without a value perspective to guide them to what their community would consider and encourage as "normal". It is this "stuckness" that typically brings people to psychotherapy (Peck, 1997).

Prayer and Psychotherapy

The crucial experiential aspect in prayer is the attitude one takes: it is contrary to the attitude of "dignity" and "pride" which is usually associated with rational debate, where we fight for our opinions and views and desire to prove them correct as opposed to others'. In prayer, being "right" does not matter at all: what matters is attracting the mercy of God, namely admitting one's own faults and fallacies and showing as broad as possible an openness to God's intervention, whatever that intervention might be, including our own death. Only such an attitude in prayer leaves the person susceptible to change sufficiently to experience a miracle.

One of the paradigmatic examples of the attitude in prayer is that of King David in the Old Testament. Having suffered the problems of arrogance and overextended ego that are characteristic of almost unlimited political power, having betrayed his closest friend whom he had sent to die in a hopeless battle in order to seduce his wife, the beautiful Bathsheba, David finds himself surrounded by enemies from the outside and from inside his court and weeps to God. David's Psalms of the Old Testament are used as everyday prayers by Jews and Christians, for their tone of submission and repentance (Ginneken, 2014: 1–13). In them, David relates every trouble and illness he faces to his transgressions of the law of God (and of moral law). In the Psalms, the most powerful man of Israel sounds like the humblest servant of God (Psalms, 38: 3; 38: 18; 51: 3–5; Leviticus, 26: 39–40—The Holy Bible, 1988). They are the classic example of the attitude in prayer that Jews and Christians believe is a prerequisite for the prayer being answered by God. Even if the prayers are said and the rites performed perfectly, an attitude or thoughts of self-importance or any kind of arrogance will annul them in the eyes of God. This attitude of submission that arises from an awareness of one's own fundamental inadequacy calls into reality new modal worlds, new sets of circumstances in the vision of God's mercy. It is the expectation of change, or forgiveness, or a blessing that increases the quality of life of those suffering, while the same dispositions create the conditions for the emergence of a "clearing" mentioned earlier on.

There is obviously an ethical element in the attitude of submission in prayer, where the idea of one's own limitations and impotence to address life's challenges necessitates a respect and reverence for God as the source of both redemption and specific salvation from daily calamities. This type of ethics is highly practical in psychotherapy, as well, because it enlightens the therapeutic process with an awareness, both by the client and by the therapist, that there are limits that they can achieve as individuals. The client has, typically, already tried everything in their power to solve the problem prior to arriving for therapy. The therapist, on the other hand, is aware that the array of interpretations and interventions that he or she possesses are of limited value if the process remains in the hands of the therapist alone. What they both ought to expect is the creation of a new psychological reality within the therapeutic process, like the attitude of expectation and submission that characterizes prayer, which would then allow the emergence of change. Neither the client nor the therapist know exactly how that change will occur and what its exact nature will be. Their work is largely in the dark, and they rely on a common attitude of looking for a conceptual and psychological clearing, while cultivating their relationship in good faith. There is a remarkable similarity between the attitude that characterizes the therapeutic expectation and that of prayerful waiting for God.

A related and perhaps more fundamental aspect that connects prayer and psychotherapy is that of *insufficiency*. In most cases, it is the sense of insufficiency and inadequacy that brings individuals to therapy. Their inability to resolve their existential difficulties by their own personal resources faces them head-on with the deep-seated insufficiency of their personalities, or what Jacques Lacan calls "lack" (Verhaeghe, 2008). It is the sense of lack that moves us in life, seeking to secure the "missing object", or the object of satisfaction where the very nature of the game is pursuit itself. Paul Verhaeghe describes this game as a puzzle where the very ability of the pieces of the puzzle to move is predicated upon the absence of one piece of the puzzle. In life, it is practically impossible to completely fill the puzzle, and even if it was possible, the puzzle would become useless as a game, because no piece would be able to move any more. However, the perception of the lack, or insufficiency, especially of the inadequacy of personal resources to deal with pain and frustration, has the form of suffering; it is the complaint most often heard in psychotherapy rooms. The nature of psychotherapy is not to remedy the lack, or to fill the puzzle, thus making life itself devoid of dynamism and movement, but to make the client, and the therapist alike, aware of the mutual insufficiency. Thus, where insufficiency brings the client to therapy on the one hand, on the other the recognition of the mutual insufficiencies of the client and therapist generate a situation of prayerful expectation of an opportunity to make an inroad into an otherwise insoluble situation. The client and the therapist recognize each other's insufficiencies (Vallas & Cummins, 2014). The cultivation of a therapeutic relationship, based on such recognition of insufficiency, but marked by mutual dedication and preparedness for sacrifice (of time, attention and energy, at least), is what heals, rather than any "technique" or "intervention" (Eigen, 2014).

One way in which we tend to compensate for our insufficiencies is by identifying with larger identities that make us feel less inadequate and incomplete. This process of identification with groups, ideologies, and even with objects, which thus become seemingly inseparable parts of our lives, is what Jung made famous as "participation mystique" (Jung, 1966). The subjective sense of lack is compensated for by participation in larger relationships. This is why individuals tend to find spouses who compensate for their own inadequacies or exhibit qualities that they themselves feel they lack, and at the same time it is why the passion with which we tend to adopt ideologies, join various schools of thought, or embrace particular moral values or aesthetic taste tend to correspond with the intensity of the felt internal insufficiency. The applications of Jung's theory of participation mystique are potentially vast and can especially usefully address issues of human conflict, ranging from interpersonal psychological conflict to warfare (Fatic, 2023b).

The prayerful nature of psychotherapy is closely connected to the concepts of lack and insufficiency, in at least two ways. First, it is the quest of a missing object or satisfaction, or the broader sense of insufficiency, that is required for personal change, including that through the psychotherapeutic process. Without a feeling of inadequacy, no amount of psychotherapy or counseling can lead to meaningful personal development. Secondly, and more importantly for my present context, the sense of insufficiency points to a structure of power that is displaced from the very therapeutic process and made vertical, like in prayer. In their joint quest for an opportunity for change and for therapeutic success, the therapist and the client relinquish the idea that they have the power to effect such change. The psychotherapist does not believe that he or she has the capacity to change the client, or that the client can change themselves. Rather, both direct their expectation of change to the outside of their relationship, in the belief that the relationship itself will create the psychological conditions for a modal logical switch of modal worlds, for the onset of internal and external circumstances that, for the client, will make possible what at present seems impossible. It is this expectation that is constructive, active, and filled with a joint investment of belief, energy, and time in the creation of an organic therapeutic community that typically creates major specific inroads into situations that the client and the therapist often do not even discuss explicitly. The very structure of psychotherapeutic training that is based on modal logic reflects this emphasis on bringing about a real change in the problematic circumstances and the client's life flow, rather than being limited to a mere reinterpretation of the events and to a modification of one's subjective reactions to what is a given "external world" (Institute for Practical Humanities, 2023). The novelty of the perception of psychotherapy as based on the dynamics of modal logic as opposed to that which traditionally rests on propositional logic is in part this bringing together of psychotherapy and the prayer-like attitude of an active therapeutic alliance in the expectation of a modal change that is effected by the organic community between the therapist and the client.

The Quest of Normalcy as Seeking a Transcendence

While the concept of normalcy is the construct of our community, our values and, above all, the projections of virtue that our community adopts as its social ideal (the closer one is to that social ideal, the more "normal" or healthy one is considered), it also shines a light on how psychotherapy resembles prayer and spiritual practices more generally in seeking to help individuals attain normalcy and mental health. The general attitude in psychoanalytic, and later in most other psychotherapeutic schools and circles, that the less of a "master discourse", or dominating, "doctorly" approach there is in psychotherapy, the more effective the therapeutic relationship tends to be in bringing about the normalcy that is sought through the process, is at least suggestive of deep methodological and phenomenological similarities between psychotherapy and spiritual practice, primarily prayer. Perhaps the most important such conclusion is that the therapeutic alliance in successful psychotherapy acknowledges the fundamental insufficiency of both participants in the therapeutic relationship—the client, and the therapist—and positions them side-by-side on the task of establishing a sincere, devoted community, while expecting an opening, a "clearing", whereby an opportunity will shine from above and allow them to move toward a solution to the problem. Thus, the therapeutic relationship pictures two persons, both proverbially "full of holes", aware of their insufficiencies as human beings, soldiering in solidarity while awaiting a break, or blessing, from above. Once the light comes, it transforms both the client and the therapist. They are often lost for words and rational arguments as to what just happened, and this is often reflected in debriefings after successful therapy (Yalom & Leszecz, 2005: 285–295).

While the concept of normalcy may be described in more or less static and simple terms, as an offshoot of the society's projection of virtue and ideal community membership, the psychotherapeutic process, which is supposedly predicated upon the need to attain or regain normalcy where it is clouded or obstructed, either subjectively, for the client, or intersubjectively, as the society's perception of the individual, is more complicated. It is the quest of normalcy through psychotherapy that elucidates the pitfalls of the assumption that one person is sufficient to change another person through a type of "professional" intervention that resembles a medical cure. The very structure and dynamics of successful psychotherapy reveal a layered process whereby the inadequacies and incompleteness of both the client and the therapists are recognized and built into a humane and empathetic relationship that strives upwards. There is an element of expectation of modality, or possible world that makes possible what is currently impossible for the client. Such a modal world is called into reality by a spiritual-like practice performed jointly by the client and the therapist. This practice is in fact an organic community-building in the therapeutic process. It is the cultivation of psychological conditions for a modal logical change that the therapist envisions, and helps the client to expect, however that neither the therapist nor the client can determine, precisely describe, or control. This prayer-like position of the client and therapist is one where, side by side, they look above the current modal worlds, or sets of circumstances that determine the client's experience and the psychotherapist's limitations, believing in the psychotherapeutic process as a fundamentally transcendent one. In this process, the boundaries of the current modal world that the therapy starts from will, at some stage, shift and transform, in ways largely unfathomable to either participant, however in a manner that is brought about by their commonality and solidarity in their effort to meet and welcome the new reality.

The Normative Context

What is normative in the concept of normalcy is socially construed, and what is normative in the therapeutic process is construed through the organic relationship between the therapist and the client. This latter construct is obviously determined by the former: the client and the counselor cannot simply agree on antisocial values and goals as a matter of their intersubjective consensus. This means that psychotherapy is fundamentally a social discipline; it rests on social structure and depends on the development of a healthy sociality in the client. Such sociality might be disturbed for a variety of reasons. In some cases, where serious psychiatric disorders are at stake, the injury to sociality might result from psychological or cerebral issues. *Vice versa*, in many cases, mental suffering arises from a disturbed sociality. Thus, it seems that the normativity of the concept of normalcy, or of any of the goals of psychotherapy, depend on a complex interplay of the various visions of values and of the modal worlds, or sets of relevant circumstances, that are created by the society and, to some extent, by the client's own decisions.

The ambition of MIP to change modal worlds as the precondition for personal improvement renders it even more "social" than many traditional psychotherapeutic approaches, which place a heavy emphasis on personal experience and shy away from addressing society or externality in the philosophical sense. Our externalities, however, typically determine our internalities. Living in an unhappy, depressed community will likely preclude the personal development of a sunny and optimistic worldview, and a way to address this in therapy might not be to work on changing one's perception of the community, but by changing the community. The angle at which we view our experience is determined by the position of our body or mind; once we move our bodies, and thus, often, our minds, a different vantage point is acquired. What was impossible in one position will become possible in another. However, things that were possible previously will cease to be possible once the modal world is changed. This change requires the juggling together of many variables and immersing oneself as a therapist deep into the philosophy of life and values of the client, participating actively in that philosophy and in the client's work to move and change. A degree of responsibility is inherent in this process: while ultimately it is the client who is responsible for their own decisions, the therapist is not entirely innocent of the gains or losses incurred in the process of change. This responsibility further accentuates the crucial need for the therapist and client to cultivate a close alliance, an intimate relationship where the therapist's understanding of the client can only be compared to that characteristic of close organic communities as we know them from the past. The therapist should not be surprised or distanced when the client, having changed their circumstances externally, finds that the desired change, even when it is fully achieved, is deeply dissatisfying or threatening; likewise, the therapist is not barred from partaking in the joy and psychological benefits of the client's basking in a newly achieved modal world that they now find has transformed their life for the better. The therapist is part of the story, part of the narrative of the modal change. The therapist is also a key element of the client's modal world, and so is the client for the therapist. They agree on the "normalcy", functionality, satisfaction, and other values that they seek, and they place a psychological and philosophical stake each in a process that is governed by modal logical principles that they can understand and call for, but that they cannot control, either "professionally" or through methods of techniques. It is a process which is both highly normative and deeply characterized by a sense of lack and personal insufficiency in all arreas other than cultivating informed expectations. This brings the process close to what we are used to regard as spiritual practice.

References

Cambray, J. (2009). *Synchronicity: Nature and psyche in an interconnected universe*. Texas University Press.

Chopra, D. (1993). *Ageless body, timeless mind: A practical alternative to growing old*. Harmony Books.

Damasio, A. (1994). *Descartes' error: Emotions, reason, and the human brain*. Avon Books.

Eigen, M. (2014). Variants of mystical participation. In M. Winborn (Ed.), *Shared realities: Participation mystique and beyond* (pp. 130–143). Fisher King Press.

Fatic, A. (2023a). Modal logic in integrative philosophical practice. *Philosophy and Society, 34*(3), 424–437. https://doi.org/10.2298/FID2303424F

Fatic, A. (2023b). Participation mystique in warfare. *Socialitas* (online). Retrieved September 24, 2024, from https://aleksandarfatic.net/participation-mystique-in-warfare-draft-paper-for-comments/

Fatic, A. (2024). Climbing Jacob's Ladder: Collective action and humility in philosophical practice and psychotherapy. *Revue Romaine de Philosophie, 68*(1), 183–194. http://www.institutuldefilosofie.ro/e107_files/downloads/Revue%20roumaine%20de%20philosophie/Tome%2068,%20Nr.%201%EF%BB%BF,%202024/ALEKSANDAR%20FATI%C4%86,%20Climbing%20Jacob%E2%80%99s%20Ladder.pdf

Fatic, A., & Zagorac, I. (2018). The methodology of philosophical practice: Eclecticism and/or integrativeness. *Philosophia, 44*, 1419–1438. https://doi.org/10.1007/s11406-016-9770-3

Freud, S. (1964). *New introductory lectures on psychoanalysis.* In J. Strachey (Ed.), *The standard edition of the complete psychological works of Sigmund Freud: 1–182* (Vol. 22). The Hogarth Press (Penguin Random House) and the Institute of Psychoanalysis.

Frunza, Sandu (2018). Philosophical counselling and the practices of dialogue in a world built on communication *Postmodern Openings* 9, 3:1–19. https://doi.org/10.18662/po/33

Ginneken, J. (2014). *Psychology of power: Temptation at the top.* Palgrave Macmillan.

Hadot, P. (1995). *Philosophy as a way of life: Spiritual exercises from Socrates to Foucault* (C. Melden, Trans.). Blackwell.

Institute for Practical Humanities. (2023). Training in modal integrative psychotherapy. Retrieved January 15, 2024, from https://iph.edu.rs/?page_id=1575.

Johnson, R. (2005). Literary epiphanies, the pleasures of recognition, and María Zambrano. *Revista Hispánica Moderna, 58*(1–2), 185–203. http://www.jstor.org/stable/30203793

Jung, C. G. (1966). *Two essays on analytical psychology* (2nd ed.). Princeton University Press.

Keany, D. N. (2018). An examination of the Book of Common Prayer as technical writing for an oral-aural culture. *Journal of Technical Writing and Communication, 50*, 1. Online. https://doi.org/10.1177/0047281618799103

Kernberg, O. F., Yeomans, F. E., Clarkin, J. F., & Levy, K. N. (2008). Transference focused psychotherapy: Overview and update. *International Journal of Psychoanalysis, 89*, 601–620.

Leal, M. M., Nwora, E. I., de Melo, G. F., & Freitas, M. H. (2002). Praying for a miracle: Negative or positive impacts on health care? *Frontiers in Psychology.* https://doi.org/10.3389/fpsyg.2022.840851

Legault, M., Bourdon, J.-N., & Poirier, P. (2021). From neurodiversity to neurodivergence: The role of epistemic and cognitive marginalization. *Synthese, 199*, 12843–12868. https://doi.org/10.1007/s11229-021-03356-5

Lewis, T., Amini, F., & Lannon, R. (2000). *A general theory of love*. Random House.
Marinoff, L. (2002). *Philosophical practice*. Academic Press.
Martin, M. (2001). Ethics as therapy: Philosophical counseling and psychological health. *International Journal of Philosophical Practice, 1*(1), 1–31.
Moncrieff, J. (2018). Against the stream: Antidepressants are not antidepressants – An alternative approach to drug action and implications for the use of antidepressants. *BJ Psych Bulletin, 42*(1), 42–44. https://doi.org/10.1192%2Fbjb.2017.11
Musalek, M., Bernegger, G., & Scheibenbogen, O. (2022). Social aesthetics and mental health. *The Journal of Kitsch, Camp and Mass Culture, 1*, 143–152.
Peck, S. (1997). *The road less travelled and Beyond. Spiritual growth in an age of anxiety*. Simon and Schuster.
Radulescu, I., Dragoi, A. M., Trifu, S. C., & Cristea, M. B. (2021). Neuroplasticity and depression: Rewiring the brain's networks through pharmacological therapy. *Experimental and Therapeutic Medicine, 22*(4), 1131. https://doi.org/10.3892%2Fetm.2021.10565
Searle, J. (1983). *Intentionality*. Cambridge University Press.
The Holy Bible. (1988). Zindervan.
Vallas, S., & Cummins, E. (2014). Relational models of organizational inequalities: Emerging approaches and conceptual dilemmas. *American Behavioral Scientist, 58*, 228–255.
Verhaeghe, P. (2008). *On being normal and other disorders*. Karnac Press.
Yalom, I., & Leszecz, M. (2005). *The theory and practice of group psychotherapy* (7th ed.). Basic Books.

CHAPTER 3

The Subject of Psychotherapy: Nominalism and Realism in Understanding Psychic Processes

Abstract This chapter discusses the relationships between the nominalist nature of psychiatric diagnoses, as described by Paul Verhaeghe, and the modal logical context of psychotherapy. The nominalist view portrays psychodiagnosis as storytelling, rather than medical diagnostics, and offers various narrative and, by extension, metaphysical possibilities for the inculcation of logical modality in the conceptualization of psychotherapy, including the idea of changing modal worlds, or possible worlds, as key elements in Modal Integrative Psychotherapy.

Keywords Modality • Logic • Storytelling • Psychodiagnostics • Subjectivism • Realism

In one of the most precise descriptions of how various states of affairs exist at the same time, and how they harmoniously provide opportunities for the shifting between various modal worlds or existentially relevant sets of circumstances that determine what is possible and what is actual or real, Arthur Schopenahuer writes:

> the coexistence of many states constitutes in fact the very essence of reality, for through it permanence or duration first becomes possible. Permanence is knowable only in the change of that which exists simultaneously with what

A. Fatic, *Modal Integrative Psychotherapy*,
https://doi.org/10.1007/978-3-031-91934-3_3

is permanent; but also only by means of what is permanent in variation does variation receive the character of change. (Schopenhauer, 1966, p. 10)

Imagine a typical therapeutic experience. A person comes into the consulting room disoriented, full of questions, pained by experiences they cannot metabolize, initially seeking at least temporary relief, reassurance, an insight to cling on to until they can mobilize more of their internal resources to really deal with the situation. They arrive with the goal to cope, to survive the moment, and once they do, the therapeutic relationship develops into a process where the person seeks long-term understanding and acceptance by the therapist and starts to perceive therapy and the therapists as life resources in themselves. Ideally, the very "possession" of psychotherapy improves the client's life, quite regardless of any resolution of their other problems that may be the substance of psychotherapeutic work.

Initially, very few people come for consultations in a balanced, curious state, seeking meaning in life as such: by the time they come to us they have usually tried everything they could do on their own to reduce their psychic pain. They have tested everything their culture had taught them to do when they were existentially stuck: they put on paper the pros and cons of various decisions, analyzed their situation, the behavior of others, and their own actions. Nothing helped.

All the actions typically taken before resorting to psychotherapy are reasonable. In ordinary, relatively easy resolvable situations, they should help. When seriously in pain, people rarely miss opportunities to address their problems responsibly. At least this is the case with people who undergo psychotherapy, who by and large tend to be intelligent, emotionally well-articulated and compassionate individuals. Many have had encounters with self-help literature, and some touch the helping professions through their own occupations. In many cases, they start with the exclamation that "they have tried everything humanely possible to solve the problem".

Indeed, in many cases, rationally, logically, conventionally, the problem appears insoluble.

This is the striking feature of many of the issues we deal with in psychotherapy: we face many generally highly capable, discriminating, sensitive individuals who arrive for counseling and bring along problems that, conventionally speaking, are insoluble. The question for the psychotherapist is what to do with this impossibility and how to turn it into a resource for the client. This is perhaps the core question for all psychotherapy, and it is where psychotherapy invites modal logic.

Consider an example.

During the writing of this book, I was selling my apartment. At one stage, a potential buyer, let us call him Barnie, an artist in his mid-fifties, appeared with an agent. He liked the apartment, spent several hours inspecting and filming it, and then decided to come again a few days with his wife, who was pregnant with their first child. Barnie worked in the entertainment business, as an events organizer. He was articulate but over-reflective and very verbal.

On his second visit, Barnie was late, although the appointment was in the evening. He was accompanied by an elderly woman whom he introduced as his aunt. His wife did not come along. Both he and his aunt looked carefully around the apartment, set down, and Barnie informed me that his wife did not like the apartment based on his video and that he had a problem convincing her to agree to its purchase. He pointed out that all of the money to be invested was his, and then continued to tell me the details of their financial arrangement, moving on to issues in their relationship, the problems associated with having a child, and the assisted pregnancy process that they had undergone. To the surprise of everyone present, Barnie mentioned that he might leave his wife because they had fundamental misunderstandings, mentioned that she was "seriously bipolar", and then, suddenly, dialed her number and handed me the phone. Surprised, I said hello and had a brief, awkward conversation with his wife. When I handed the telephone back to Barnie, he said to his wife to speak freely and then turned the speaker on, so that we could all hear the very confrontational and, in many ways, inappropriate, aggressive manner in which she related to him. He then ended the conversation and, with a sense of exhibitionist joy, commented: "My life with her is hell".

Over the next two hours, Barnie engaged in a self-disclosure that revealed what seemed to me as histrionic personality issues, displaying a sense of unsustainability of his own marital life, with a partner he seemed quite unable to accept. He had lived with his wife for four years "on and off" as he said: they could not agree on a kind of place where they liked to live: he liked central, urban environments, where he had grown up, and she liked the periphery and more relaxed surroundings with greenery. He was looking forward to having a child, but it seemed that he saw parenthood more as the achievement of another life goal than as a part of an organic, emotional relationship. He ended up suggesting that his wife did not love him, but that he "could not live without her" because he thought she was physically beautiful. He proceeded to show me her photographs, and the women shown on them appeared to have a facial convulsion which seemed to be the result of either an injury or a neurological problem. There was a marked discrepancy between the tone of the woman's voice and his (inconsistent) narrative about their marriage, as well as between the photograph and his perception of it. Barnie was fundamentally in an extremely challenging situation. He had tried to solve it by spending time separately from his wife, living in his apartment which was similar to the one I was selling, with her living in an urban periphery, in her parents' house. In addition, he believed that people who had failed marriages in their lives (divorced people) were "deeply problematic" and did not want to be one of them. His options all seemed closed. Yet, he was desperate for a solution. When I mentioned that some people found it workable to live separately and take care of a child from their own positions of identity and personal preferences, without necessarily heading to divorce, he was immediately enlivened, but did not say anything or affirm such a possibility. It was difficult to end that session that started as a potential flat buyer's visit and turned into an unexpected psychotherapeutic encounter. He mentioned during our conversation that he might become a client of mine.

What the therapist deals with in the type of situation that Barnie is in comes down to a change of meaning. In this process, there are several meanings that need to be clarified and changed.

The first meaning to change is the meaning of a solution to the problem. If the issue is unresolvable by conventional cultural means (resolution of a conflict, of emotional frustration or blockage, or of a dysfunctionality in the relationship), the first step we take is to address the meaning of a potential resolution. In Barnie's case, he was completely focused on the choice of an apartment and was trying to reconcile his views with those of his wife so that the area and type of accommodation would be acceptable to both of them, while she did not want to compromise. He saw his quest for an apartment (he mentioned that he had looked at close to 40 apartments already) as a way of addressing his marital problem. His wife's reaction that I witnessed over the telephone made it clear that the problem could not be resolved in Barnie's way: she had no interest in compromising over the apartment and wanted Barnie to follow her preferences entirely. When I suggested to Barnie that the apartment might not be a resolution of his problem and that he may wish to look into the nature of that problem in more principled ways, he seemed energized. This was a mild suggestion of change of meaning that had an immediate effect on him.

A part of understanding the meaning of a solution to a problem is in considering whether leaving the problem as it is might be a solution. In some cases, not solving impossible situations might be a solution that allows the person to move on with life. Sometimes the unresolved problem that is left in the past can be integrated seamlessly into one's overall life experience. In other cases, a more dramatic "facing up" to the problem and the people involved is required. For various people, the meaning of a resolution in this sense can differ. When I suggested to Barnie that "some people just live in different locations and maintain a romantic and parenting relationship", gently touching on the possibility that a "no solution" might be a solution, this elicited an energised mannerism, but no explicit response from him. He saw a resolution as affirmative action where he would either stay with his wife and live together with her or leave her. When, in the end, I asked him directly, Barnie was explicit about this.

The next meaning to examine is that of one's underlying values and the resulting life strategies, namely what the cognitive behavioral therapists would call "patterns" in decision-making and action which, more often than not, after having served the person well for large swaths of one's life, start proving inadequate in addressing the new and contextually changed circumstances. A typical example is the narcissism of youth: when teenagers gradually become adults, parents often try to make sure that they receive enough support and confirmation to develop sufficient self-confidence in their future life. When this kind of supportive behavior goes too far, and there is too much of it, various forms of destructive and debilitating narcissism set in. Thus, sometimes, a young girl, who as a teenager took pride in her good looks, which were always praised and emphasized by her parents and other family members, grows into a 30 years old adult who continues to conduct her social life by looking at her photographs and admiring her beauty, while missing real issues and challenges the everyday adult life brings. Unnoticeably, such a person finds herself immersed in depression after the first emotional rejections or betrayals. She starts to perceive her own personality as "not of this world", incapable of dealing with the environment which challenges her value despite her beauty. The old pattern, which had got her through her teenage years relatively successfully, is now proving to be a source of pathology, because she has outgrown the pattern, but has failed to reject or modify it.

An ageing philosophy professor may become dysfunctional in an environment full of younger colleagues because his patterns of thought, his previously successful strategies, might collide with the mentality and prevailing spirit of the younger group, leaving him in a position to either sink into isolation or to seek to transform the old patterns. Examples of the principle are innumerable.

In Barnie's case, his strategy of being "egotistic" as he described himself, "letting down many women in his life", seemed to him to have generated a "karma" as he called it, where he now found himself in an impossible situation: he either had to accept life with a demanding woman who had strongly divergent values from his, or he had to risk his parenthood and the future relationship with his child by "sticking to his guns" in terms of his values. Barnie needed to change, to become a different person, in order to make his marriage work, or he needed to give up the marriage. No other solution was possible other than a complete transformation of his life strategy; a change of meaning of his very values and life goals.

The transformation of a life strategy is at once a practical, therapeutic process, and a value-based one. Its therapeutic achievement marks an interface between practical philosophy and traditional psychotherapy. In fact, most of the critical junctures of personal change that make up the very crux of successful psychotherapy are exactly such interfaces, or portals, into value-laden issues, where lasting change requires a modification of the philosophical outlook on life. This is the reason I consider all psychotherapy to be a form of philosophical practice.

I mentioned at the beginning of this chapter that clients arriving for psychotherapy are typically distraught. Barnie did not intentionally arrive for counseling; however, his visit transformed into counseling. He was distraught. When his internal conflict is observed from a logical point of view, what causes him pain is the coexistence of conflicting states of affairs in his value system at the same time: the complexity of his life-world that makes up his experiential reality. He is in love with a woman whom he perceives unrealistically, with whom he is in a structurally serious conflict, where, fundamentally, he does not see a future with her. He has focused his dilemma into an obsessive process of looking for an apartment to buy, which should embody the desired state of affairs in his marital relationship:

a convergence of personalities, an agreement, understanding, and a compatibility of values. All of this appears absent from his real, actual relationship.

The cognitive and emotional congestion which clients in psychotherapy face with various, tensely crowded together, internal states of affairs (various commitments, emotions, values, diverging projections of action, energy, problems in decision-making, and the resulting issues for well-being) tears the person apart between a *permanence* (remaining in an unpleasant situation characterized by strong ambivalences between different states of affairs) and a *desire to change*. This is Barnie's present situation. Logically viewed, it is a simple and stable structure; however, for him, "his life is hell" as he puts it.

In the described structure, personal change is conceivable only as a jump to a *different structure that is relatively stable*. One must move from one relatively stable state of affairs to another relatively stable state of affairs. Moving from a current stable "hell" to a passing solace, such as, for example, having an affair, does not address the problem and is likely to additionally complicate it. The solution must be logically sufficiently radical. Both factual situations between which the person moves (in Barnie's case, his current marital stalemate on the one hand, and a potential decision to adopt a different structure of the relationship, on the other) are characterized by what Schopenhauer considers "permanence". However, permanence also applies to the process that might address such statically unresolvable situations: only a structured, ordered, permanent change as a flowing, but predictable sequence of events can carry Barnie out of his Platonic "cave" of life structure. Barnie needs to change his modal world and changing, or choosing, the apartment of his liking may be a part of that process, but in itself it is merely a compensation for the need for more radical self-change. We are naturally predisposed to cling to permanence and to avoid unpredictability, and this is the main reason for the inertia that prevents so many people who undergo psychotherapy from making the "jump" to alternative modal worlds. In order to make such a jump, Barnie needs not just to select an apartment that is his authentic choice, but to abandon his views of marriage, the structure of the power relationship between him and his wife, and his fixed representation of parenthood. In this process, he is likely to suddenly face a change of his perception of his wife as a person, in all of the ways in which he currently idealizes her, and this last aspect of change might be the most dramatic. Barnie must be very brave to make this jump, and this is why people typically cannot face the need for modal change without therapy or something that effectively substitutes for therapy (a deep and engaged relationship with someone playing the role of a therapist, deep philosophical self-questioning, or a transformative life experience that induces a serious tremor to one's current modal world).

To make a change in the moment, to step out into a different, new set of "permanent" features of our existence, is somewhat like stepping into a waterfall: it involves a sense of losing oneself for a while. Such a step is a conscious effort to jump from one modal world to another; both worlds are defined by permanence. This entails an inner change which occurs through decision-making.

The concept of decision-making in the described sense is more dramatic than it is usually thought of. There is always an element of death and relinquishment in a decision: to decide means to leave one modal world and choose another, to leave some beliefs, values, and people behind and embrace new ones. Any decision involves a moment, or period, of loneliness, whether for an instant, when the person moves from one modal world, from one set of permanent circumstances, to another, or a longer time, if one lingers between the two modal worlds. Decisions are like small divorces, or small deaths: by deciding, we relegate one modal world to the past, or to death, and embrace another, which we never fully know or understand. Thus, we leap into a partial unknown, informed by what we have of the facts and by our hope, or at the very least by our inability to withstand what we are leaving. Each major change of life along the described lines thus involves a change of our own identity. This is both a personal change, characteristically sought by traditional psychotherapy, and a change of life perspective from a cognitive and value point of view, which is the province of philosophy.

The existence of various, mutually compensating states of affairs or potential life-worlds is exemplified by the different thought-worlds in the same real or actual circumstances. Shortly before I started writing the very first version of what was eventually to become this chapter, I had a brush with death from illness, where expectations by doctors were that I would not survive. In the weeks and months afterwards, I lingered in a state of fear. My everyday routine, marked by isolation and intensive medication, included frequent checks of temperature, oxygen saturation, intense self-monitoring, and a fright that things might go wrong at any moment. Every cough, the varieties of which I could unmistakably identify as more or less troubling, triggered thoughts that reduced my quality of life. But parallel to this thought-world was another: one of courage, acceptance of the consequences of the illness, and a projection of constructive and stabilizing thoughts, primarily related to my work and outstanding obligations and deadlines, which promised to reduce fear, draw my attention away from the preoccupation with illness and death. This was the modal world that rehabilitated me. Importantly, this modal world was not merely an interpretative frame of my experience; it was an identity change. While I was still in hospital, I wrote an article for a local newspaper calling for a radical response to the government, in a country whose democratic credentials and those of tolerance of critics were not great, and I continued with a changed public and personal demeanor because I had experienced the fragility of my own existence. My preferences and strategies in my personal relationships changed markedly. These changes resulted in a different social context in which I found myself, acting more assertively, and this resulted in threats that were issued by the government in response to my political views, which, after the experience of near death, did not really shake me. My new thought-world was different from the one I had resided in prior to the illness.

When we switch between thought-worlds, and thought-worlds are modal worlds, too, there is a point in time when the two thought-worlds exist simultaneously, either's reality is no less than that of the other's. What is required, then, is for the person to initiate a chain of causality, as Schopenhauer calls it, and travel in one's mind and through one's actions from one world to the other; in my case, from a world of fear and self-restraint to one of greater personal stability and propensity to take risks. The two modal worlds are both characterized by permanence. They are both there, as real possibilities. One is actual, but the other is no less possible, though, for the moment, less "real", and the "jump" from one to the other is essentially a matter of decision, which will change the actor's identity. What changes our identity are structural decisions, not ones made in order to adapt to an existing modal world. Divorce is a structural decision. A major change of career is another one. The adoption of different values and sensibility is also a structural change. In all these situations one's "take" on one's problems and life in general shifts: what was impossible becomes possible, and conversely, some things that were possible are no longer so. A different person, with a different identity, has different options and different problems. That is what MIP comes down to.

Having considered the above, how ontologically "real" are the two modal worlds prior to one's making the jump from one to the other? Their inner dynamics, their existential "taste" and presence, consist primarily in the thoughts that make up the corresponding patterns of experience. Are these thoughts "real", verifiable, measurable? If the thought-world is different from the physical world in that it lacks the capacity for empirical measurement and verification, if it is not "real" in that crude, "scientific" way, is it ontologically less real?

There appears to exist no convincing reason to assume that suffering because of thoughts is less real a life experience than suffering because of physical pain, although, admittedly, physical suffering can greatly surpass mental suffering in intensity. The idea that subjective experience can be "objectified" through tests and psychometrics seems as absurd as ideas come in the history of science. The greatest psychotherapeutic "findings" have been the result of methods of introspection and observation, many of which would be considered "non-scientific" by the standards of empirical sciences based on quantification. Consider Freud and his observation of his patients, his interpretations of dreams and his formulation of the first psychoanalytic principles, most of which have withstood the scrutiny of time and experience since, and now have the status of accepted knowledge in psychotherapy. Consider Lacan and his speculations about speech and psychosis, almost all of which are now parts of the standard methodology for psychoanalytic, and even positivist psychiatric diagnosis, where the connection between the structure of language and psychological processes is considered a part of the "evidence based" diagnostics. Finally, consider Jung and his work on his own unconscious dynamics, which he considered scientific research, and which has changed psychotherapy so profoundly and established the entire paradigm of "analytical psychology". It is impossible to accurately quantify spiritual or emotional pain, just as it is not possible to measure the amount of resilience a person is able to muster under certain extreme challenges. The human person is not entirely measurable: it is rather relatively interpretable, and only so if one decides to allow oneself to be interpreted or "diagnosed". The reality of personal suffering is a logical, and not a scientific category. It is a feature of modal worlds, including thought-worlds.

Psychodiagnostics as Storytelling

One of the key features of psychiatric diagnostics which attract critical attention is that such diagnoses cannot be objectively verified in the way that is considered essential for all other medical diagnoses. They cannot be observed by imaging equipment, confirmed by biochemical tests, or in any way empirically verified. They are simply phenomenological tools which describe individual experiences through a relatively standardized language, in much the same way as does the storytelling narrative. Psychiatric diagnoses are interpretative tools. They are not scientific categories. A description of a state of affairs is not by itself a diagnosis in the strict medical sense: it is merely an interpretative narrative. For an interpretation or description to become a diagnosis, it must satisfy certain scientific criteria of independent empirical verification. Such verification is obviously unavailable in psychiatric diagnoses. Furthermore, psychiatric diagnoses are not even particularly specific descriptions of the mental states that they purport to normatively capture. While in creative storytelling the writer describes an experience by trying to make the description unique, thus at the same time making her work original, the psycho-diagnostician describes an individual experience of the client, or patient, with the opposite aim to that of the writer: the clinician tries to describe the unique internal reality of the client or patient in as unoriginal and standardized way as possible. This is called "classification". While classification in itself is not a diagnosis, it is a crucial part of diagnosis. The full psychiatric diagnosis includes both a classification and a description of the patient which links the patient's individuality and individual presentation to the terms of the classification.

Classifications of psychiatric disorders are consensually postulated concepts that are supposed to stand for certain experiences and mental states that the clinician *supposes* the patient undergoes or possesses. They are phenomenological aids to describe individual experiences in as recognizable and approximatively acceptable manner as possible. This is why psychiatric classifications alone are not considered diagnoses; nevertheless, they are the essence of diagnoses, which then expand into broader descriptions of the patient's troubles. In other words, psychiatric classifications are the core of standardized and unoriginal story telling about the mental states and experience of others that the diagnostician cannot gain access to directly, or in any other verifiable medical way. Such diagnoses are fundamentally descriptive narratives; however, because they rest on classifications and are standardized, they are by definition *uncreative* narratives.

It is not difficult to see the problem here. The obvious methodological query is how a description based on a fundamentally arbitrary classification which, at best, only approximatively captures the phenomenon it tries to describe, could possibly have the status of "diagnosis", where there is no objective way to verify it. The problem further grows when one considers the fact that in most cases the same group of symptoms in psychodiagnostics meets with different "diagnoses", even different classifications, offered by different clinicians and different institutions. The phenomenology of experience and behavior which, for one clinician, represents bipolar disorder, or latent schizophrenia (if he happens to be a Lacanian), for another clinician will clearly signify Borderline Personality Disorder (BPD). For a third diagnostician, the same phenomena might involve both mentioned classifications, as well as some others, as comorbidities.

The habit in psychiatric institutions is to string new diagnoses on a person whenever a particular clinician sees in the patient something that appears to him as warranting a different diagnosis from those the person already has. Then, rather than absolving the victim of the previous diagnosis, the clinician typically simply adds another one to his list of the person's mental dysfunctions. I once met a person who had been a long-term patient in a psychiatric institution, and who at the time led a non-governmental organization tasked with offering assistance to the "survivors of the mental health system". She told me of the way they used to joke while in the psychiatric word, whenever somebody would be invited for diagnostic interview by a new clinician. Inevitably, the interview would result in at least one new diagnosis, and the common comment by the other "inmates" upon the person's returning would be that "they didn't need to collect all diagnoses like Pokemons", referring to the popular game. At some point, the name-giving to the clinician's impressions of the patient assumes truly bizarre forms and proportions, such as in the described examples. It is almost as though the clinicians believe that the more diagnoses the person receives, the better treatment they will get, or that giving new diagnoses will help them and others understand something about the patient's phenomenology that would otherwise be unfathomable. In fact, the need to develop psychiatric diagnoses to describe every pathological or otherwise problematic mental phenomenology suggests the awareness by psychiatry that something is lacking in its grasp of the substance and ontology of mental states. One of the problems here lies in the apparent lack of exactness and clear meanings of terms, which is quite uncharacteristic of medicine. However, a greater problem is the fact that the interactive field between the diagnostician and the client is not neutral: *it is an experiential space wherein both the client and the clinician articulate their own issues and projections*; thus, the often considerable differences in diagnoses and classifications given by various clinicians do not merely reflect the methodological inadequacies of psychiatry as a discipline, but, specifically, *the personality of the clinician* (Verhaeghe, 2008, pp. 228–229). The diagnosis takes place in a transferential relationship between the patient and the clinician, where both sides in that relationship contribute to the diagnosis. This is why a diagnosis is structural, and not strictly medical, where in the Lacanian tradition "structure" stands for an interpersonal relationship. Verhaeghe thus points out that the psychiatric diagnosis does not exist outside the relationship: a patient cannot be "disordered" on their own; their pathology is always constituted through an interaction, and a part of it rests on the pathology of the Other. Such a pathologising Other can be a significant and intimately close person, the society as a whole, or the diagnosing clinician himself.

In the interactive field of psychodiagnostics, and in psychotherapy, just like in the philosophical discourse, the interaction between the two interlocutors brings out the unresolved issues of *both interlocutors* to the surface. This is part of the reason why not every therapist is appropriate for every client, as therapists are predisposed in various ways to react and assume normative attitudes towards various aspects of their client's life and experience. The idea that the "training" of psychotherapist can be a substitute for this irreducible human character of self-recognition in the variety of problems and issues presented by the client is extremely naïve. While the psychotherapeutic training equips the therapists to relate to their clients in ways which do not impede self-disclosure and self-discovery, no conscientious psychotherapist will claim that they are able to withhold their own personal viewpoint from their interaction with the client. After all, this personal viewpoint is an integral part of the therapeutic relationship, and it is one of the main reasons clients find therapy empowering and satisfactory, or, alternatively, decide do move on to working with a different therapist. Clients in psychotherapy do not seek an impersonal, machine-like, normatively structured and relationally castrated therapist whose personality is amputated from the highly intimate process of building a therapeutic alliance. To the contrary, a successful and dynamic therapeutic process rests on the personality of the therapist as much as it does on the personality of the client.

In the described context, at least at times, it is difficult to say who is the client and who is the therapist; the actions and choices of each reflect their personal values and projections, including the clinician's perceptions and evaluations of the client. What the psychotherapist says about the patient is at least as indicative of the psychotherapist's personality as it might be about the client's issues. This is a methodological stumbling block that appears unsurmountable if one insists on viewing psychodiagnostics (and, by extension, the psych-professions) as science. To say that psychiatric diagnoses are nominalist categories means exactly that: these categories exist only in the mind of the diagnostician; they are not external realities, "illnesses" in the sense in which real medical diagnoses capture ontologically strong concepts: a tumor is something that can be scanned, measured by various indirect tests and removed, if necessary. The same goes for inflammation, which can be fought by drugs and the effects will be shown in tests. Psychiatric diagnoses do not "exist" in this way: a schizophrenic person is so in the mind of the psychiatrist and those who share their views, and this often includes the schizophrenic person herself. For other psychiatrists, the same person might be borderline, and for others they might be extremely creative, depending on the presentation of the psychosis. When we say that someone is "mentally ill," we do not really mean that they are ill: what we are saying is that the person is sufficiently unhappy, dysfunctional and odd that, according to certain criteria that we have put together to deal with such situations, they could be labelled as mentally disordered. People can be unhappy, dysfunctional and odd without being mentally ill, and they can be so quite consistently, across a prolonged time. There is no *necessary* connection between the nominal diagnostic criteria of a person exhibiting certain behavioral characteristics consistently, over a protracted time, on the one hand, and mental illness, on the other. The connection is fundamentally *arbitrary* in ways in which medical diagnoses of physical illnesses are not arbitrary, but unequivocal, as is the medical treatment and recovery in most cases. There is thus an element of realism in proper medical diagnoses: they exist outside the mind of the diagnostician, and they refer to actual states of affairs that correspond to observation and measurements in more or less uniform ways, whoever does the measurement or observation. Psychiatric diagnoses are fundamentally different: they are *nominalist concepts* that may be useful in describing and treating various individual difficulties, but these concepts do not actually refer to anything specific that exists in the patient in ways that most other people would have to agree with. In other words, according to Freud, a psychosis is merely a theory of reality; what makes it "pathological" is merely the fact that the diagnostician and a number of people who share the diagnostician's view do not agree with that theory (Verhaeghe, 2008, p. 52).

Nominalism is a view which stipulates that concepts exist merely as entities in our mind, that they don't necessarily correspond to any kind of "hard reality" outside the mind. This does not make nominalist concepts useless; they could be extremely helpful in many practical contexts, but one must always be careful not to assume that just because one takes a particular attitude towards something or someone that is based on a nominalist concept, and that attitude seems to produce the desired effects, the concept itself designates something real. Perhaps treating someone as a psychotic client and offering them the tolerance and understanding based on the assumption that they are delusional is indeed highly therapeutic for the person; it would be so, too, for someone who might behave in delusional ways without being mentally ill. The fact that our nominalist assumptions may be useful in practical contexts is not an epistemic confirmation that they can be treated as realist hypotheses.

I have recently worked with a young woman who was hospitalized several times because of her self-harming behavior, with a diagnosis of Borderline Personality Disorder. On her fifth hospitalization, the doctors seemed desperate as very strong therapies consisting of two antipsychotics, an antiepileptic, a sedative and an antidepressant seemed to wear off very quickly and her mental status degraded repeatedly. They resorted to lithium, and her mood stabilized to some extent. Some of the doctors then concluded that this was a diagnostic gamble, which proved that the girl was actually (also) bipolar. The fact that a drug is used to treat a particular diagnosis does not mean that it will stabilize moods only in people with that diagnosis, nor does the fact that this drug has a certain effect on a certain person mean that any assumption about the person's psychiatric diagnosis is thus confirmed. Such reasoning is seriously logically fallacious, but that does not change the fact that the particular treatment might be helpful and indeed necessary regardless of any realistic diagnosis. Nominalism does not imply that a concept should be dispensed with just because it does not designate anything outside the diagnostician's mind.

Realism, on the other hand, suggests that concepts are ideas which correlate with objective realities. Realism is based on a Platonic understanding of ideas as living essences, as the definitional characteristics of reality, so that all reality approximates ideas as its internal purpose. This would then mean that realistic concepts designate aspects of the external reality that are "mirrored" in the observer's mind, although imperfectly and in a distorted manner. Realism assumes that the reality is primarily external to the observer, that it is "objective", where the observer grasps the reality in an imperfect way, through one's limited epistemic capacities. This type of conceptualization of illness is appropriate to physical ailments, whose objective and bodily reality appears verifiable independently of any particular observer. That is why Paul Verhaeghe insists on the distinction between diagnoses in physical medicine, which are realistic, and psych diagnoses, which are nominalist, where psychodiagnostics exhibits what he calls "epistemic impotence" (Verhaeghe, 2008, pp. 46–56).

The two perspectives are methodically very different, but practically this difference tends to fade into insignificance, because of the overall subjective character of psychic experience.

Given that psychiatric diagnoses are not really medical diagnoses, but merely "words", which we seem to need as denominators for the currency of psychic life in a troubled individual, Verhaeghe concludes that the best we can contend with is the nominalist view (Verhaeghe, ibid.). Such a view implies that one works with classifications and psych-diagnostic descriptions as approximations, descriptive and interpretative narrative tools; however, one must always remind oneself not to take them too seriously. It is doubtful whether there is anything "out there" that corresponds to those words other than our own perceptions and interactions between our own projections, frustrations, values, and evaluations of our experience of our clients.

Psych-diagnoses, or stories that these diagnoses tell, are structural compensations within social relationships. On the one hand, given that each diagnostician reads into their diagnoses much of what they feel inside their own person, the psych-diagnosis tends to be partly a self-diagnosis of the diagnostician, in much the same way as the way in which a person speaks about others is to some extent a reflection of their opinion of themselves. We read our own issues into whatever we do and say. More importantly, however, psych-diagnoses compensate for various social structural inadequacies, in the sense that they are needed by various social actors who inhabit the space around the person who is diagnosed. This structural fact is witnessed, for example, by the widespread experience that families of psychotic patients often appear unprepared to accept the person's post-psychotic normalcy and functionality: they refuse to accept that the person has been healed, or that their psychosis is "in remission", and continue to treat the person as ill. They seem to "need" their family member to continue to be ill (Estrade et al., 2023). The story that they tell themselves and others about their family, their personal experience of their close ones and their difficulties has become an entrenched part of who they are in the community where they socially exist: changing that narrative once a post-psychotic improvement has occurred and the person seems well changes their own sense of self, and that experience may be highly unsettling. The family member's "staying ill" helps avert that painful self-transformation. Similar considerations apply to diagnosticians. By diagnosing others, clinicians tell stories about their views of mental illness, their own perceptions of their patients, and their relationships to them. A change in the diagnosis shakes the narrative, with consequences not just for the patient, but for the diagnostician, as well.

Logical Issues with Diagnoses

One of the general assumptions about most diagnoses of mental disorders involves the characterization that they are "lasting patterns of behavior and perception". One wanders here what a lasting pattern is, in light of the principle, mentioned in the Introduction, that each present reality, or modal world that we experience, is a balance of various contemporaneous states of affairs, some real, some less-than-real, all of which are more or less accessible to us. If the very concept of constancy is based on holding on to a particular state of affairs, it only makes sense against the assumption that there are alternative states of affairs that one could opt for: to be constant means to be opposite to being in change, and being in change requires the availability of change, namely a different state of affairs to which it is possible to change to from the current state of affairs. The same balance of various possibilities, or modal worlds, as various possible states of affairs at the same time, all of which are relatively accessible to the subject, accounts both for constancy and for change.

A "lasting pattern" of behavior and perception is nothing other than constancy in certain views, positions, attitudes, and mental processes and situations, which only makes sense against the assumption that a different pattern, or indeed the absence of any pattern, is equally possible and more or less accessible to the person, at the same time. The logical possibility of choosing A requires the availability of B. In other words, lingering in a particular mental state in a "stable and unchanging manner" simply means choosing not to change to a different mental state, which is the complementary logical possibility. Thus a "lasting pattern" means very little: it is a contingent fact that the person lingers in one mental situation, and the very distinction of that situation from what would be the alternative implies a possible alternative modal world. In order to classify someone's schizophrenia as a "stable, unchanging pattern", we automatically, logically assume that there is an alternative pattern, or indeed the absence of a pattern, which the patient could choose, in which case he would leave his current pattern, but the patient "chooses" (in some sense, and on some level, at least, though for psychotic patients such choice is far from obvious) to stay in this reality, though it is merely one of the possible realities. The patient thus makes the current reality "stable". There is an implication here that the person might at any moment choose to depart from a condition such as, e.g., schizophrenia, in which case their psychosis would no longer represent a "stable and unchanging pattern", and it is unclear whether in such a case the person would be clinically deemed to no longer have schizophrenia, namely how this departure would be interpreted in light of the "stable and lasting pattern" diagnostic ideology.

The above clinical conservatism with regard to abrupt recovery from psychosis in light of the assumption of lasting and stable characteristics of psychosis is similar to the conservatism of the narrative of family members of psychotic patients who sometimes refuse to accept their post-psychotic recovery. The clinician's term for distrust in the ability of the stable and lasting patterns to dissolve abruptly is "remission". The concept of "remission of psychosis" is predicated upon the assumption of psychosis as a stable and lasting pattern that is not easily changed or abandoned. In modal logical terms, psychosis is a modal world where the patient lives, and logically speaking (though this is of course practically more difficult), the patient can leave that modal world when certain conditions obtain. "Remission" is a concept contrary to modal logic: it assumes that leaving one modal world occurs against a tendency to return to that modal world. The same modal logic applies to families who distrust that their post-psychotic relatives are well. It is not easy for a psychotic person to get well in the eyes of either the close ones in their everyday life or of their diagnosticians, and a large part of this practical difficulty lies in the type of logic that we use when we think about psychosis.

One way to proceed with a consideration of the phenomenology of mental illness, instead of asking about the stability and unchangeability of the pattern of behavior, is to ponder on *the value of that pattern for the person* and their close ones. A related query is what alternatives there are for the person, and what is required for their "jump" to another, perhaps more optimal modal world, in terms of psychic realities, emotions, experiences, which might warrant them a generally better quality of life. With this type of questions, the proper modal understanding of the other person begins.

A particular type of compensatory pathology that is widely known is that associated with political clientelism. In politically corrupt systems, what makes numerous individuals support a destructive political party of elite tends to be a compensatory self-perception where morally problematic policies, views, and decisions are supported because the benefit to one's otherwise deficient sense of self-worth arises from one's association with the structures of power. Lacking internal structure and resources is easily compensated by access to or association with external power, including political power. Thus, individuals who, privately, condemn political decisions that are destructive act the opposite when it counts, namely when voting, voicing their opinions publicly, or deciding whether to join community initiatives. In some countries, such behavior is used to consolidate corrupt political decisions that lead to major environmental degradation, threats to human health or human rights. When individuals who act in a contradictory manner as reflected in their private views and their public persona or institutional engagement are observed in continuity, they basically satisfy many of the criteria typically attached to psychotic disorders. They have an unstable sense of self, distorted picture of reality, inconsistent views and values of others and of the society they live in. One wonders what kind of difference exists between someone who votes for the opening of a toxic mine in the vicinity of their community, where signs of pollution to the air, soil, and water abound and one is aware of them, while the same person privately expresses grave concerns over the health of one's family, friends, and neighbors should the mine open, and someone who beats their spouse and children, wages legal battles over child custody, and inflicts serious trauma on their children, while at the same time, privately, claiming that the wellbeing of their vulnerable family members is a top priority for them. Psychiatrists and psychotherapists often have a role in the latter type of cases, offering expert opinions typically based on "best interest of the children" or the vulnerable, where various parties to the conflict, claiming that protection of the children is their top priority, pursue strategies that directly victimize their children. There is always a reason behind such actions, where a tacit benefit for the person overrides the declared values and priorities the person espouses publicly or privately. In many cases, it is the sense of power that motivates individuals to act in ways which, when part of a complaint in the psychiatric office, would normally elicit a diagnosis of mental disorder. Our "disorders" are our strategies to deal with our modal worlds. Rather than shifting to a different modal world, one chooses the road of personal compromise and injury to one's integrity and that of one's community in order to "stay on top" of one's modal world. In large part, diagnoses are descriptions of such strategies to master the otherwise unpalatable modal world one finds oneself in.

From the point of view of Modal Integrative Psychotherapy, running in a circle of labels and diagnoses is often the wrong approach in the described sorts of cases. Where in the latter type of case, with child neglect in family issues, especially in divorces, diagnoses are often used as value-anchors to decide which parent is more suitable to exercise child custody, the real task of counseling and therapy in such cases is to philosophically, morally, ethically, and behaviorally rehabilitate individuals. In the latter case, diagnoses are largely useless. Such an approach requires discrimination and moral judgement. One's "mental disorders" are only nominalist descriptions of one's behavior, sensibility, and actions. They are merely depictions of the various modal worlds in which one lingers at one time or another. The real normative meaning of therapy is to set apart those modal worlds in which one would be a healthy, happy, productive, decent person, and identify strategies that are likely to lead one to jump to those modal worlds. Such is a strategy of guidance, discipline, and, indeed, moral treatment, effected through the mechanisms of therapeutic transfer and authority that permeate any quality relationship between a client and a therapist (Charland, 2015). On this view, a mental disorder is fundamentally a deficiency of one's sociality that is predicated upon one's modal worlds. The restoration of that sociality is therapy. Lacan considered sociality as the root of psychological normalcy. However, our interpretation of the client's or interlocutor's sociality depends on *our own sociality*. Once the discourse of pathology is translated into a discourse of values, two types of sociality, that of the patient and that of the diagnostician, come into direct contact. It is the interaction of these two styles and value structures of being social that trigger a fundamentally philosophical dialogue that Philippe Pinel and Luis Charland consider the crux of the moral treatment involved in talk therapy. This is why psychotherapy is always a philosophical discourse first of all, whether the therapist and the patient/client are explicitly aware of it or not (Verhaeghe, 2008, pp. 74–76).

Evil as a Disorder

One of the questions which come to mind when the value perspective is seen as the primary referential frame for psychotherapy is whether evil is a diagnosis, whether moral corruption is a mental disorder, and to what extent it factors in more commonly occurring mental problems. For example, the great prevalence of personality disorders faces us with this question particularly strongly. Are Cluster B Personality Disorders, which Charland considers exclusively moral, and not clinical disorders, ones that embody moral evil? Should individuals with such disorders be treated as somehow "disturbed" or mentally "disordered" because of the moral deficiencies inherent in such conditions? Is the evil of their actions a potential diagnosis?

This question is the juncture point for a potentially completely different way of thinking about psychiatric diagnoses than the traditional one. Psychiatry usually connects the existence of a mental disorder with some kind of personal experience which is painful, odd, and inhibiting for the person's social relationships. This way of interpreting especially psychoses has been challenged by modern Lacanians on different accounts, notably on what may be called "the subjectivity dimension of pathology". Jonathan Redmond thus argues that subjective psychic experience need not be a necessary criterion for the diganosis of schizophrenia, because there are numerous somatic schizophrenias, manifested only through bodily symptoms, such as automatisms in movement in cenesthesias (Redmond, 2014, pp. 1–2). Redmond draws on research by Eugen Bleuler about the so-called mild schizophrenias, which may later develop into a full-fledged schizophrenia, complete with delusions and hallucinations (Bleuler, 1987).

In the modern classifications, mild schizophrenias have been eliminated and a new category of personality disorders included instead, where in particular Borderline Personality Disorder or BPD has replaced mild schizophrenia (Gunderson, 1979; Redmond, 2014, p. 3). However, my challenge to the diagnosis of psychosis is the question of whether evil is the subject of psychotherapy. and whether evil can constitute the diagnosis of pyschosis, or any other mental disturbance (personality disorders are particularly apt candidates).

Given that the psychotherapist is a teacher, freely chosen, but still a teacher, with all the prerogatives of authority and leadership, normative judgements are inherent in any psychotherapeutic relationship, just as they are embedded in any philosophical discourse. Philosophy cannot ignore evil, and consequently, psychotherapy works with evil as a therapeutic problem.

One can define evil in different ways, either as malignant narcissism (Peck, 1983) or as intent to harm others, or even as enjoyment of inflicting pain and deprivation on others, and potentially on oneself. There is myriad of ways to formulate evil, but one element is common to them all: the element of *malignancy*, or some kind of darkness harnessed by the person's choices whereby the person becomes insensitive to others' suffering or to one's own responsibility for anothers' pain.

Malignancy is associated with a lack of value judgement of one's own choices. One's proneness to "bracket out" judgements about oneself facilitates malignancy. Just as Modal Integrative Psychotherapy, unlike some schools of traditional psychotherapy, rejects any kind of normative neutrality or a priori acceptance and encouragement of the client's value system, it also rejects the medicalization of evil which renders it morally neutral. Evil is not a medical condition. It is a moral deficiency. The malignancy in evil is the malignancy of values, not a physiological malignancy, like that of a tumor. The conceptualization of *evil* remains in the domain of *personal identity*, which is based on personal values.

Unlike serious psychoses, which appear to destroy the subjective identity narrative and hamper any consistent relationship between the self and the world, evil does not require a disturbance in the systematic relationship between the subject and the subject's world (Freud, 1924, 1957; Miller, 2009). However, there is still a disturbance in the substance of that relationship. The reason evil is traditionally not considered a mental disorder is that mental health and mental illness tend to be defined in functional terms, the former supposedly involving a coherent, non-contradictory, functional relationship with others and with one's society, while the latter tends to be seen as some kind of inability to be functionally effective, to systematically, consistently maintain an identity, a job, a set of relationships with others, etc. Thus, the systematic nature of a person's relationships with others appears to be the key to mental health, traditionally concerned. Conversely, a jammed, torn, or tangled narrative, which lacks structure and stability, is considered a sign of mental disturbance.

The problem with the above traditional view of normalcy is that various values, including malignant ones, can be solidified into a stable narrative. Various villains throughout history, and especially various well-organized groups of villains, have had very stable narratives, highly structured and predictable relationships with others, to the extent of maintaining a rigid, militaristic ideology of crime and systematic infliction of pain on others, while at the same time these same malignant individuals, in their private lives, were seen as reliable husbands, parents, sons, and daughters. In other words, there is nothing in a stable personality structure that guarantees the health or vitality of the substance of that stability. Evil can be stable, just as virtue can be unstable. In fact, it is doubtful whether stability is a desirable value in general: people change and grow because they are unstable. Stability stifles growth and leads to a calcification of the same old normative structures. A stable evil is more damaging that an unstable evil. Structure without substance does not necessarily lead to beneficial results; the question is obviously what it is that is well structured, and thus made stable. A stable problem is a persistent problem.

The value of instability in psychotherapy comes across in one additional aspect of it: in order to change, a person must first be *uncomfortable* with the way they are. One must be *troubled* by one's ways in order to seek help and develop a desire to change. This trouble manifests as an instability and may present a mental illness as its phenomenology. Such mental illness is much better, and much more constructive for the person's future, than the mental "health" and stability of an evil person. Thus, to change someone, one must first create conditions under which that person would start to be uncomfortable with the way they are. This is a part of how child upbringing works, where intervening upon undesirable traits in a child's behavior requires making the child uncomfortable, first with the consequences of that behavior (various sanctions or changed communication by the parents) and subsequently with the behavior itself. Importantly (and this is often neglected) the process of change requires affirming and praising the desirable behavior, not just taking it for granted. The relationship between a psychotherapist and a client is very similar to the described aspect of the parental relationship. This structure of relations stretches throughout society: we become socialized by social affirmations and, conversely, by social negations of our choices and values. In life partnerships the process is the same: we socialize ourselves into relationships by a system of affirmations and denials. This mechanism goes beyond the simple conditioning: it is a socially mediated structure of self-perception where the other person is a gateway to values that become our own.

In Lacanian psychoanalysis, the primary Other is the fatherly figure as the key agent of socialization and at the same time the constituent of psychological normalcy. Though Lacan is generally a structuralist, his account of normalcy as proper socialization is substantive. To be mentally healthy, one must be socialized through the main signifier—Name of the Father—and conversely, all mental disturbances result from either the *blockage* of Name of the Father (neuroses) or from the *absence or removal* of Name of the Father (psychoses) (Redmond, 2014, pp. 20–23). Structure serves to solidify and stabilize the substantive values, and it is the nature of these values that primarily determines whether a person can be considered healthy or unhealthy. The Father, in Lacan's context, makes us healthy or unhealthy for it is through the eye of the familial, fatherly other that we articulate ourselves.

When faced with evil, the psychotherapist intervenes by reasoning, however in a way which will destabilize the evil. Where the person is content with an evil structure of values (such as a narcissistic system of values, indifferent to others' emotions, interests, and condition), the most obvious sign of effectiveness of the therapeutic intervention will be an initial worsening of the person's psychological situation, namely the crumbling of the structure which keeps the person stable. This is at once contrary to the person's desires and interests at a particular point of time (the person suffers as a result of the "treatment"), and it is also in the person's long-term interest, much the same as a surgical intervention in medicine causes pain and displeasure at present, initially leading to a worsening of the patient's situation (the patient walks into the hospital for surgery, but is wheeled out after surgery and requires intensive care until they recover) in order for the patient to get better in the longer term, or to prevent them from getting much worse. The evil person is similarly destabilized in order to re-develop a different normative structure in the future, one they can then rely on. This is the militant part of therapeutic intervention which, while potentially discomforting in appearance, is logically soundly established: until one structure (in this case, structure of evil) is dismantled, no new structure can be erected in its place.

Some early accounts of psychosis, especially schizophrenia, mention the "absence of authenticity and depth" of feelings and perceptions of the world and one's social relationships as the most destructive aspect of psychosis, even when the person is otherwise stable and can establish functional routines and communication patterns that keep them afloat in interpersonal relationships (Deutsch, 1942).

The fact that somebody knows what they are expected to feel and say in particular situations does not substitute for one's spontaneous perceptions and feelings of the situations one finds oneself in. Acting out one's emotions is not the same as having emotions. Thus, one wonders whether an evil person, who narcissistically fails to empathize with others who suffer, and who in fact inflicts pain on others, might be considered psychotic, for such persons clearly lack authenticity and depth of feelings, especially of social emotions such as solidarity, trust, or empathy. It is no wonder that persons who are rational calculators of interest with no capacity to dampen such calculations by feelings for others, less fortunate than they, are sometimes colloquially described as "monsters". There is something uncanny and frightening in a purely selfish rationality which is not offended by the pain and agony of other people: it is in fact very close to Helene Deutch's account referenced above.

Reaching out to others, in feelings and in action, is what keeps us away from the darkness of our narcissism and our potential disregard for the dignity of another person. Hence, such social emotions can be considered the spring of mental health. Moral corruption, on the other hand, tends to arise from an enlarged focus on ourselves and our own needs, with the concomitant diminution of others, their rights and interests. In other words, malignant narcissism is inherent in moral deviance. If such narcissism, and the evil which envelops actions arising from narcissism, can be seen as a pathology, then moral faults would also be definable as pathologies. Such faults, if they are radical, are described in social sciences as "social pathology". Much of the argument that Luis Charland puts forward for the moral treatment of personality disorders (and Pinel talks about the moral treatment of all psychopathology) is based on the idea that a disregard for externality, for the others and for the society, forms the morally critical core of much psychopathology (Charland, 2015). The sense of common virtue, which determines the identity of a community and, correspondingly, crucially articulates the individualities within that community, is darkened in at least large swaths of psychopathology overall (Fatic, 2016).

"The good life"

One of the more general goals of psychotherapy is what ancient philosophy describes as achieving "the good life". While conceptualizations of the good life differ widely, generally the ancient schools associate it with a life of inner satisfaction. This means that, while psychopathology as a cause of psychic pain retracts from the quality of life, the role of psychotherapy is not limited to addressing psychopathology, because even healthy persons can be unhappy, lack satisfaction in their everyday efforts, and live a life that is less good than it could be. Thus, psychotherapy is a logical and philosophical structure within which values of the good life are discussed, at least as much as the complaints associated with psychological and broader experiential issues. MIP is a form of psychotherapy that places the entire realm of psychotherapy, both that focused on addressing pathology and that striving to attain the good life, in a modal logical perspective. Such a logical perspective on the entire psychotherapeutic process is relevant both methodologically, because it helps us to critically examine our own methods and interventions in light of the logical principles that govern our approach, and existentially. The way in which we interpret our experience and reality is inevitably predicated on some kind of logic, whether we use it consciously or unconsciously, and the ability to invoke a powerful logic explicitly in one's decision-making and interpretation of one's experience is existentially highly empowering. Modal logic is particularly capable of triggering personal change because it layers the reality, or our circumstances, without limiting us to what is actual or "real", thus facilitating decisions and life strategies that might shift the entire logical plain on which we encounter a particular life issue.

The various modern ideas of the good life also incorporate suffering. From the infamous story of Epicurus, who died surrounded with friends and stated that he was about to have a good death because the pleasure of conversations with friends was greater than the pain of illness that killed him, to the more recent accounts of the good life being lived even against the most extreme experiences, such as that of a concentration camp, suffering has been incorporated either into a composite concept of "pleasure overall", where pleasure exceeds suffering, as in Epicurus, or into an alternative view of "meaning" as inclusive of the suffering that "makes sense" (Frankl, 2006; Rist, 1980). A good life can be a life of sacrifice, a life of pain, which the person chooses and embraces. In such a life, the person makes sacrifices for a value which one feels gives meaning and value to one's life. For many people, sacrificing themselves for the welfare of their children means living a meaningful life. Others make sacrifices and accept difficulty in order to advance justice. A life permeated with meaning is often interpreted as a good life, regardless of what that meaning is, as long as it is fulfilling for the person and beneficial to society. The ancient Greek interpretation of this interplay between suffering and joy within what is generally a good life was mediated by the concept of virtue. On this reading, to possess virtue means to be able to navigate between various values, so that one is both personally satisfied (or happy), at least on some level, and socially recognized as a valuable member of the community. For Ancient Greeks, virtue included both the enjoyment of life and the observance of moral standards of one's society. Thus, virtue involved prudence and a certain skill in living one's life and was always predicated on the values of the community (Fatic, 2016).

The ancient understanding of the good life cuts to the very core of psychotherapy: the aim of therapeutic intervention is to increase the quality of one's life in ways which, at the same time, contribute to society. When the psychotherapist works with evil, such labor is corrective and, along Pinel's lines, requires a "moral reformation". However, in most cases psychotherapy is a leadership exercise, where both the client and the psychotherapist explore the conceptual and practical underpinnings of virtue, both as a moral normative standard and as a practical skill in living a good life. It is *virtue as the practical implementation of values* that we seek through psychotherapy. Virtue, in the broad, composite sense, encompasses both a responsibility to others and the talent and skill to balance life's satisfactions. While our whole picture of the good life may be just a nominalist narrative, where our personal experiences may not correspond to anything "real" outside our own mental coordinates, this does not change the relevance of the experiences themselves. As long as we don't pretend that what we feel or perceive is "real" in the ontologically strong sense, as something that gives rise to our sensations, rather than our perceptions and ideation being a narrative of its own, this nominalist perspective allows us to weave the good life in whatever way is both satisfying to the individual and socially acceptable. This means that our "diagnoses" in psychiatry are nominalist labels relating to the narrative, not to "objective", "measurable" realities. While an inflammation or a tumor, as I mentioned earlier, are something that verifiably gives rise to various narratives in various individuals, within various cultures, but invariably requires treatment and does have an "objective" ontological core, psychiatric "diseases" are diseases of the narrative itself; they do not venture outside the moving pictures of our subjective perceptions of what may or may not be the "reality" in any objectively recognizable sense.

One of the most illuminating modern philosophers who spoke about the good life in the context of a balance of perceptions is Schopenhauer, who sees life as a series of objectifications of the general will that moves the world, where the insatiable desire to achieve, move, and change is the subjectively felt work of the will in the human being, powered in turn by a desire for satisfaction (fulfilment of wishes and desires, a sense of power and ability to reach the targets of the will) and the experience of pain (the sense of absence, what Lacan called "lack"). According to Schopenhauer, the latter (the inability to attain fulfillment) is a source of pain, and it occurs when the will cannot attain its immediate striving; however, the successful completion of a quest, after an initial experience of satisfaction, eventually also leads to pain, because the absence of want, of desire, causes boredom, as it is also contrary to the will's internal impulse to constantly exert itself, to move and change. Thus, a good life, or a reasonably happy life, would be one where instances of achievement followed by want and desire would occur sequentially and frequently, so that boredom has no opportunity to set in, and yet the pain of failure to achieve the immediate goals of the will does not occur, because one's tasks are relatively easy to achieve, yet sufficiently significant to give one satisfaction (Schopenhauer, 1966, pp. 315–320). Schopenhauer's strategy for counseling would be to educate the client that there is a predetermined capacity for satisfaction in every person (Lacan would call it *jouissance*), and for suffering, as well, and that this capacity largely depends on individual character. Some individuals react more joyfully to bright events in their lives and more sorrowfully to the dark ones than other individuals; the intensity of this reaction, according to Schopenhauer, depends on the strength of one's "will to live", on one's existential energy and zeal. Whatever our capacity to be happy or to suffer, it will not change in the course of our lives: once a particular reason to rejoice or to grieve disappears, another will move into the same "slot". Thus, the present difficulty or pain is, in a sense, a vaccine against another type of pain, which might be more hurtful, given that every pain is a frustration of the will to live from flowing smoothly and attaining its aims. Schopenhauer is thus close to the Stoics in arguing that keeping pain at a minimum, while balancing one's satisfactions, is as close to the good life as possible.

The various attempts throughout philosophical history and modern psychotherapeutic theory to capture the good life have largely determined the values of the respective therapeutic approaches. Perhaps one of the most significant perspectives in modern social theory and psychotherapy is the one that sees the social dimension of one's existence, namely the dependency of the good life on good social arrangements and functioning institutions, as decisive in achieving a relative personal wellbeing. That is why social arrangements are irreducible elements of effectiveness of psychotherapy.

Too often, psychotherapeutic interventions insist on remaining blind to the dependency between the individual good life and the surrounding quality of social arrangements, as though it is somehow obviously possible to live a good life amid bad social arrangements. Indeed this might be possible, but more as an exception than as a rule. For example, it is possible, temporarily, to have a "good life" amid the ruins of extremely bad social relationships and culture, if one is, for example, in love, and thus oblivious to the general degradation that surrounds them. However, such temporary states of elation despite the surroundings tend to pass quickly and the reality of the conditions in which one lives comes back into the picture with a vengeance. Society is the context of our life, just the same as personal relationships are the very structure of our mental well-being, which cannot be separated from our social well-being.

MIP disagrees with the normative subjectivism that is characteristic of much traditional psychotherapy, whereby it is assumed that the norms that individuals chose for themselves are psychologically "valid" merely because they have been "freely" chosen by the subject. This idea, which is intended to support the autonomous identity of the subject is fundamentally flawed. The subject must consider a world of which the subject is only a part. Even if one adopts philosophical subjectivism, one still must consider the ramifications of a universalization of one's personal choices. Subjectivism is a form of ethics whereby we make our own norms, *as long* as we would be prepared to live in a modal world *where everybody else would choose and follow the same norms.* Sometimes, this type of subjectivism is also called "subjective universalism" (Fishkin, 1984). Subjectivism in applied ethics suggests that our choices of values and actions, which presumably lead to a good life for us, if made identically by other people, would also contribute to what we would consider a good life for us. This is an important element of universality which makes subjectivism socially relevant; otherwise, it would merely be a form of relativism. It is a normative context in which most traditional psychotherapy operates.

While the psychotherapist works with the individual choices and values of the client, they maintain a degree of critical judgement as far as the normative choices made by the client must be able to be acceptable to the client *if others made the same choices.* Just like with general subjectivism in ethics, this gives traditional psychotherapy social validity.

MIP goes further and sees subjectivism as insufficient for a lasting change, or for moral reformation, re-education, or even for the general education of the interlocutor in psychotherapy towards achieving a good life. If the realization of the good life is dependent on society, then the MIP therapist will address both the experiential processes, on a subjective level (including the normative conceptualizations of social reality and the client's choices), *and at the same time the social processes* which cause misery. This is a broader task: for example, in a case of discrimination, the MIP therapist will work with the victim of discrimination, but will also address, in public, or through other available forms of exerting influence, the social pressures that help generate and maintain the structures of discrimination. This positions MIP as a therapeutic approach both for individuals and for the society as a whole. Like in MIP, for most ancient schools, philosophy was a therapy for the person *and* for the society; this was considered self-explanatory as otherwise philosophy as a mere theoretical discipline aimed at perfecting arguments would have been considered superfluous (Nussbaum, 1994).

MIP's focus on the good life, in addition to addressing psychopathology, brings ethics into the substantive picture of therapy in a prominent way. It makes MIP close to the affective psychotherapy of Pinel because it positions a quest for virtue at the very center of the psychotherapeutic process. The concept of virtue involved here is not a restrictive one, associated with judgmental attitudes about the person's preferences and choices; it is the ancient concept of virtue that combines a skill to balance one's satisfactions and one's pain, on the one hand, and to contribute to society, or at least, live in a broad alignment with society, on the other. The virtue at stake is a skill and a sensibility, or a style of sociality—not a standard of judgement.

An interesting event occurred with regard to the concept of the good life and the ancient concept of virtue during the 2024 Paris Olympic Games, which were ongoing during the writing of this chapter. In a women's boxing bout between Imane Khelif of Algiers and Angela Carini of Italy, the latter boxer quit after just 45 seconds of the match, after receiving the first blow. She then sat on the mat and burst into tears exclaiming that "this was not fair" and that Imane Khelif was in fact a transgender man who was allowed to fight as a woman. A salvo of public condemnation was triggered against the Olympic Committee and Khelif herself, even as information surfaced proving that Imane was neither transgender, nor a man. As it turned out, Imane Khelif was born a girl, raised a girl, started training as a girl, competed in Algiers as a girl, won the Algiers national women's championship, competed with a number of women in the international arena, and was defeated by several of them. The controversy at the 2024 Olympics was sparked by Khelif's apparently heightened levels of testosterone and biochemical tests that had caused the discredited International Boxing Federation to disqualify her from a previous competition. One of the boxers who had defeated Khelif, Amy Broadherst, came to her defense saying that the hate against the Algerian boxer victimized an innocent person, as Khelif acted in good faith and had previously been beaten by nine women, which clearly showed that she had no critical advantage over other women (The Independent, 2024).

The controversy, which saw a considerable amount of hate speech aired against the Algerian athlete, marked a confusion about how society sees one's life narrative and one's entitlements to pursue what one sees as the good life. A person who has lived her whole life as a woman was suddenly questioned as to whether she was really a woman because someone found her punches "too hard" and, perhaps more likely, because to many people she did not look sufficiently "womanly". Hence, science was called to aid, to count her blood cells and her chromosomes, to establish whether she had more or less testosterone than another woman she fought, and to disqualify, degrade, and derogate her successes and her very identity publicly. While equality in the sports has different faces, ranging from the limitations of sex, weight, and discipline to issues of the use of stimulants, including testosterone, once the issue of inequality of natural ability is pushed too far, it militates against an individual's freedom to pursue their vision of the good life. The fact that someone finds a woman, who has lived her whole life as a woman, in a culture that is anything but tolerant of trans-sexuality, too "manly" for their taste to compete against other women, encourages the acting out of public infantilism, where an Olympic boxer receives a single punch and then sits on the mat crying that it was "too strong". Such infantilism makes it possible, and in some way publicly "proper", to victimize those who do not fit in. It is telling in this case that no psychotherapists voiced their opinion on this scandal. The political arguments flouted in public raged unabridged and created an atmosphere of lynching the Algerian athlete. Her life narrative, her identity, her community, family, friends, her career, and her emotional wellbeing were all victims to someone's decision to sit on the mat and cry against a superior opponent. Such a social setting destroys the prospects of the best athletes and infringes on their mental health, because it turns out to be more important to fit with the political correctness of the time than to train, hit hard, and excel in the discipline. Even someone's existence is, in a way, questioned by such militant social discourse that easily leads to the canceling of individuals based on how they look and whether they are more or less "manly" or "womanly" in the eyes of society.

In the perspective of MIP, the above is an example of how society can need psychotherapy as much as an individual person might, and of how the need for involvement of psychotherapists in public discourse in such a case borders with political activism. It is a sensitive but important topic. Can and should psychotherapy involve political activism as a form of psychotherapy and standing for the values of the psychotherapeutic calling?

For philosophers, the answer to this question has never been controversial; it was an unequivocal "yes", and many have paid a heavy price for their public exposure and courage to advocate values contrary to those endorsed by the masses or the powers that be. With psychotherapists, the situation has been different: it remains a largely open question whether a psychotherapist's mission is to speak publicly on social and cultural matters, and whether such speech is considered collective therapy or not. Freud, of course, saw his mission to criticize the culture and society as an integral part of his psychoanalytic work and his life path, and so did many other psychotherapists of the older generation (Adler, Jung, and others). More recently, however, psychotherapy has at least partly shied away from public activism and has tried to find a refuge among the narrow and strictly "professional" vocations, huddling particularly closely to psychiatry and psychology. Many a destructive period in recent social and cultural history has passed without a major psychotherapists' public outcry or critique, including, infamously, of course, the Nazi period, and afterwards the long decades of communist abuse of psychiatry to detain and destroy political opponents, followed by the current raging controversies over the new forms of political correctness and the resurgence of nationalistic state and the racist and apartheid politics. One wonders if it is possible to pursue a good life in an environment where one civilized state abhorrently ignores any international order or human rights and systematically kills tens of thousands of civilian people, destroys universities and the infrastructure of an entire society, or where a culture arbitrarily victimizes athletes because of their physical appearance, their femininity or masculinity in appearance, and threatens to undermine the very rules and value guarantees embedded in the Olympic games. How can we speak of psychotherapy without being vocal about the social conditions that make psychotherapy not only impossible, but bizarre?

Any social engagement by a philosopher, and likewise by a psychotherapist, is Socratic in the sense that it carries an inherent risk to the philosopher as an individual, and hence, represents a personal sacrifice, either potential or actual. This sacrifice, at the same time, is a statement of the therapist's, or philosopher's, own values. The fact that voicing an opinion about a particular culture might lead to someone's being "cancelled" from one's profession, whatever that opinion might be if it is against the culture, then the cancelation might come from within that culture, and if it is in favor of a culture (such as a culture of tolerance or affirmation of particular rights), then the cancelation might come from the newly rising nationalistic and racist right wing politics—should not prevent a philosopher or a psychotherapist from making one's views public if one believes that this issue has psychological consequences and exerts a relevant impact on individual and collective wellbeing. However, the cancelations, professional or broader, moral and social, are a continuation of the repressive sanctioning of dissenting views. Addressing such practices is a part of the psychotherapist's public role, just as it is a part of the philosopher's role. In this context, MIP is an activist modality, or school. While the narratives that the MIP therapist works with are fundamentally, ontologically nominalist, the social conditions within which these narratives unfold are not nominalist: they exert a real and tangible influence on the subjective pictures of reality of all those involved. A society that is pathological or toxic, as many contemporary societies are, presents a challenge to the psychotherapist as much as to the social scientist. As Freud made it obvious, working with culture is a part of working with individual people.

References

Bleuler, E. (1987). The prognosis of Dementia Praecox: The group of Schizophrenias. In J. Cutting & M. Shepard (Eds.), *The clinical roots of the Shizophrenia concept* (pp. 59–74). Cambridge University Press.

Charland, L. (2015). Moral treatment. Wiley Online Library. Retrieved September 15, 2024, from https://doi.org/10.1002/9781118625392.wbecp094

Deutsch, H. (1942). Some forms of emotional disturbance and their relationship to Schizophrenia. *Psychoanalytic Quarterly, 11*, 301–321.

Estrade, A., Onwumere, J., Venables, J., Gilardi, L., Cabrera, A., Rico, J., Hoque, A., Otaiku, J., Hunter, N., Keri, P., Kpodo, L., Sunkel, C., Bao, J., Shiers, D., Bonoldi, I., Kuipers, E., & Poli, P. F. (2023). The lived experiences of family members and carers of people with psychosis: A bottom-up review co-written by experts by experience and academics. *Psychopathology, 56*(5), 371–382.

Fatic, A. (2016). *Virtue as identity: Emotions and the moral personality.* Rowman and Littlefield International.

Fishkin, J. (1984). *Beyond subjective morality.* Yale University Press.

Frankl, V. (2006). *Man's search for meaning.* Beacon Press. Originally published in 1946.

Freud, S. (1924, 1957). The loss of reality in Neurosis and Psychosis. In J. Strachey (Ed. and Trans.). *The Standard Edition of the Complete Psychological Works of Sigmund Freud, XIX*: 181–188.

Gunderson, J. (1979). The relatedness of borderline and schizophrenic disorders. *Schizophrenia Bulletin, 5*, 17–22.

Miller, J.-A. (2009). Ordinary psychosis revisited. *Psychoanalytic Notebooks of the European School of Psychoanalysis, 19*, 139–168.

Nussbaum, M. (1994). *The therapy of desire: Theory and practice in Hellenistic ethics.* Princeton University Press.

Peck, S. (1983). *People of the lie: The hope for healing human evil* (2nd Touchstone ed.). Simon and Schuster.

Redmond, J. (2014). *Ordinary psychosis and the body. A contemporary Lacanian approach.* Palgrave Macmillan.

Rist, J. M. (1980). Epicurus on friendship. *Classical Philology, 75*(2), 121–129.

Schopenhauer, A. (1966). *The world as will and represenation* (E. F. J. Payne, Trans.). Dover Publications.

The Independent. (2024, August 2). Boxer who beat Imane Khelif at 2022 World Championship speaks out about Olympic gender controversy. Retrieved September 10, 2024, from https://www.independent.co.uk/sport/olympics/imane-khelif-boxing-gender-controversy-olympics-amy-broadhurst-b2590060.html

Verhaeghe, P. (2008). *On being normal and other disorders.* Karnac Press.

CHAPTER 4

The Context of Psychotherapy: The Geometry of Motivation

Abstract This chapter discusses the structure of motivation, including the balance of motives, developing a comprehensive account of motivational and behavioural compensations. An overarching principle of the geometry of motivation is that of symmetry, where experience, values, and sensibility all play a part in how a person will approach what could broadly be considered a life project and how one will address important individual situations faced in life. The key role of modality and modal thinking in general in understanding the symmetry of motivation is reflected in the particular choices a person makes seen as geometrical outcomes or an interplay of various motivational directions. In psychosis, where a disturbed reality defines the person's experience of the world, a particular geometry of motivation remains as basic structure.

Keywords Motives • Decisions • Symmetry • Values • Sensibility • Choices

Motives and Decisions

There is a popular saying among psychotherapists that "healthy people come for help, while sick people get brought in for treatment against their will". This general experiential view, mainly by hospital psychiatrists (private psychotherapists cannot treat anyone against their will) has

A. Fatic, *Modal Integrative Psychotherapy*,
https://doi.org/10.1007/978-3-031-91934-3_4

ramifications in the field of what motivates us for choices that later become a source of our troubles that lead us to seek therapeutic help.

The dissatisfactions that mark the beginning of any successful process of self-change in psychotherapy are motivated by a desire to delve deeper into oneself. Somewhat deceitfully, this desire is sometimes called "self-change", while in fact, in most cases, it is a drive to peel off the layers of inauthenticity that the society has placed on the individual through the process of socialization and to establish an understanding and acceptance of one's own values. While, on the one hand, our values are shaped by our socialization, on the other they are predicated upon our individual sensibility whose articulation is largely arbitrary. This is what is often called "neurodivergence": individuals who are born and raised in the same society and under similar conditions and values tend to be vastly different in their innermost emotions and propensities to choose a lifestyle, if they are not too strongly pressured by the prevailing societal norms. This is obvious in liberal and laxly regulated societies, where various types of alternative life-styles flourish that, in more strict and conservative societies, may often be deemed deviant. In many ways, the psychotherapeutic process shows that our own self-discovery is predicated upon the accumulation of considerable life experience, whereby we discover who we really are, what our individual, private sensibility is, and even what we believe or disbelieve within the range of publicly recognized values.

The described process of "pealing the onion" through experience—one that ought to result in greater self-knowledge—sometimes leads the person to look with disapproval at their past decisions or to feel difficulty in relating to them. For example, having acted in a conformist way before might become repugnant to a person who, through various life experiences (various relationships, health issues, and sometimes a brush with death), has pealed much of the onion of one's Self, under which their character is hidden. The continuity of their life narrative becomes threatened by such experiences and they sense difficulties in relating who they feel they are to their earlier choices, actions, and perceptions of them by other, important people in their lives. One particularly clear-cut situation of this type is when a person, living one's whole life in an apparent harmony with one's neighbors, family, and society, survives a life-threatening illness and emerges from the hospital a changed person, with entirely different priorities. The experience has made it barren to them just what their most important values are and to what extent compromising those values in order to satisfy the society, the family, or someone else reduces the quality of their (short) life. This is a narrative we often hear in therapy from those who have recovered from major heart surgery or from cancer survivors. When these individuals return to their families and their communities, they often induce a degree of disarray of the established relationships, in much the same way as a post-psychotic person, having recovered, disturbs the balance of roles and power in their familiy and is often not recognized as a fully functional, responsible members of the family or the community. Similarly, recovering from hypocrisy is always disturbing, whether one was aware of the hypocrisy or not, for society is based on well-structured hypocrisies in order to maintain stability. We pretend to like our neighbors and smile when we meet them even if we do not like them, or even resent them; we do the same to the traffic officer who stops us for a banal traffic infringement while we are facing a terribly bad day and are on our way to attending to another important and possibly stressful task. We do not tell our wives, husbands, girlfriends, or boyfriends that we do not love them anymore, unless particular, exceptional circumstances motivate us to do so. We do not tell our governments that their pressure on democracy and free speech is sickening, unless, in statistically very rare situations, several catalysts accelerate social discontent and turn it into mass demonstrations or revolution. At any synchronic moment, our motives tend to be insufficient and unclear when we move against our own hypocrisy and that of others. However, in a diachronic perspective, over time, through personal development, the process of pealing the onion or moving deeper into our character inevitably exposes a myriad of micro-hypocrisies that we have been a part of, sometimes without noticing it.

What we discuss as personal change, thus, tends to be a process of self-discovery, rather than the invention of a new self. Even in situations where a seemingly new life is forged, the essence of such "change" is a return to the deeply embedded sensibilities and desires that often, subjectively, make the person feel as though one has "come home". This experience is perhaps the most obvious in individuals who choose the monastic life at a mature age. Often, new monks arrive in the monastery from a life of excesses and a sense of emptiness. They spend some time in the monastery preparing for their vows, with a daily routine that is dramatically different from what they are used to. Yet, those who stay experience a strange sense of finally having arrived home. They gradually "invent a new Self" when they begin to spiritually motivate and structure their lives and the lives of those who seek advice and guidance from them. Their inner experience is one of having allowed a deeper core of their desires and values to surface through, and often against, the long learned structures of behavioral patterns, beliefs, and habits that had solidified by repeated social practice in their families and communities. The psychotherapeutic process is very much the same in principle, where what others perceive as major personal change is usually subjectively experienced as having left the "inauthenticity" of the life previously lived. Yet, the social structure of our self-perception (its dependency on relationships with others) is so strong and pervasive that even the triggering of such a move toward self-discovery depends on fortuitous social conditions.

To delve deeper into personal exploration, the person must experience discomfort in the present situation that is not muted or distorted by the social structure one is immersed in. For example, if one is trapped in a non-stimulating environment or group, with bad, low standards, even corrupt practices, with abundant superficial satisfactions and little incentive for reflection, the chances for change are slim. If the community sets low standards, or if it openly encourages impropriety and degrades opportunities for critical reflection, both public and private, then the prospects for improvement of its members will be greatly hampered.

The above is obvious with individuals working in bureaucracy and committing the so-called administrative evil. People who conduct their administrative business in groups operating through protocols that are below standard, but demand less effort, often reach retirement age without ever questioning their practices toward others and their very relationships with themselves. Again, good examples are those bureaucrats who serve in the authoritarian regimes that inflict immense suffering on innocent people. Many of those people are ordinary individuals, good neighbors, gentle parents, and, generally, community members who do not see themselves as instrumental to any wrongdoing. They are cushioned in an evil that, from the inside of the evil bubble itself, does not even seem evil. Their propensity for self-examination and self-discovery is anaesthetized. When the rude awakening comes, usually after dramatic social changes, in the form of trials or lustration policies, only then do they discover the moral status of their coalescence in evil. The structural stability of a normative system can irritate or hystericize individuals into self-change or, to the contrary, cushion and insulate them from on critical thought; this depends on their positions in a stable social structure, their sensibilities, and their interests.[1] Even in the most authoritarian circumstances, the free spirits were not soldiers, prison guards, or government bureaucrats, but those who had the free time and fortuitous professions to unbox themselves from the confines of ideology and repression by state institutions: philosophers, psychiatrist, artists, activists.

A person's identity is based on the their values and sensibility. The values and sensibility are mutually connected and articulate each other (Fatic, 2016). Self-change is thus a delving into the deeper structures of values and the process of discovery of core sensibilities that require both a degree of discomfort with the present identity and a sufficiently stimulative, or at least permissive, social and existential circumstances to assume a critical stance toward what is the case, namely the current modal world, and to venture on a calling of a different modal world into one's reality. This is easier for free spirits than for those caught firmly in the grips of institutions or state interests. Philosophers and psychotherapists will find it easier, in general, to envision alternative modal worlds than policemen or bureaucrats (exceptions granted); they thus tend to be the movers of change for others. In fact, psychotherapy and all forms of personal counselling are largely a structured induction to envisioning a different modal world for many.

[1] At least in psychoanalysis, the successful analysis typically aggravates the dormant issues in the analysand and thus "hystericizes" them, to use Freud's concept. Without this initial disturbance, it would be difficult to expect that unconscious content could be brought to light, becauses the reason it is unconscious, i.e. repressed, is that it is disturbing or unacceptable to the person. A similar principle applies to any in-depth process of self-discovery. What one discovers about oneself in therapy is what one is normally unaware of, and the reason for this lack of awareness is that the content is usually incompatible with one's self-imposed views, roles, values, and other normative positions. Such positions are a part of our socialization. The suggestion of MIP is not that by "peeling the layers" of one's inauthenticity (what Winnicott calls one's "false self") one undoes socialization, for socialization is a pillar of our psychological normalcy. To the contrary, the peeling process allows one's internal reorganization in a way that does not impede one's sociality, but rather in a way that allows the person to more freely choose the modalities of articulating and implementing that sociality. For example, one's ability to change jobs, places of living, or views on important aspects of life can take place within one's high level of social functionality; in fact, such a self-discovery can increase one's sociality by making the more authentic desires and sensibilities more impactful on how one contributes to one's community. A person who, proverbially, resigns a job in finance and moves to rent out boats on a remote island does not become less social by doing so: in fact one increases one's deep understanding of what kind of sociality best agrees with one's authentic sensibility.

Given all of the above, how does modality actually operate on the level of motivation? The process of adoption of values is social; we learn values from our society. The same person would likely adopt different values if one is raised in a society with significantly different normative signifiers. It is in this sense that we are indeed "social constructs". However, there are factors associated with character and individuality that play a part in the balancing of various possibilities, choices, and decisions that occur within the process of socialization. The dynamic principle behind this balancing (the attachment of various values to the same choices by different individuals within the same social environment) is *geometrical* in nature.

It is in the nature of modal logic to see reality as a balance between different possibilities. Various modal logics elaborate logical principles and relationships that pertain to the various ways in which these possibilities are defined, or to the various dimensions of such possibilities. For example, the logic of probability quantifies possibility (as opposed to necessity) in terms of probability. Thus, a logic of probability would additionally qualify various modal worlds that are potentially available to the person at the same time as other modal worlds by attaching to them the quantifier of probability. Again, probability might be defined in various ways, and it usually includes a variety of different factors, such as the person's preferences, the time and effort required to move from one modal world to another, the complexity of the current and potential alternative modal worlds, the person's ability to operate in a different modal world, one's courage to take risks, etc. However, every modal logic rests on a concept of *balance between diversities*. Likewise, the various modal logics are various possible logical explanations of the same phenomenon. The constancy of remaining in one modal world (for example, one type of motivation, based perhaps on a desire for security) is opposed to a change to a different modal world (which is the complementary alternative possibility, such as, for example, a desire to move to a different culture, start a new career, or envision life with a new spouse). Without the modal world of constancy (sometimes also described as stability), logically, the other possibility (that of challenge, change, discontinuity) would not be conceivable, and it would thus be theoretically and practically impossible. A change would not be a change (as opposed to constancy) if there was no constancy as a real possibility. This basic geometry of possibilities is at the very foundation of modal logic. We make most of our decisions within this logic of geometry, with balances and counterbalances, which do not need to be entirely symmetric, but practical modal logical thinking factors in some kind of a balancing act. The way in which this balance is defined and redefined is the reason we stay in a particular modal world or move to another.

When the principle of geometry is applied to motivation, it implies that one type of motivation reciprocally determines other types of motivation. In practical therapeutic work, understanding this modal nature of motivation is perhaps the single most important aspect of successful counseling. By successful counseling, I mean the counseling that leads to a lasting change in the interlocutor.

If I understand that my motivation to write late at night is only one type of motivation, which is reciprocal to my motivation to get enough sleep, to maintain a healthy timing in my waking and sleeping, or to simply rest, watching sports, my view of the various aspects which contribute to, or detract from, my leading a good life will be more accurate and practically better for me. By understanding that in weighing the various reciprocal motivations I have decided to write now because I don't want the ideas that I have at the moment to vanish by the morning, I will be able to evaluate my actions and integrate them into my life-script and my general experience more accurately and more usefully than if I simply follow my whim to write so late in the night, while at the same time feeling guilty because I am not getting enough sleep. Doing something with awareness of what it means and how and against which other possibilities one has chosen to do so is not the same as doing the same thing unthinkingly. One takes risks in making everyday decisions, and the quality of life that this risk-taking is a part of depends, to an extent, on how aware one is of all the dimensions of the risks: making a sacrifice for someone else, someone we love, may be a source of pleasure and satisfaction, while acting in the same way without giving the action a meaning might be perceived as mere suffering. This seemingly obvious distinction between a choice that is made with awareness and one that is made unthinkingly can make a major difference in our ability to integrate our choices into our overall experience and our identity.

Another aspect of the geometry of motivation is that it implies that the increase in one type of motivation requires, for the psychic balance to be maintained, a corresponding decrease in any incompatible type of motivation. This principle overcomes any ambivalence, and let us not forget that ambivalence is a potentially highly damaging dynamic that drains psychic energy and often incapacitates individuals from making decisions. The existence of ambivalence suggests that an internal reworking of the geometry of motivation is required, whereby the therapeutic or counseling work ought to be focused both on increasing one type of motivation and on decreasing another. The latter is often overlooked in traditional psychotherapy. Practically, in sorting out ambivalence, the therapist articulates his or her own view of the client's ambivalence, deciding which side of the dynamic equation should be strengthened, and which one should be weakened. We know what we would like the client to do and we consciously control our expression of this normative position; we do not push the client to do what we believe is right for them. Another thing that an observant therapist usually knows, typically from the start of the process, is what the client actually believes is right for them despite the ambivalence. In most cases the ambivalence occurs on different levels of motivation. For example, a person has a moral dilemma as to whether to move one's elderly parent into a retirement home or continue caring for them, while balancing their own family life and a number of personal issues. Given the circumstances, the therapist believes it would be the wrong choice for the client to proceed with the parent's transition because the parent is unlikely to live much longer and the client is likely to suffer from guilt if the parent dies soon after being pressured to move from their own house. The client, on the other hand, is tired, under pressure from their own family, and "falling apart" inside. They have come, fundamentally, for a psychological license to make the transition for the client's parent, but the client remains torn by the ambivalence and feelings of guilt. The initial session reveals that, although the client says that he is torn between the two potential decisions and does not know what to do, and although he says that the reason he has come for counseling is to make the decision, in fact he appears to have arrived seeking a psychological license to make the transition for the parent, which he has already subconsciously decided on. Ideally, the therapist controls the expression of his or her own view on the matter, which is obviously morally loaded and associated with the therapist's experience of the client's character (countertransference). It is essential here that the therapist portrays to himself the client's situation as a geometrical problem of motivation. Through the process, the therapist adds or detracts weight from the various sides of the motivation scale to explore where the client's authentic decision lies and to reach beneath the client's defenses to help him reach the geometrical outcome that is likely to be stable. Many times, the process leads to surprising results. Motivation is a mathematically structured process, and the therapeutic process in MIP involves a modal logical balancing of numerous modal worlds so that the person in therapy can see which modal world is their emotional home—their core choice. The process is not one of interpretation of framing and reframing, as is usually the case in traditional psychotherapy: it is a process of peeling off the onion of identity, and that, often, involves unleashing the deeply buried reserves of energy to make large, sometimes sweeping decisions and changes in one's entire life world. Where in traditional psychotherapy the client would likely balance one's options within the context of one's current modal world (job, marriage, kids, house, friends, health status, quality of life given all the relevant circumstances), in MIP it would not be inconceivable for the client to emerge with a desire to change the entire modal world. Such changes would likely be discouraged in many traditional psychotherapeutic modalities, while MIP does not shy away from supporting the client's decision to break down the entire geometrical structure and build a new balance, assuming the change of modal worlds is ethically sound regarding the interests and wellbeing of vulnerable third persons (in this situation, likely, the children). While personal change and the acceptance of one's inner self do not depend entirely on the person or on the psychotherapeutic process (certain factors that are not easy to rationally grasp must also obtain—a certain "fullness of time" must be achieved and a number of external circumstances need to be at least permissive of such personal transformation)—MIP generally accepts the method of "shaking the entire structure" in order to reshuffle the possible and the impossible by switching the modal worlds in the client. This approach seems controversial, while in fact it is based on stable principles of logic. The subjective sense of shaking one's reality to the core may, and in fact often does, coexist with a rewarding experience of personal change, a set of internal processes that unfold in the logically most constructive direction, with most benefit to the person. Dealing with such reshuffling of modal worlds, which is the everyday reality of MIP, may be unsettling at first, and may, in appearance, differ from what most traditional psychotherapists do, with their gradual questioning of the client's assumptions and their worldview.. MIP tends to be more abrupt: the very movement of modal worlds, the inclusion of potential changes of the external life world for the client in order for his internal world to articulate a new perspective, with different possible and impossible choices, is at the heart of the deepest spiritual and emotional thirst of most people. The possibility of escape (from the current modal world) is as badly needed as hope.

The key geometrical principles of motivation are those of symmetry and reciprocity. Just like a building whose construction does not obey the principles of symmetry, balance and the reciprocity of forces that operate on it from the ground and air, such as ground solidity that allows the building to resist the winds without the foundation sliding or cracking, a healthy, good structure of motivation must be based on the logical and geometric principles of symmetry. In one structure of symmetry, e.g. where a person is primarily oriented towards one's career as one's foremost goal, certain other life goals such as having a family at an earlier age become impossible, because the achievement of a career requires the commitment of time and energy that would otherwise be spent on raising a family. If a person disturbs this structure, they decompensate: they fall ill, become a psychiatric patient, have slips of attention and they make serious mistakes in life's key decision, etc. This situation is trivially familiar to most people. In such a modal world, important things one desires might be impossible, because they are not a part of the geometrical equation of the modal world one currently inhabits. However, the entire geometry may change by switching to a different modal world, not internally, or merely psychologically, as a change in the interpretation of events and experiences, but externally, through concrete decisions that will change one's life world. One abandons one building and moves to another one, so to say. In the different geometry, where the desired outcomes that were previously impossible become possible, some outcomes that used to be possible will inevitably become impossible. One might establish a more joyful life by setting up a family and establishing a small business to support that family, but one will not be able to become a high-powered executive and have a top-tier career that one might have opted for before. Changing lives involves choosing both the possibilities and the impossibilities. While this sounds familiar and trivial, in psychotherapeutic practice it can be quite a dramatic perspective, when individuals face the reality of their situations in terms of having to change more than just their views, perspectives, and frames of perceiving and interpreting their (external) experience. The idea in traditional psychotherapy that we do not change the client's world, but rather the client's *relationship* to that world, does not apply to MIP. We change the client's world as a precondition for a change of the client's logical structure of life, where completely new experiences become possible. That is what the practical application of the difference between propositional logic and modal logic results in. Propositional logic is concerned about the truth conditions for specific beliefs (and beliefs give rise to emotions and desires) within a given modal world that traditional psychotherapy does not infringe on. Modal logic focuses on how the conditions of possibility vary between the different modal worlds, and how the client might achieve what is currently impossible by abandoning, and, often, shaking, undermining, and weakening the constraints of their current modal world, not merely psychologically, but fully experientially, as an agent in society, within one's Lacanian "structure", that is, the system of one's relationships.

A healthy reciprocity in our motivational structure corresponds to the reciprocity of our reality, where even space and time are structured on geometric and complementary relationships: to fill the bottle of water from 1/2 to 2/3 means to decrease the amount of air in the bottle from 1/2 to 1/3, otherwise (if the bottle is sealed and additional water forced into it under pressure while all the air is kept inside) the bottle will break.

Symmetry and reciprocity operate in all kinds of modal logic, from the simple Kripkean one where modal worlds are seen as equal to sets of circumstances that make the truth of certain propositions possible or impossible, to the more sophisticated modal logic of probability: the increase in the probability of a person adopting, or attaining, one modal world corresponds to the decrease in the probability that the same person will attain another modal world. This simple principle, when applied to motivation, leads to a modal understanding of decisions and actions: they are the materialization of a person's geometric proportionality of motivation in the form of causality. Once a constellation of motivation is changed by increasing one and decreasing another type of motive, that creates an abstract situation, a psychic disposition,, which sets off a chain of causality of action. However, the symmetry of our motivation is not only internal: it is influenced by external factors, by our world. We might feel an inkling of motivation to move in a certain direction, while being objectively prevented from developing a full-fledged conscious drive to do so by a variety of cultural or other normative influences exerted on us by our society. To develop a motivational disposition to act or decide in a certain way, the person must first be able to envision a modal world in which such a disposition would be possible, reasonable, and, perhaps, desirable. Social conditioning operates across modal worlds, and the main tool for individuals to move from one modal world to another is their imagination. While imagination allows us to "bracket out" or abstract certain social conditions and constraints and is a freer and more creative faculty than reason, imagination, too, has its limits that are imposed on us by social conditioning. In certain, particularly limiting social conditions, some modal worlds are unimaginable for most people. To be able, or to dare to imagine, presupposes a social permission to do so, at least to an extent. We are taught how to think about our experience by our very world, by our society, by our modality of existence that is mainly shaped by our society; likewise, the reach and strength of our imagination is influenced, to various degrees, by the frame of the window through which we look out into the world, where that window is defined by society.

The disposition created through a geometry of motivation expresses itself through causality, or action. A motive causes an action, and conversely, our chosen actions, in retrospect, reveal the structure of our motivation. While this principle seems trivial, it practically illustrates an important axis of counseling work, with many clients in therapy who have issues with expressing their motivation and making decisions. We discover motives based on actions, not on the rationalizations of our motives. Individuals do not make decisions accidentally, at least not in most situations for which they seek counseling. Such situations are deeply embedded in their important social structure, or relationships, and when decisions are made within such structures, they spring from deep subconscious sources and reveal important values and the corresponding motives, whether the person consciously agrees with them and embraces them or not. The two axes (increasing/decreasing motivation and expressing motivation by setting in motion a chain of causality resulting in action) constitute the foundation of dynamic counseling, or dynamic psychotherapy as it is traditionally known.

The practical meaning of the above principle is that, if motivation was endless, then all kinds of mutually incompatible motives could coexist at the same time with no need for proportionality. However, the limits of psychic energy, of one's time and space in which one lives one's life, cause the incompatible motivational factors to militate against one another and cause experiential difficulties, or complaints. There is conflict between possibilities, or modal worlds, when they contract through limited time, space, and energy. In fact, our decisions are, metaphysically, a contraction of modal worlds through the limitations of time, space, and our limited psychic abilities. Our energy and the space in which we live our lives are limited. This is what makes the geometric proportionality of motivation a law of our existence. Any illusion with regard to the limits of our energy or space (and we are all occasionally prone to such illusions of grandeur) disturbs our inner economy of emotions and causes anxiety or ambivalence, from which all kinds of other experiential complaints may follow. This is particularly obvious in an inability to make decisions and the existential consequences of such an inhibition.

Consider a fairly common situation in psychotherapy. An ageing person, nearing retirement, senses a decline in their physical and mental prowess to control and operate their property. The person owns several pieces of real estate, all of which require the timely payment of taxes, bills, dealing with tenants, repairs, etc. In addition, this person has a fairly intellectually demanding job that is also time-consuming. They strive to maintain their friendships and social circle, all of which takes most of their time. They are torn between the need to streamline their life at an older age by reducing the number of assets which they must take care of, on the one hand, and their desire to leave some property to their children so that they can have an easier start in life. They decide, at one stage, to sell several properties and buy just one, higher quality one, where they will live, which they will be able to maintain, and which they will then leave to their children, where the value of that property will be higher than the individual values of the various properties they possess now. In the process of sale, however, they develop second thoughts. They are not sure how the process of consolidation of the properties will unfold financially, given the changes in the real estate market. Their kids are used to using one of the houses to spend time with the parent, or with friends, and have memories there. Thus, the internal conflict escalates as the time of the sale nears, and the person allows the opportunity to fall through, postponing the entire process. Obviously, at a later stage the person will be older, less agile, and overall, the transaction will be more difficult. The commitments continue, the financial and cognitive exhaustion continues. At one stage, the roof in one of the properties leaks seriously, and major investments are necessary. One's child decides to go for schooling abroad. One is left with the properties that are financially taxing and practically suboptimal for the person. He then enters therapy with symptoms of anxiety and depression; he "no longer wants to live his life", needs to "move to a distant place", and wants to "leave everything behind". In this situation, the person has not been able to compress space, time, and motivation in a material articulation of change, and the existential consequences are debilitating for his quality of life. This is the well-known story of indecision as a problem in psychotherapy.

Indecision is in fact the result of asymmetry, rather than symmetry, of motivation. Where various desires, or drivers of action, are involved, such as in indecision, the modal world within which the desires operate determines, to a great extent, which desire will be causally operative, or as Frank Jackson puts it, "the strongest desires". Jackson further describes the phenomenon of weakness of will as a situation where one's strongest desire, the desire that ends up being the operative driver of choice and action, "has not sufficiently evolved in light of the person's reason" (Jackson, 1984). In other words, Jackson sees weakness of will as a person's inability to act in accordance with one's reason. This implies that the ultimate driver for action is desire, not reason, and that in the case of "weakness of will" there is a regret on behalf of the person that they did not act in accordance with reason. However, this is an only too familiar situation in psychotherapy, which for long has known that reason, alas, has little to do with the way we act and make decisions. When one regrets one's choices as not being "reasonable" by one's own lights, one merely recognizes that consciously, one believes that one ought to have acted otherwise, while subconsciously, emotionally, where it really matters, one actually acted the way one's sensibility, of which one may not approve rationally, dictated them to act. Our decisions and actions take place based on an alignment of mainly emotional, dynamic drivers, and this structure is fundamentally geometric. As with the alignment of vectors, the strength of various desires or drivers yields a resultant vector or driver, which articulates the action both in its intensity and in its direction. This is a mathematical equation; assuming that one could, theoretically, establish the exact intensity and direction of the particular desires involved in the internal conflict, one could, theoretically, calculate the actual resultant vector of the eventual action. The client who let the opportunity to sell his property slip away is insufficiently aware of the very intensity and direction of his own desires, and he merely acquiesces in indecision, because he senses, on a subliminal level, that neither of the drivers is sufficient to determine swift action to sell his properties. There is a stifling balance of drivers in his motivational structure. So how is this balance disturbed and action triggered? MIP's response is that this is achieved by switching modal worlds. In another modal world, the drivers are different, and the resultant vector of action is also different. What are the potential elements of that new modal world? Well, perhaps the client could take action to anticipate or even accelerate any decisions his child might take; he could proactively seek to help the child to go abroad for further schooling, thus removing one important inhibiting factor for the sale of the properties (the child's habit to use the particular property to spend time with the parent and friends). Alternatively, the client could envision a speedy switch of properties with a fast sale of all his properties and their a quick consolidation into a single property that would be useful both for his parenting role and later in his life, for his own use. Both courses of action would have changed the objective elements of one's situation that would alter the motivational equation; they would switch the modal worlds that determine what is possible and what is not with regard to this particular decision.

When I suggest that the change in modal worlds that MIP typically seeks is not merely an "internal" but also an external change, an "objective" repositioning of the person vis-à-vis the real circumstances and facts of life, which also change in a changed modal world, this includes changes in one's bodily cognition and processes. In fact, the role of the body in psychotherapy has generally been greatly underestimated, apart from the bodily equivalents of certain psychiatric disorders. The general role of our bodies in all our psychic processes, however, is far greater and more comprehensive than just the psychosomatic connection. In a way, one could argue that all change, including personal change, is inevitably mediated by the body, and thus also partly a bodily process. We experience change by starting with perceptions, and in interpreting our perceptions in terms of the causality of events we start from the effects of change and proceed to its causes. It is through this backtracking process that we decide that we have changed. Invariably, the immediate awareness of the effects of any change that happens around us is that on our bodies. We sense time, space, comfort or discomfort, as well as most other psychic experiences through the body. It is our bodily processes that cause us to feel "anxious", or "apprehensive", or fearful. When we are depressed, this clearly shows in our bodies and a growing research suggests that even the causes of depression might be connected with very specific bodily issues, such as gut microbioma(Radjabzadeh et al., 2022; Liu et al., 2023). The body is the fundamental and first instrument with which we engage the world; it is the seat of all our experiences.

Our body is what Schopenhauer calls "the immediate object" (Schopenhauer, 1966, p. 11). Through this immediate object we gain representations, or knowledge of all other objects, all of which are "mediate objects". Schopenhauer makes what could be regarded as a programmatic statement for psychotherapy: the world is perfectly real as our representation; this representation is held together by the law of causality (Schopenhauer, 1966, vol. 1, p. 3, 15). Our experience represents our reality, our nominalist world, which is nevertheless fully real for us. It is dynamized by the causality of all the actions and decisions we and those around us make. These choices are instantiations of compressed motivation, time, and space. We influence our experiential reality to the extent that we are able to freely choose how to compress time and space and make decisions. Thus, although decision-making does not exhaust our psychic life, nor is it the only aspect of our life that psychotherapy works with, it is a materialization of our motivation in the limited space and time in which we find ourselves. By the decisions we make, and the subsequent causal backtracking of the way in which we have made those decisions, we can judge our motivation and our very identity, in the same way as we judge our world through the effects of various causes on our body and the experiences that we thus gain. Furthermore, our choices, which sometimes surprise us, are a way to discover our own character, or what we are made of (Schopenhauer, 1966, vol. 1, pp. 287–230). This is why MIP starts with the body, intuition and desire as the bodily projections of our values, where values can largely be identified with motives. We are motivated by the true values that constitute our character, whether or not we are conscious of such values, or perhaps believe that our most important values differ from those that truly drive our decisions. That is why the process of making decisions, based on the sensibility and actual drivers within our character, according to Schopenhauer, are the only way to discover our authentic values as motives for our actions (Schopenhauer, ibid.).

The geometry of personality through the looking glass of motivation explains, from yet another angle, the social nature of normalcy and, more fundamentally, of identity. Any change in the personality of an individual undergoing psychotherapy must rest on social factors as much as on the psychotherapeutic process itself. By adopting certain values, people give up on other values, and by accepting one type of normativity in life, they scale down or abandon their commitment to other norms. This change in priorities is likely vital for their ability to live a good life. The MIP psychotherapist always bears in mind the geometrical principles of motives and desires, so that when a particularly pronounced desire is identified in the client, they assume that there is a deficiency somewhere on the other side, somewhere in the dark, hidden corners of the same personality. This insight allows a better grasp of the entire structure of values and desires at the very outset of psychotherapy.

The same geometry applies to differences in values and desires between various social groups, ranging from bearers of various collective interests in the social contract to generations in the same society. "The generation gap" has several different dimensions, one of which is the occasionally dramatic change in the values between older and younger generations. This theme often comes up in therapy and counseling. The generation gap perfectly illustrates the geometry of motivation and values. Often the choices prevalent in a younger generation were "unimaginable" in an older generation, not only in light of the frequent complaint in parental counseling that members of the younger generation routinely do things that older people consider improper (engage in promiscuity, seek easy ways to finish their studies without adequate learning, see the use of recreational drugs as normal). Taking one perspective corresponds to favoring one set of values, and taking another perspective on life, with different values, requires becoming less sensitive to the previous one. The generation gap is a gap between different mentalities, which articulate their motivational options, space, and time in different contractions of context, that is, decisions. This is why, when one generation's choices are questioned by another generation, little argument ensues other than a general disagreement about the criteria by which to even judge one's choices. The values are different, and this means not only that one generation has values that the other generation doesn't, but that each of the generations have also blocked out different values. There are all kinds of value-systems available to us at the same time, as modal worlds; however, choosing one means rejecting the others. Every choice of identity means a rejection of the reciprocal identity. This does not mean that one cannot return to the reciprocal values one has once rejected: they continue to linger in the vicinity as alternative modal worlds.

Choices as Geometrical Outcomes

Our motivation is a proportion between various motives potentially coexisting at the same time, a kind of alignment of decision-making vectors governing our choices. This proportion resembles a distribution of content in a limited space. Jack Smart once described human beings as "buckets" into which happiness can be poured (Smart, 1991, p. 361). Imagine the human being as a container for various choices: there is a single vessel or psyche, a single "bucket", whose ability to take new content depends on the empty space within it. A full bucket cannot take any more content, just as a person deeply immersed into and attached to one's current modal world cannot make a shift to different life realities. This is a simple fact that many clients in counseling forget: to make a new choice, create a new reality in one's life, one must first make space for it. Only too often, we deliberate about the best choices that we might make without first creating the practical preconditions to even make any choice: people dream of a new lover while they are still in a relationship and have not freed the room where a new lover could settle in their lives, or they make plans for a new career where they are still caught in the values, practices, and habits associated with their old career. This is like trying to jump up with shackles on one's ankles bolted to the ground. To make a decision, to initiate change, one must first create a space for change, and this means leaving, or at least being prepared to imminently leave, the current modal world where one finds oneself.

One common problem with the inhibition to leave the current modal world is fear that, once the "bucket" is emptied and ready to receive new content, no new content might be forthcoming, and the bucket might stay empty. A typical example is fear of solitude. If one creates a space to find someone to love, this does not guarantee that one will find a lover. One may end up alone, for a long while, experiencing oneself as an empty vessel. Thus, because one fears the emptiness, one tries to juggle the impossible. One stays in the modal world where the things one needs or wants are impossible.

The Missing Object

The psychoanalytic concept of the missing object is closely connected to my understanding, inspired by Schopenhauer, of the contraction of space, time, and motivation in decision-making and the dual aspect of change based on the attainment of new content of desire and, equally importantly, the removal or abandonment of the previous content, or the rejection of the current values for new ones. The two aspects are analogous to the reciprocity of change in space: an action to change a state of affairs (or modal worlds) at any point in time, just like moving in space, requires room, and given the limited mental space, just like movement in limited physical space, some bulky content blocking that mental space must first be cleared out.

I mentioned before that Paul Verhaeghe uses the metaphor with a puzzle toy consisting of sliding tiles, where various tiles slide in different directions in order to achieve a particular constellation or pattern. This was an early version of the Rubik's cube. The toy consists of a board to which various tiles are attached so that they can slide in a straight line in all directions. One tile is missing, leaving an empty space, and the goal is to manipulate the tiles using this one empty spot to get them in the desired order and positions. As Verhaeghe points it out, the key is the missing tile, for if all the tiles were attached to the board, no movement would be possible and the toy would be useless. It is the missing tile that renders the toy functional, and as long as the toy remains interesting and useful, the missing tile can never be attached to "complete" the number of tiles. This is the role of a missing object in human motivation, although the missing object is typically a source of common neuroses (Verhaeghe, 2008, p. 54).

The tile puzzle game illustrates the role the subjective sense of a missing object plays in the way our psyche operates. We are motivated by a sense of lack; this sense is an important part of our fundamental human condition. However, the lack instills dissatisfaction, which causes individuals to seek to attain the missing object. In doing so, various constellations of thoughts, ideals, and motives occur, just like in moving the tiles within the tile puzzle. The missing object makes possible the various constellations of psychological "tiles" that change their order, sequencing and overall meaning, just like changes in values and normative directions change a person's sequencing and order of thoughts, resulting in different worldviews and overall perceptions of meaning of one's choices and life as a whole. This process of change of order of thoughts, emotions, and motives, and the resulting switching between different modal worlds, leading to personal change, is called "*displacement*".

While the concept of displacement, or disruption to the original, unproductive or unhelpful structure of thought, is at the core of any apparent change in our decision-making and general behavior, its reach is limited in achieving a change in everyday life. Our ideas, cognitions, and decisions are determined by our sensibility, or character, on the one hand, and by our environment and circumstances, on the other. The disruption in thought that is a displacement, especially when it is triggered by psychotherapy, can induce the person to change their circumstances, to switch to a different modal world. This happens when the disruption is sufficiently radical. A major loss (illness or a brush with death) or a major gain (unexpected job offer, for example) can cause a displacement in one's ordinary chain of thought that leads to decisions that will call into reality new and different modal worlds and make possible what was hitherto impossible.

Absent such major events, it is the role of psychotherapy to subvert the limitations of the current modal world of the person undergoing therapy. Psychotherapy achieves this effect in a variety of ways, perhaps the most straightforward of which is the establishment of a strong transfer with the therapist, who then introduces various new challenges and ideas to the client, causing a displacement of thoughts. These inductions are implicit, but powerful as far as the transfer is strong. The very fact that the person "has" psychotherapy is a major change in one's life; developing a strong sense of alliance and therapeutic community with the therapist further increases and strengthens this changed reality of one's life and empowers the person to make the decisions one might never have thought of without therapy.

One particular way in which this change of life due to the presence of therapy works is by shifting the person's focus of thought. With therapy, the person will think about different things and in different ways that one used to do prior to therapy. They will think about the therapist, the content of the session, the ideas broached in therapy, and about the unexplored areas of decision making and life planning that the therapy session might have offered a glimpse into. This thinking will replace the otherwise prevalent rumination about a former partner, job loss or personal predicament, thus inducing a displacement into the person's ordinary pattern of thought. This displacement, then, consequentially, leads to the emergence of different feelings, sense of personal resilience, and, perhaps most importantly, the springing to the person's conscious life of new ideas, concepts, and creative ways of articulating and understanding one's experience. Even if the therapist does not do anything particularly creative or effective, other than help build a strong transfer and develop a sense of security and empowerment in the client, this very structure of life where one has therapy as a stable element of one's everyday experience will induce displacement and therapeutic change. That is the inherent subversive role and value of psychotherapy that unfolds through displacement.

The missing object is a precondition for displacement, and this is the psychoanalytic way of saying that change requires an empty space to occur. The contraction of time, space, and motivation to produce an event of change requires a location which must receive such an event. This location in the mind, just like a location in physical space for a physical event, must be secured prior to the event actually taking place. The missing object is a precondition for any action to occur. It is in place of the missing object that our important decisions take place: they are driven by what is missing, by the desire which arises from a built-in lack of our everydayness. The differences in the decisions we make arise from different missing objects, and from differences in our fundamental desires, far more than they arise from the substance on which we decide. In this sense, decisions are responses to desires associated with the missing object, that free space in the mind where contractions of time and space occur when the sparks of decision-making happen; they are thus inroads into our fundamental values, especially when they are made in a way that requires considerable rationalization to reconcile the decisions we make with what we consciously believe to be our values and principles. When decisions are contrary to our conscious principles, they are cognitively the most useful to us in understanding our subconscious register, where the actual dynamics of the missing object and the connected desire occurs. Acting contrary to one's best rational reason, following a drive that removes our capacity to act otherwise, is the best inroad into understanding what really drives us. As I have already recalled in Schopenhauer, our actions, regardless of our concepts (or rational thought) show us what kind of persons and characters we are.

Given that the missing object is not simply a lack which can be filled by obtaining the object, but rather an existential condition which cannot, and ought not to be filled, because if one missing object is actually found, another one will have to appear for the psychic life of an individual to continue, the very concept of the missing object in psychoanalysis, and in psychotherapy, helps distinguish between the therapeutic and everyday dialogue, between a healing discourse and a friendly one.

The therapeutic, or analytic discourse does not focus on attempts to attain a missing object. Instead, it seeks to make sense of the missing object as an opportunity for personal development. The "hysterical" or everyday discourse is a collaborative effort where one person tries to help another person achieve their missing object as a (misunderstood) condition for attaining the good life.

The two types of discourse may seem similar in tone and format, but they rest on entirely different perspectives. It is this difference in perspective that accounts for the difference in longer term effects of either. The friendly discourse may actually help the other person attain a missing object, but this will inevitably lead to another object being lost (the missing tile in the tile puzzle), otherwise all psychodynamics would be destroyed. The conquering of one missing object may cause a false sense of achievement, which may carry over into attempts to attain another missing object; however, in the longer term, the missing tile will prove inevitable. Once the person realizes that there is always a missing object, and that chasing after it is futile, they usually show up for counseling. A focus on the missing object often leads to a perception of structural neurosis in the person, one that we all seem to harbor.

The problem with neurosis, according to psychoanalysis, is that it is our existential condition. We are all neurotic by definition. Given that neurosis is linked with the missing object, every person psychologically alive is unavoidably more or less neurotic, and the way to address the serious neurosis which presents as a complaint in therapy is first to elucidate this principled, universal nature of neurosis to the client. The next step is to work with the role and meaning of the missing object in a more holistic manner, thus helping the client to gain a richer understanding of what is required for them to progress towards a better life, while at the same time reducing the subjective difficulties associated with the neurosis caused by the missing object. The inevitability of a lack, once it is understood as the existential condition of all people, ought to reduce the neurosis to a more acceptable level of the subjective experience of discontent. Once a fundamental lack is seen and accepted as the source of dynamization of one's psychic life, its militant edge against the person's inner peace and quality of life is blunted, and its potential as a space for the making of constructive, novel, and exciting decisions about personal change can be harnessed. In other words, it is the acceptance of our structural neurosis that opens room for change, rather than attempts to remedy or cure it.

It is essential here to articulate what, in the context of psychotherapy, could be considered a major Schopenhauerian point: psychotherapy speaks about *causation* in the creation of psychic phenomena, and this suggests a degree of realism in assuming that if events cause psychic phenomena, then this implies the assumption that "events" and "things" exist as objects in a "real" world, which then causes effects in the subject (the person and the person's psyche), or vice versa. This would seem to contradict the nominalism that I sketched as a sufficient and reliable foundation on which to philosophically understand the appropriate metaphysical context for discourse therapy. The mistake that suggests a realism in the above argument is the almost automatic assumption, when we speak of causality, subjects and objects, that causality is the relationship between the subject and the object. Schopenahuer points it out that *causality only operates between objects as our representations*, namely between our body (the immediate object) and events and things other than the body as mediate objects.

Thus, the world of causality organizes our representations, which are our (nominalist) reality. Such a reality is sufficient for psychotherapeutic purposes. For Schopenahuer, this nominalist structure of representations is also sufficient for broader philosophical purposes.

When I say that the missing object causes our neuroses, I am talking about experiences, or representations. The yearning for a missing object (a feeling based on a representation, thus a mediate object, conveyed to us through bodily sensations, like all feelings) causes the representation of neurosis. On this account, neurosis as an experience is not part of the subject; it is in fact a representation, an object which the epistemic subject, the "I", experiences. The subject is abstract without experiences, but experiences are not parts of the subject, they are the subject's world of which we speak as the reality of our lives. Once we understand our neuroses as objects in much the same way as our car is the object which we drive or our emotions are objects to which we relate, this additionally clarifies the modal perspective that I briefly discuss in the first chapter. Some objects I can do without easily, and others seem so deeply and intricately associated with my very core self that I cannot imagine living without them. However, in principle, the objects, including our feelings, are our experiences; philosophically, they are the content of our perception, and not a part of our subjecthood, our "I" which experiences those representations. If I am in love, I participate in a socially structured relationship with another human being, and I experience the emotions that arise from that relationship. The "I" who experiences these emotions is not the same as the emotions one experiences: although the emotions occur within my psyche and my body, and in that sense they are parts of my corporeal "I", they are not epistemically parts of my subjecthood. I can thus relinquish my emotions and still remain the same "I" who experienced those emotions. I may be able to do this with more or less difficulty, but the principle that emotions are separate and can be removed from my subjecthood without changing the integrity of the "I" remains.

With neurosis, it is somewhat different, because neurosis is, indeed, an experience, similar to emotions; however, it is structurally tied to our psychic existence, so we cannot really get rid of it completely. We can control those neuroses that are particularly debilitating, but we cannot change the intentional nature of our mind that it seeks a missing object, and in fact that it needs the lack, embodied by the missing object, in order to stay alive and active. Thus, neurosis is the only mental state that we can't seem to remove from our subjecthood, despite the fact that it is not a part of that subjecthood, because it is experienced by the "I" as the content of representations.

In the above sketched geometry of motivation and the dynamics of the missing object, neurosis is a situation where the person is "stuck" to the missing object and loses sight of the broader picture. This is a narrow perspective to which most people succumb much of the time, and thus the psychoanalytic pronouncement that "we are all neurotic" or "we are all hysterical". Neurosis, or "hysteria", is this unrelenting focus on a problem, on a missing object. It is the sort of thinking we are conditioned to in the western civilization: we first think about problems that must be "solved", and only afterwards about other, finer things in our lives that are not a problem. It is this type of hysterical or neurotic thinking that causes so many people to report in counseling that they spend their day "putting out fires", leaving their real creative work for the evening, when they come home, when they should normally rest, spend time with their families, or engage in hobbies.

The neurotic culture in the modern world has led to people "paying their dues" (largely imagined, not real) to the day, the society, the employer, by focusing on the lack, whatever the lack might be (a problem that must be solved at work or in private life), while leaving the creation of new things, the creative aspect of their jobs, for a later time. My colleagues in the academia thus report that they "start their academic jobs" in the evening, when they sit before their computers and start writing, creating new value, which is their job, while during the day they do things which, as they report, "they can't even describe, because they are insignificant", such as attending meetings, spending time in traffic, and dealing with petty workplace issues. This neurotic structure of the working day became obvious with the onset of the Coronavirus global catastrophe, which started in 2019 and continued for several years, forcing most people to work from home. It suddenly became clear that almost everything in jobs like those in academia could be successfully completed from home, without attending to so many superfluous activities (coming to work, spending many hours there, seeing students in person, etc.). The pandemic, in addition to taking so many lives, has made even more obvious the neurotic structure of our organization of everyday life.

The various rituals, including those, as it turns out, unnecessary activities such as going physically to the workplace, engaging in debates with colleagues which don't really produce any palpable results, driving to different places to do things one can do from one place, etc., are in fact *rituals* created to generate a sense that we are paying our dues to our societies, or institutions, or that we are doing something of public value, where in fact what really matters are things we could do completely differently. In the academia, we can develop valuable relationships with others by meeting colleagues and students in quite a different setting from formal scheduled meetings, and we can teach creatively at a distance, so that we don't have to travel to summer schools or conferences, wasting unnecessary funds, time, and energy.

There is, of course, a cost to the change: one doesn't get to meet the people, enjoy the new countries and cities and get a sense of physical mobility; however, there are benefits, as well: in the same amount of time one can participate in more events, one can spend more time preparing one's lectures, and one can better document one's performance and comments by others by recording sessions, receiving statistical feedback from the internet meeting platforms, etc. The neurotic missing object will always be there, our efforts will feel incomplete, but changes in the activities themselves, forced by external threats such as the pandemic, reveal the surplus rituals which we have built around our jobs and our social interactions.

The problem with interventions to address neurosis is that, given that the missing object cannot be lastingly attained, these interventions focus on making sense of the fact that the missing object makes motivation possible and on rearranging the structure of motives (through displacement) so that the space belonging to the missing object is used for personal development. However, if the quest of a missing object, or the value that makes up its substance (such as affluence, power or security) is too engrained in the person's personality and has driven the person for too long, making sense of the permanent and structurally necessary nature of the missing object will only produce limited and temporary effects, and the person will soon revert to their usual behavior and way of thinking. One can change one's life setting and one's modal world. One cannot, however, change one's character through therapy. This is why we sometimes refer to "hopeless clients" in psychotherapy. When the focus on a missing object has solidified particularly strongly in the person's very sensibility and emotional structure, it is a far-fetched expectation that in such a client either a dynamic transfer with the therapist or a reinterpretation of the role of the missing object will address the pathological dimensions of neurosis. In an important sense, again, our character is, indeed, our psychological destiny as it poses limits to what psychotherapy can achieve.

Psychosis

The above discussed way in which the missing object generates neurosis is direct and occurs on the level of immediate experience of "reality" (Lacan's concept of *jouissance*). The therapeutic intervention in neurosis takes place *at the very juncture* between "reality" and the onset of personal processing of the missing object. However, the connection between the missing object and psychosis is *indirect* and requires an additional step of development of what Freud calls *"a mistaken theory of reality"*.[2] While there are numerous ways to develop a psychosis, one that is relevant to the concept of the missing object is that where a person experiences a missing object in such a focused way that it "sucks in" their overall perception of reality. Their entire theory of reality is thus bent around the missing object. Paranoid ideation and delusions of grandeur are often psychotic superstructures built above the missing objects of security and respect. Maslow's hierarchy of needs posits the need for security (and, I would add, the need for privacy as a related need) at the very bottom of the structure of needs, making it a basic, psychologically primitive need, while the need for "esteem" is positioned towards the top of the hierarchy, making it more sophisticated and culturally dependent (Maslow, 1943). Axel Honneth's more modern interpretation of human sociality in general (Honneth believes that this interpretation derives from Hegel) focuses on the need for respect and concept of mutual respect (Honneth, 2007). These two needs are likely at the core of the psychotic presentations of paranoia and grandeur.

In Lacanian psychoanalysis, a somewhat more complex view of neurosis and psychosis is adopted. The assumption there is that neurosis and psychosis are structurally fundamentally different phenomena, where the difference rests on the status of the primary factor of psychological well-being,

[2] The idea that psychosis is a theory of reality just like any theory, and that it differs from non-psychotic theories simply by a consensus of most people on the latter, is perhaps one of the epistemically most interesting aspects of Freud's theory of psychosis (Verhaeghe, 2008, p. 67). Psychosis as a theory, according to Freud, is fundamentally infantile and substantively narcissistic. In fact, Freud describes psychosis as a "narcissistic neurosis", where the person is incapable of object relations, but remains neurotically charged toward oneself. One of the reasons Freud did not consider psychotic patients good candidates for psychoanalytic treatment was because he considered them incapable of object relations, and thus also of developing a transference with the therapist. The transference itself, however, is the foundation of a particular type of neurosis, that can be productive for treatment, one that Freud calls "transference neurosis" (Freud, 1912, pp. 18–23).

the Primary Signifier, Name of the Father. Where Name of the Father is suppressed, neurosis is the outcome. However, when Name of the Father is cancelled, or abolished, the result is psychosis. Thus, Lacanians insist that a structural difference must be established between neurosis and psychosis prior to any treatment. One of the arguments put forward by Johathan Redmond is that the tendency in psychiatry to treat mild symptoms as neurotic and more severe symptoms of the same structural type as psychotic is a diagnostic error that results in the wrong treatment. Redmond insists that "mild" or "non-manifest" psychoses should still be diagnosed as psychoses, and this includes, according to him, most of the diagnoses of Cluster B personality disorders, primarily BPD (Redmond, 2014). The idea that modern personality disorders ought to be included into the class of psychoses is attributed to Kraepelin's early classification of mental disorders (Kraepelin, 1968).

The procedure for the initial psychiatric interview according to Lacanian protocols is to look for any signs of psychosis first (this would presumably involve the non-manifest psychoses), because spotting these signs early on facilitates a treatment that might prevent them from turning into full-fledged, manifest psychoses. Once a fully manifest psychosis has developed, Lacan's understanding is that it cannot be cured; the cancelled, absent Primary Signifier can only be temporarily compensated for by developing a compensatory symptom; thus the treatment of psychosis, according to Lacanian theory is symptomatization: the development of a symptom that is sufficiently strong to compensate an internal disintegration, and at the same time sufficiently socially and functionally acceptable to be bearable, to allow the person to live an optimum quality of life with that symptom. Verhaeghe generalizes this paradigm to argue that a symptom is typically an "economically efficient" method for the patient to deal with dysfunctionality and pain, and that symptoms, in most cases, produce "more gain than loss", thus suggesting that the role of psychotherapy, unlike that of medical treatment, is not automatically, or most of the time, to remove symptoms; sometimes, removing a symptom can plunge the person into a far worse and less manageable condition (Verhaeghe, 2008, pp. 16–18).

While there are many virtues of understanding psychosis in Kraepelin's way, a shortcoming of Lacan's view of therapeutic intervention in psychosis appears to arise from his belief that the construction of a symptom around the real experience that cannot be psychologically metabolized is the sole principle of stabilizing psychoses. Rather than addressing in depth the idea that psychosis is a mistaken theory of reality, by questioning that theory and seeking ways to rectify it, Lacan and the Lacanians are content with establishing *a temporary and fragile equilibrium* that patches up the problem, while harboring no hope that it can be solved in a lasting way. This patch or symptom makes the experience of psychosis psychologically bearable to the subject by provisionally making symbolic sense of it, in the absence of authentic normative structures established by Primary Signifier, Name of the Father (Verhaeghe, 2008, p. 200). However, it seems that therapeutic experience shows this assumption to be false. Many psychiatric patients diagnosed with psychosis, including very severe forms of it, have in fact lastingly recovered, despite the conservative views and vocabulary of psychiatry relating to psychoses, which, as I mentioned earlier, are reflected in the use of terms such as "remission" rather than recovery. In fact, Lacan himself notes that psychosis ought not to be stigmatized, or seen as a particularly threatening situation, given that most healthy people experience psychotic episodes of varying degrees of severity as transient experiences in their lives (overview of the Lacanian views of psychosis in Redmond, 2014).

The above discussed dimension of psychosis as theory opens up room for discourse therapy. Both Verhaeghe and Redmond develop more narratively woven views of psychosis than the initial structural description offered by Lacan, where in the latter description the very idea of "foreclosure", or complete absence, of the key symbolic structure that determines one's perception of the Other (Primary Signifier Name of the Father) factually incapacitates the person from genuinely recovering from psychosis.[3] Peter Raabe has perhaps been the modern pioneer of philosophical

[3] Lacan develops his theory of psychosis by building on Freud's theory of neurosis, which rests on the mechanism of repression. According to Lacan, while neurosis arises from a repression of Name of the Father into the unconscious, in psychosis the person finds oneself in a situation where one is unable even to register and recognise Name of the Father. Thus, one simply has no recourse or tool to even symbolically structure one's relationship to others, leading one into a psychotic compensation for what Lacan describes as a "hole" in one's personality (Lacan, 1958/2017). Such a situation occurs, in a very simple form, when, for example, a child is brought up with a mother in a family that militantly negates the child's need for a father, or even the existence of the father, insisting on developing the child's compensating behavior by developing unusually, and abnormally, strong relationship with the women in the family (mother, grandmother, aunts, etc.). The child is thus left without a symbolic resource to understand the role of a man in the family, or the role of maleness in society, with all of the consequences for the child's understanding of complex social relation-

counseling with psychotic clients, which is a particularly conceptually and logically demanding form of psychotherapy (Raabe, 2013). The narrative and discursive approach to psychosis is a logical development of the idea that psychosis is a compensation of the symbolic lack of key structure. The theory of reality that determines our relationship to the Other depends on the symbolic ingredients of the narrative that we are equipped with; the removal of a key symbol, such as Name of the Father, impacts the person's internal story telling about the world and redirects the narrative in a direction that society considers a mistaken theory of reality, or a psychotic one. Assuming that the symbols within a structural architecture of normalcy are anchors for the development of a personal narrative, the psychotherapeutic interventions make sense as a way of influencing the psychotic theory, disturbing the psychotic narrative and the symbolic structure on which that narrative rests. It seems that this is the main development of Lacan's theory of psychotherapeutic intervention in psychosis that later Lacanians have elaborated by describing psychosis as an epistemic, rather than merely clinical, or nosological, phenomenon (Redmond, 2014; Miller, 2009; Grigg, 2011).

Assuming that ordinary psychosis, or a deviation of the narrative to compensate for deficient or missing symbolic structure, is generally prevalent among not only psychiatric patients, but also healthy individuals, and that it is often a transient state that never reaches the "fully manifest" form of psychosis, as Redmond describes it, one wonders why such a "warping" and pathological proliferation of the identity and experiential narrative of oneself and the world should be limited only to individuals. A disturbance to the fundamentally geometrical, symmetric structure of the symbolic toponyms of our thought that causes psychotic ideation can be equally consistently ascribed to collectives and collective thinking as it can to individuals.

Freud's idea of psychosis as a mistaken theory of reality implies that psychosis is omnipresent not only among individuals, but also among groups, corporate entities, and institutions. This idea leads to questions about whether psychiatric diagnoses ought to be ascribed to collectives, as

ships. This creates a symbolic "hole" in the child's psyche, and as he or she grows up, they increasingly develop compensatory mechanisms to phantasise about a substitute for the father, or for maleness, or for authority, or whatever other symbolic function maleness plays in the particular society. This phantasy occurs in what Lacan calls the Imaginary Register or realm. Gradually, such abandonment of reality and compensatory creation of an imaginary world becomes a full-fledged psychosis (Lacan, 1958/2017).

well as to individuals. Any theory can be adopted both by individuals and by collectives, just as any symbolic symmetry of meaning and relationships can be disturbed on a collective as much as it can be pathological on an individual level. Both individuals and groups can adopt mistaken views about the reality compared to those held by the majority of other individuals or collectives. If it is possible to argue between various individuals and groups about any theory in general, there is no principled reason why it should not be possible to argue about a psychotic theory, assuming that the psychotic subject is capable of at least implicitly theorizing about reality. The therapeutic discourse, in each case, is a meta-discourse: it seeks the missing object in one's psychosis and interprets its role in the development of pathological ideation. This missing object can be fundamentally neurotic, in the sense Freud had in mind when he described neurosis as a prevalent existential condition for most of us, or it can be symbolic, as in Lacan's understanding of psychosis. In each case, there is a lack that is geometrically, and symmetrically, compensated by motivation and meaning associated with the pathological phenomena, or what Verhaeghe describes as the most "economical" way to manage the lack, namely the development of a compensatory symptom. The same dialectic applies to communities; they can also develop a psychotic ideation, where the psychotic ideas are induced in a large number of individuals who make up the community, and the "inductor" is a collective lack. This may happen because of an unstable sense of collective identity, or of self-worth, or simply because of a deep-seated lack of quality of life in the community that is then ascribed to external conditions, various real or imaginary adversaries, international politics, etc. Sometimes, such collective psychosis assumes aggressive paranoid forms and results in abominable destruction. Consider Rwanda or Bosnia. In both communities, the sense of collective victimization was induced as a type of psychotic compensation for a shaky sense of national identity (the Tutsies, the Hutus, the Serbs, the Bosniaks, etc.); instead of being the stabilizing reflection of one's own community, the Other (the other ethnic communities) were warped within each community's narrative into the villains who threatened the identity of one's own community, interests, land, or history, and the defensive paranoid behavior ensued, resulting in mass atrocities. The logical paradoxicality of the psychotic ideation in these cases was obvious because no changes to either community's history, identity, or the land they lived on were possible by civil conflict: in most cases, such as in Bosnia, people fought over the land that was already theirs, whose fruits they had already enjoyed.

The territory remained the same after the war, with the difference that the relations between the communities were deeply scarred. This situation is structurally the same as that of a psychotic patient who acts out one's psychotic paranoia on one's family members, only to be left with the same relationships, in the same home, with diminished and scared loved ones and a simmering resentment of oneself (Fatic, Bachmann and Lyubashenko, 2018: 1–58).

If one of the challenges of a healthy personality is to integrate a structural, permanent lack, then psychosis, among other ways, could be described as a situation where that structure of internal integration crumbles. One way in which psychosis can develop is through a progressive failure of the person's psyche to compensate for everyday lack. The effort required to get up in the morning, to shave, to prepare breakfast, bathe, do the house chores and work, when it is devoid of a unifying meaning (life goal), especially in people who live alone and have limited social interactions and opportunities for personal validation, can, in time, become too much for the person. Such an individual might resort to devising various phantasms as their alternative modal worlds, some of which might be damaging to their wellbeing. For example, they might stop grooming themselves and maintaining a basic hygiene of their living space; many switch day and night, sleeping through the day and spending nights awake; they run debts through unpaid bills and become closer with their pets than with their relatives; eventually, if they are lucky, they become hospitalized and get treated, or, if they are unlucky, become homeless and die in the street. There have been thousands of such examples of individuals who, at some point, decided, even if subconsciously, that the everyday effort required to compensate for the numerous (and constantly challenging) missing objects was simply too much for them. It is at this point of potential departure into psychosis that meaningful relationships step in and offer solace, solidarity, and a sense of beauty or friendship, empathy, or love. These values and relationships are so important to us because they replenish our enthusiasm for life when the constant need to compensate for structural lack would otherwise deplete that enthusiasm completely. This is the meaning behind the phrases that "home is one's refuge from the world", that "love is a cure", etc. I think that this is also where the key significance of the organic community lies. A community that heals is one that matters the most; a regulatory, distributive, or restrictive community, one organized through institutions and formal rules, can never substitute the actual, immediate community, which is one of solace, mercy, empathy, self-sacrifice, or at least self-investment in the wellbeing of others, and of fellowship. Much of the modern benefits of psychotherapy arise from the mere fact that the psychotherapeutic community is a particular fellowship, an organic relationship forged in a society that is increasingly formal, detached, institutionalized, and cold.

When the sense of the existential lack becomes too much, and the healing influences are absent, the crumbling of a person's internal structure is almost inevitable. I would say that instead of Lacan's concept of Name of the Father, whose foreclosure precipitates psychosis, what actually leads to psychosis is the foreclosure of any expectation of Another engaging us in an organic relationship that enthuses and heals us. It is the absence of an actual community that precipitates psychosis, in structurally the same way as, for Lacan, the absence or deletion of the Primary Signifier does.

Depending on the extent of the crumbling of one's symbolic world, or the tear in one's ability to integrate one's view of reality as a meaningful narrative—the tear that starts when it becomes "too much", and no human and social cure is forthcoming, the psychosis will present different degrees of severity. When a person's symbolic world is fractured, this impacts their entire interpretation of reality. In mild cases, the person will exhibit what is often described as a "highly functional psychosis", namely they will be able to maintain a job and social relationships, including a family; however, this will require a high expenditure of energy to maintain the inner balance and will occasionally present as "oddness". A careful observation of the person's behavior in the long term will reveal a "crack" in her overall view and understanding of reality, of her representations of others and her relationships with them. Just like with any other structure, if no help is rendered, the initial crack will widen and impact the stability and "statics" of all other parts of the construction that we call a person. This will then lead to the emergence of more drastic and broadly familiar symptoms of psychosis such as delusions, erratic behavior, and open intrusions of symbolic distortions into speech and broader linguistic behavior.

The more profound the disorganization of the structure of personality, the less coherent it is to speak of a "missing object" or "lack", because the context for a lack is compromised. In psychosis, a lack, the driving force of personality, cannot be adequately articulated. This, at the same time, is the reason individuals with advanced psychotic disorganization have problems articulating a psychiatric "complaint". Their issue is *the whole reality*, which overwhelms them and causes them pain, and the response to that pain varies: it could involve the invention of a new, psychotic reality, seeking refuge in temperamental and cognitive withdrawal, or in medication.

The experience of the world can no longer be psychologically metabolized, because the person's internal symbolic resources no longer have an effective structure: the symbolic interpretation of experience shifts, dissipates, and bends in various mutually incompatible directions, thus deepening the rift between the person and others and making the world an even scarier and less accessible place.

This is the place where Freud's concept of theory of reality can be philosophically used in therapy, for to cure someone who has a psychosis, a new symbolic structure of experience must be built. Such a structure is very close, if not identical, to a theory of reality: understanding the world and one's perceptions of others in their systematic mutual interconnectedness requires powerful symbolic meanings to both generalize from experience and analyze empirical content. This work can be done through the building of philosophical views of reality and the normative ordering of values. It is a job for philosophers and psychotherapists at once, a job that shows just how theoretically charged psychosis in fact is. Such a therapeutic process where the missing theory of the world and of life is re-built turns the patient into a student and collaborator. Unlike an academic theory, this personal theory of reality is of existential significance for the psychotic person. It can redeem their disintegrated life narrative in crucial ways and lift them from a victimhood in life to a stewardship of at least their own interpretations and values.

The Aesthetics of Proportionality in the Geometry of Personality

When my daughter was 12, she told me about this dream of hers, which I wrote down verbatim:

> *Important*
>
> *March 2021*
>
> *When I opened my third eye I was near a lake full of beautiful blue, purple, pink, white… fish and stones, full of crystals. I saw my spirit-guide Claire, whom I had summoned with my ring. She welcomed me and called me a tiger. I walked deeper into the forest, which was near that lake. I saw a little fox with a white collar and her tail was fading away in sparkly shades of blue. I also saw my second spirit-guide Charlie.*
>
> *She looked like she was around 40 years old. She led me into the cave full of blueish purple crystals.*

We were walking as I asked her some questions as though I talked to her through my ring. I asked her if she was really my spirit-guide, if she could make it possible for me to talk to people who have passed away. She said "yes".

We walked until we saw a snake. She asked me if I had a fear of snakes and I answered no. The snake had a bright light full of colours on her stripes all over her skin because of the light that reflected against the crystals.

Charlie asked if I had a fear of the dark and my answer was also no.

Then she asked me if I considered myself a brave person, and my answer was still no.

Then she said "Well... These two fears are the most common fears and you don't have them; still, you don't consider yourself a brave person?"

I didn't answer that question because I was confused.

Then Charlie said that she didn't understand why people had a fear of the dark.

I said that they don't have the fear of the dark itself; they are just scared of what is inside the dark.

Then Charlie said something really smart: "Here is the thing... if there was a dark in this cave you wouldn't see the crystals and you would be scared. But if the lights were turned on you would see the beauty outside of the dark. And for the snake, her glowing stripes on her skin wouldn't be so shiny and colorful without the light reflecting on the crystals, so people would be scared of the snake in the dark, but they wouldn't be scared of the snake when the lights are turned on, because she looks innocent and under the lights you see the beautiful outside of the fear... so they have a fear of the unknown... almost all the fears are actually fears of the unknown."

Actually, she is right. I don't have a fear of snakes because I know that they are more scared of us than we are of them. Snakes have a reason for their fear, though. People kill innocent animals every day because "they could harm us". Well, we do harm them. We give them reason to attack.

Another example: I have a big fear of sharks even though I know we are not sharks' natural food, but I never had a fear of water. Being afraid of sharks, jellyfish, fish... usually grows into a fear of water. Water is something where I find my peaceful zone so this proves my theory that there are more terrifyng things that we don't fear than those we do fear, because we have got used to some things, and others are still unknown to us.

The metaphors of light in the cave, ornamental crystals reflecting the light onto a snake (a threat), thus transforming the threat into an object of beauty, show the work of a healthy consciousness working to symbolically process the Lacanian "Real" of her fears and insecurities. The transformation of threatening objects to those of beauty shows the self-balancing function of the geometry of a healthy mind that is often associated with optimism.

The "I" of the narrative is never free-standing and self-centered, the references to ego are always related either to a higher authority (the spiritual guide in the form of a fairy) or to a general principle, knowledge, or wisdom (the idea that people should transcend their traumatic experience by looking at its beauty from the outside, etc.). Ksenija shows an inner struggle, which is particularly obvious when the narrative is interpreted psychoanalytically. The narrative itself is full of powerful psychoanalytic symbols (the dark, the snake, two supernatural beings—the two spiritual guides, fairies, the cave, the lake, the forest).

Ksenija's desire to transcend her experience is exhibited throughout the narrative indirectly, but perhaps most directly at the beginning, through the idea of "opening her third eye". The symbol of the third eye in the dream is the equivalent of the principle, perhaps most clearly formulated by Deepak Chopra, that understanding our reality, and resolving any issues that the reality poses before all of us, is only possible by actually transcending that reality. In this integrative logical sense, no question has an answer on the level on which it is posed. To truly address any question, one must go beyond it; one must enter a logical metalevel at which the question is viewed differently that it is from the vista from which it is initially experienced, or at the level at which it is posed in the first place (Chopra, 1993).

In the note about her dream, Ksenija fights for beauty, for the light, for a transformation of anything that is conventionally regarded as threatening and ugly (the snake) into a different meaning and thus into a symbolic asset. After I had given her to read this passage, in this very book, about her own dream, she remarked: "I want you to write down that I am not one of those who fear snakes!" Her protest against the threatening object was her statement of an optimistic philosophy of life, where the conservative, almost consensually adopted symbol of threat, evil, and sin (the snake, especially in the psychoanalytic tradition) is symbolically (and practically) transformed into an aesthetically pleasing life content. This dream is an example of integrative thinking; it is the vision of how choosing a modal world might manifest in choosing and integrating symbolic meanings. The dream contains "ornaments" to everyday experiences that make the overall experience of life better; this is a particular aspect of philosophy of optimism that is embedded in symbolic interpretation. On a level of decision-making, focusing on particular ornamentally enhanced meanings that are attached to life experience and on general symbols that we as humans use to interpret our experience in general leads to a changed context of decision-making, a changed value matrix, where one decides from a position of beauty and benevolence, rather than from the common position of need and exigency (Robbins, 1992).

The view of the role of ferries in the dream largely reflects the way in which we learn, as we grow up, to perceive others: we see them either as angels and benevolent wizzards who can help transform our lives into brighter and better tales, or as witches and evil sorcerers who are there to torment us. In the liberal ideological contextualization of society and social relationships, it is the latter concept of others that predicates our efforts to prioritize our privacy, our boundaries, and our personal space in the face of an onslaught by others—an onslaught seeking to capture as much as possible of the presumably limited space, limited resources, limited privileges and social capital within a society perceived as a distributive and competitive machine, where strategies to protect oneself are limited only by the right of others to protect themselves. A different, healthier view of others is that characteristic of children: others are fairies, princes, and princesses; they have the capacity to magically transform our lives through love, companionship, and empathy, while society is seen as a magic land where the circumstances of life are not "limited resources", but unlimited possibilities. The latter is the vision inherent in modal logic; the former is the practical way of thinking naturally associated with propositional, binary logic: according to propositional logic, only one of the options can be true, the rest are false; there is a clear and largely black-and-white distinction between what is and what is not the case, and an almost as sharp a distinction between what, in such a coarse propositional world, is possible, and what is not. Modal logic, on the other hand, does not recognize impossibility; it seeks modal worlds where the structure of possibilities is different from the current ones; it queries the magical interplay between the modalities in terms of necessity, possibility, probability, contextuality, etc. The truth there is not binary, and the external context for subjective experience is seen as no less changeable than the subjective interpretations of events and the experiences themselves.

When one considers Ksenija's dream, one sees the geometric elements of a healthy narrative embedded in the characters and structure of the dream. Other people are positive and magical; animals are friendly and beautiful; there is a sense of harmony between all the actors and all elements of the dream.

In a harmony-seeking approach to living, the logical precondition for success is our ability to accord others sufficiently important roles and places. Only a life structure which inculcates others, with their identities, dignity, and values can be balanced; any structure that focuses on self, without a distribution of different roles, some of them comforting, some supporting, some opposing, to significant others, is likely to collapse because of a disturbed inner static, just as a concrete building based only on one unbalanced architectural idea, a limb protruding in space, or a structure striving in one direction, will collapse, because its balance is disrupted. The rule of physical laws, which determine what physical structure can remain erect over a long time and what kind of structure will fall, is the metaphorical equivalent of the psychological law that a life plan and a view of life focused on one's self alone, without a distribution of "weight" to other actors and concerns, outside oneself, is bound to fail. If this psychological law is violated, perhaps the person will survive, but their psychic integrity and quality of life are likely to be severely disturbed. There is an irreducible magical element to modal thinking that brings us to believe that what we imagine will, somehow, spring to reality. More precisely, being able to imagine a different modal world is the first precondition for any further decisions and actions that might help call it into reality; the imagining itself is a form of action; it is the articulation of a new symbolic and normative context in which the structure of possibility is different from the one we face in the current "state of affairs" that we start off with.

References

Chopra, Deepak (1993). *Ageless body, timeless mind: A practical alternative to growing old.* New York: Harmony Books.

Fatic, Aleksandar (2016). *Virtue as identity: Emotions and the moral personality.* New York and London: Rowman and Littlefield International.

Fatic, Aleksandar, Klaus Bachmann and Igor Lyubashenko (2018). *Transitional justice in troubled societies.* London: Rowman and Littlefield.

Freud, Sigmund (1912). The Dynamics of Transference. The Standard Edition of the Complete Psychological Works of Sigmund Freud, Volume XII (1911–1913): The Case of Schreber, Papers on Technique and Other Works, pp. 97–108. London: Hogarth Press 1953–1974.

Grigg, Russell. (2011). *Treating the Wolf Man as a case of ordinary psychosis.* Culture/Clinic 1, pp. 78–88.

Honneth, Axel (2007). *Disrespect: The normative foundations of critical theory.* Cambridge: Cambrdige University Press.

Jackson, Frank (1984). “Weakness of will”. *Mind 93*: 1–18.
Kraepelin, Emil (1968). *Lectures on clinical psychiatry*. New York: Hafner Publications.
Lacan, Jacques (1958/2017). *Formations of the Unconscious: The Seminars of Jacques Lacan*. Book V pp. 333–349. Cambridge: Polity Press.
Liu, Lanxiang, Haiyang Wang, Xueyi Cheng et al. (2023). *Gut microbiota and its metabolites in depression: From pathogenesis to treatment*. eBio Medicine (The Lancet Discovery Series) 90, 104537. Online. https://doi.org/10.1016/j.ebiom.2023.104527.
Maslow, Abaraham H. (1943). *A theory of human motivation*. Psychological Review 50. 4, pp. 370–396.
Miller, Jacques-Alain (2009). Ordinary psychosis revisited. *Psychoanalytic Notebooks of the European School of Psychoanalysis 19*, pp. 139–168.
Raabe, Peter (2013). *Philosophy's role in counseling and psychotherapy*. London and New York: Rowman and Littlefield
Raabe, Peter (2014). *Philosophy's role in counseling and psychotherapy*. London and New York: Rowman and Littlefield.
Radjabzadeh, Djawad, Jos. A. Bosch, Andre G. Uitterlinden et al. (2022). “Gut microbiome-wide association study of depressive symptoms”. *Nature Communications 13*, p. 7128. Online. https://doi.org/10.1038/s41467-022-34502-3.
Redmond, Jonathan (2014). *Ordinary psychosis and the body*. A contemporary Lacanian approach. Melbourne: Palgrave Macmillan.
Robbins, Tony (1992). *Awaken the giant within*. New York: Simon and Schuster.
Schopenhauer, Arthur (1966). *The World as Will and Representation*. Translated by E.F.J. Payne. New York: Dover Publications.
Smart J.J.C. (1991). Utilitarianism and Punishment. *Israel Law Review 25*, pp. 360–375.
Verhaeghe, Paul (2008). *On being normal and other disorders*. London: Karnac Press.

CHAPTER 5

Linguistic Pragmatics in Psychotherapy

Abstract This chapter focuses on how language, and what Ludwig Wittgenstein calls "language games", are factored into everyday thinking, psychotherapeutic interventions, and the modal theory of therapy. The way in which psychological structures that are reflected in language are played out in the therapeutic narrative reveals not just the difficulties faced by the person in therapy, but also the moral assumptions and confusion that require a particular philosophical resolution in the intimate community between the therapist and client. The chapter discusses how the nature of therapeutic community as a value community influences the client's and the therapist's perceptions and use of language and, in turn, how the growing quality and intimacy of that community is articulated in the therapeutic narrative.

Keywords Language games • Ethics • Narrative • Community • Value change

Unlike other forms of therapy, psychotherapy is a primarily linguistic and behavioral encounter between the therapist and the client. Given psychic life's inaccessibility to immediate perception, assessment, and direct measurement, our mental experiences are reflected in our behavior, and, in the context of psychotherapy, that behavior is mostly contracted into

A. Fatic, *Modal Integrative Psychotherapy*,
https://doi.org/10.1007/978-3-031-91934-3_5

language. That is why language is of utmost importance to therapists, not only the literal content of what is expressed through it, but equally, if not more so, the structure, richness, liveliness, dynamism of the language the client uses as a form of compressed behavior reflecting their psychic life. The entire linguistic process, including the use of both verbal language and body language, and the role of the body in linguistic expression can be seen in therapy as what Ludwig Wittgenstein described as a "language game"—a particular relationship that, in its explicit or tacit rules, expectations, motives, and emotions, is reflected in the way people use language as a way of relating to one another (Wittgenstein, 1958, pp. 7, 66–67, 71, 101). According to Wittgenstein, any expression gets its meaning from a broader language game and from the rules of that game that the user of the language plays at a particular time: language is woven into behavior to such an extent that it is itself a form of behavior. This means that the meanings individuals attach to individual expressions are articulated not just by the general rules of the language, but by the particular rules and intentions characteristic of narrower linguistic communities, such as peer groups, friends, families, etc. The language game can also result in what Wittgenstein calls "private language", namely a language that is so peculiar to the particular group that the use of specific linguistic expressions by members of that group is no longer comprehensible to the other speakers of the same language who are not members of the group (Wittgenstein, 1958, p. 243).

In this chapter, I argue that linguistic games and linguistic pragmatics along the lines of Wittgenstein's view of language games can elucidate the nature of therapeutic community and the key emotions that constitute that community, such as empathy or solidarity. Language games also throw light upon the client's character. They can direct psychotherapeutic work even in cases of the so-called hopeless clients.

The Language Game of Empathy as an Organic and Therapeutic Community

Empathy has been a conceptually contested value for large swaths of early modern and contemporary history of philosophy, ranging at least from Hume and the Scottish Enlightenment to today's discussions about the role of empathy both as an emotional relationship and as an intervention tool in psychotherapeutic practice and in philosophical counselling alike

(Fatic, 2021; Slote, 2010). While I do not feel that engaging with the conceptual debate on the meaning of empathy here would be productive, I wish to argue that empathy in practice, and in principle, is predicated upon suffering and commiseration. When we speak about empathizing with someone, we always have in mind an undesirable or painful condition of the other, and our own propensity to reach out to that person emotionally and to somehow relate to their suffering. The assumption of suffering, pain, and deprivation is thus internal to the very idea of empathy. This is the first idea I develop here in some detail, primarily engaging with Schopenhauer and his views on the quality of life and will to live as relevant to any debate involving the helping professions, in particular psychotherapy and philosophical counselling.

The second idea here is that empathy as a way of relating to another's suffering is constitutive of the only morally truly valuable community, namely a healing, organic community. It is our care for others and our ability to cross-identify with the other members of our community in our capacity to suffer through the exigencies of everyday life that creates lasting, helping, and resilient communities. Any institutional regulation, or state structure, is a compromise to the organicism of a community. Early communities, some of which at least were very organic and permeated with links of solidarity, had almost no institutional structures of governance, although they did have a hierarchy of power that was articulated in organic ways (the best warrior, the best decision maker, the council of elders, etc.). Such structures of leadership have very little to do in principle with modern governing institutions. The latter are created based on mainly procedural criteria that often cause manipulation of even the most basic principles of democracy, such as the will of the majority in the constitution of government.

The two ideas, that of suffering as the foundational condition we all face, and at the same time a precondition for meaningful empathy, and that of community as a consolation, structure this discussion.

Suffering: Schopenhauer and the Psychotherapeutic Perspective

If empathy is predicated upon suffering, then the universal nature of the normative application of empathy relates to the assumption of a factual universality of suffering. The idea, championed by Michael Slote, that empathy has the capacity to be the normative foundation for an ethics that is at once deontological and consequentialist in nature (Slote, 2010) presupposes that suffering, as the logical and practical precondition for empathy, is a universal human condition. If the moral justification of an action can be argued to be based on the consistency of that action with empathy as a universal principle, as Slote argues, then suffering is presumed as a fundamental life condition of all people. This is an assumption that reverberates through much of practical philosophy and psychotherapy and is in fact deducible from several major philosophical and psychological theories.

One particularly strong early modern theory that posits suffering as the original context of our existence is Schopenhauer's philosophy of life. According to him, pain is the universal condition that determines our existence. Our everydayness is marked by the necessity of routine labor and, in a complex society, attendance to administrative, institutional, and social tasks and chores that consume most of our day. The room for any human creativity is circumcised by necessity and need. The experience we all face, one that connects us to one another, is not that of joy or jubilation, but that of frustration, acute pain, illness, death, and existential angst. Any moments of joy, according to Schopenhauer, are merely respite from the more or less continued suffering at various levels and in various ways (Schopenhauer, 1966: Book IV; Stewart, 2023). Suffering, according to Schopenhauer, is caused by desire; we are driven by a will to live; this will is in itself aimless, it merely occurs, and it manifests itself in human beings as desire and drive. Given that desire can never be completely fulfilled and that efforts to reach its object only lead to new desires and a sense of lack, the entire life, which is dynamized by the will to live, is suffering and deprivation. This existential condition facilitates empathy as the foundation of our constructive mutual relationships. A way to escape suffering is by denying the will to live its objects, by embracing asceticism, and by trying one's best to step off the wheel of causality by becoming an observer, rather than actor of social relationships. The argument is common to Indian philosophy and to much of ancient Stoicism, and Schopenhauer makes repeated references to the Indian philosophical sources.

The condition of suffering, as fundamental to our place in the world, renders us susceptible to hurt and betrayal by others, and at the same time capable of establishing powerful links with the other members of our community based on our vulnerabilities. Empathy appears to be the core emotion and relationship that facilitates organic community-building.

The assumption of suffering produces interesting value consequences for psychotherapy. Namely, the attitude required of a therapist when entering the counseling room with any client, against the backdrop of this general hypothesis about the human condition, is one of commiseration. Schopenhauer, radically, sees all human love as a type of commiseration, of feeling sorry for the other because of this inescapable condition of deprivation, lack, and insufficiency (Schopenhauer, 1966). This means that when we see someone's psychotic compensations for the unbearable pain or deprivation in one's immediate experience, we don't perceive it primarily as a pathology, but as a manifestation of suffering, and focus on the sources and modes of experience of the suffering that is endured. Empathetic intervention tends to differ from a medicalized, detached approach that sees ideational divergence from reality as a mental illness in that, in the former case, the therapist will engage the person's ideas regardless of how odd they might seem, while in the latter the therapist will most likely treat them merely as symptoms, rather than as interpretative attempts by the patient, each of which attempts holds particular symbolic meanings. The therapist's metaphysical assumptions play a crucial role in determining his or her value laden approach to any client and to the suffering involved in the complaints presented when we encounter our clients. Our optimistic, or pessimistic view of life, our understanding of it makes up the substance of our daily experiences and what drives us in making key decisions, all of which are fundamentally metaphysical. This general philosophy of life determines how we perceive other people, especially those who seek help from us. The hypotheses of suffering as the primary human condition, of commiseration and mercy as the emotions that best describe a mature relationship to others, at least on a base level of interaction, and of empathy as the normative beacon for ethics, psychotherapeutic and otherwise, determine our sensibility. They determine our method, tools, and philosophy of psychotherapy and counseling. Our view of suffering also determines our portrayal and delineation of the role of our clients in our own lives. The ethics of therapy and counseling determines how relevant and significant our clients will be for us, within and outside therapy. This also determines how professional or organic we are in our therapeutic and personal approach to our clients.

A related aspect of the therapeutic relationship and the empathy that lies at its core is that of the characters of the client and therapist. Assuming that character is a relatively stable structure around which identity is solidified, the nature or character of the client and the therapist will determine the extent of the transference and countertransference and the limits of empathetic reach in either direction. Empathy as the normative foundation of a relationship posits character at the structural center of that relationship. Not every therapist can adequately or sufficiently comprehensively empathize with every client, and vice versa. This means that a certain alignment of character is the prerequisite for a truly effective and close therapeutic alliance. A similarity of characters propels individuals towards more collaboration and willingness to reach beyond the traditional professional boundaries in their relationship (Yalom, 1996).

The convergence of characters between the therapist and client in a strong therapeutic relationship fosters the emergence of a clear and symbolically powerful private language between them. Such a language characterizes most close relationships. Lovers, colleagues at the same job or members of the same organic communities share parts of the language that only they understand. Even their use of the general language is sometimes idiosyncratic and incomprehensible to other users of the same language. Their language game, to use Wittgenstein's term, is almost entirely private: the boundaries of that language game are the normative tresholds of their very relationships. The rules, values, and emotions involved in the relationship are all parameters of the essentially private language game that unfolds between the client and the therapist, and the same is the case with any close relationship: ones with our loved ones, friends, neighbors, colleagues. Any organic relationship or organic community rests on a particular value-laden language game that defines the particular interactions between its members. Giorgio Agamben describes these significant interactions as "special actions" that define membership in a particular community (Agamben, 2013).

Assuming that our vulnerabilities, our awareness of our own predisposition to suffering as an essential life condition, determine our close, significant language games, the very special actions that take place within the language game of an organic community focus on empathy. It is the type of empathy that we show to other members of our community that largely determines the identity and nature of that community. The ways in which the members of a particular community help and support each other also arise from the modality of empathy that they share. Workers gather around work conditions, mutual solidarity and a sense of shared identity that arises from empathy concerning the precariousness of the workplace and all the existential exigency that this precarity generates. Members of various religious communities articulate their sense of collective identity through empathy concerning the values and way of life that require considerable discipline, asceticism, and a critical distance from the dominant ways of the secular society. For example, members of the Christian communities share concerns about the lives of their children, they uphold values that require considerable self-denial; they maintain a high value of the family in their worldview, refrain from promiscuous life styles, prefer to have more children. They tend to see their career in perspective, within a hierarchy of values where professional success is less important than one's family life and one's spirituality. Members of Christian communities share these and other concerns in their group. They try to assist each other in child-rearing and the instilment of the same values in their families, to the extent that they set up communes and separate settlements, hoping to reduce the risk of alienation of their close ones from the core language game that determines who they are. It is the possibility of failure, or of detachment from the language game, or of any kind of harm to their key values, that predicates their relationships of solidarity and mutual support. The language game is fundamentally embedded in empathy for the shared worries by other members of the community and threats to the community as a whole. In the history of Christianity, the whole canonical law tradition can be traced back as a set of responses by the Christian communities to the various threats to their identity and way of life. These threats emerged at various points of time in history, and that is why various canonical laws seem odd when observed from the present point of view. They can only be understood in the context of the particular situations and issues faced by the Christian communities and church at the time when they were formulated. The history of any organic group bears witness to the same structural phenomenon: concern over the threats and temptations faced by that group over time produce various models of action, rules, and principles of the language game that arise from the empathetic relations between the community's members concerning the threats and temptations that could afflict any one of them and the community as a whole. We always connect with others more deeply through our vulnerabilities, through our awareness of shared suffering as the elemental situation of life. Our language games that determine our communities are thus merely the various articulations of empathy, except in groups that are transient, superficial, and based on momentary interests or logic of executing a particular action. Deep structure is the structure of awareness of pain and vulnerability, not one of joy, power, or convenience. The psychotherapeutic relationship, when it is a truly effective and strong therapeutic alliance, thus goes beyond the professional setting and engages both or all of the participants in their deeply human capacities (Yalom, 1996).

The Community: Value Unity as Opposed to Institutionalized Group

When I speak of organic community, what I mean is a community that does not depend for its sustenance and identity on procedural and institutional guarantees. In this sense, an organized society is an inorganic group, because it is intransparent, dependent on procedures and institutions, and the members' very perception of other members is mediated by the rules and procedures. We do not know our neighbors in a large, institutionally organized town; however, we draw conclusions about them based on how well they fit in with the rules of the community: whether they are quiet, discrete, whether they park in the right spots, etc. The very concept of an "ideal neighbor" is based on an institutional vision of community, one where virtue is projected based on the adoption of shared normative structures and on daily rule following. Contrariwise, an organic community is one where members are, fundamentally, "stuck with" the community and the other members of it because they are deeply connected. Traditionally, the family was seen as a par excellence organic community; however, with the destruction of the family through an exceptionally high rate of divorces worldwide, the derogation of a hierarchical relationship between parents and children, and the loss of the family's role as the primary socializing and therapeutic community (primary socialization and therapy are now the roles of peer groups), new organic communities are needed in place of the family.

One of the critical points in the constitution of such communities is the lack of physicality and the mediation of all human relationships by electronic devices and channels. This violent imposition of electronic and global forms of communication upon any individual (it is violent because there are no viable alternatives) directly impacts the language games of empathy and solidarity that our joining together by the "hooking together" of our vulnerabilities entail. Electronic communities thus precede organic communities and are sometimes hoped to mirror organic communities in the electronic space. The language games that are played on the internet forums and in various quasi communities particularly clearly illustrate the syntactic and semantic structures that characterize the hoped-for private languages that help constitute organic groups. However, these are inescapably quasi communities, and the community languages are largely chimeras, because the full sense of another's predicament, suffering, and thus the preconditions for a full-fledged empathy are impossible in electronic communities, as they lack physicality. One can imagine the suffering of another in an electronic relationship, and more so in one that is semi-electronic and semi-traditional or physical (people meet and communicate electronically, developing their relationships on both levels, electronic and that involving physical presence); however, one can only experience the pain and vulnerability of another person through physical presence.

We suffer through our bodies and the reflections of this suffering, awareness, and, sometimes, anticipation of it, generate a meta-level suffering in our minds. Indeed, we can suffer mentally through a representation of pain that is fundamentally felt physically. Even our supposedly "sui generis" psychic pain, such as that arising from the loss of loved people in our lives, is primarily experienced physically, through the physical processes that cause us to feel unwell, to have diminished life energy, to experience a range of functional problems that all add up to an aggregate experience of "mental suffering". Our physical encounter with a person who "mentally" suffers makes it very clear to us, in most cases, that their suffering is as physical as it is psychic: their appearance, their body language, their energy, and their overall demeanor command empathy in much the same way as does an encounter with someone who suffers only physically. It is the physical human encounter that generates the full-fledged language game of empathy, because it is only through physicality that we can fully express our suffering, or fully experience the suffering of another at the level of genuine empathy. This does not mean that one cannot or does not feel sorry for someone one knows is experiencing pain when that knowledge arises from electronic communication; this emotion and the corresponding relationship, however, lack the immediacy, the wealth of information, and the unique human contact dimension of the physical encounter that offers the only opportunity to join in a full organic community of empathy.

The language games of organic communities focus on values and related emotions. The values and emotions that dynamize behavior arising from such values further project a common virtue, on which the sense of collective identity is based (Fatic, 2016). In this respect, an organic community is different from that regulated by institutions and rules, because the latter can bring together individuals with very different views of life, values, and sensibilities; such individuals can coexist in a tolerant liberal society through refraining from expressing their differences in order to respect the dominion of others—after all, this is the foundation of liberal political theory: the idea of tolerance of differences in order to facilitate the unhindered autonomous development and life of the potentially incompatible others. Organic communities are communities of destiny: they are seen as lifelong or at least very long-term collectives where members are simply destined to live together and care for each other; they do not "tolerate" others, but integrate them and strive to be one with them as much as possible. The dynamic foundation of organic communities is not tolerance, but deep acceptance. This is at once the difference between the psychotherapeutic community as an organic one and the social community that clients and therapists alike come from. When they step from their everyday communities into the therapeutic relationship, they enter a new world, where many of the norms and assumptions typical of their society no longer apply. They leave one language game and gradually, as their therapeutic relationship develops, build a new one, whose structure, meaning, and level of detail reflect the quality and depth of the very relationship.

The above-described dynamics of the therapeutic alliance lead us to controversy over the professional nature and limitations of the psychotherapeutic process in light of the empathetic relationship that marks the organic dimension of any therapeutic community. Empathy and the recognition of suffering are at the core of the phenomena of transference and countertransference. Both the client and therapist project their own structures of empathy, recognition of personality and important others into each other. In cases where there is sufficient compatibility of character and sensibility, the alliance can grow strong, and in such cases the boundaries of a professional relationship are quickly transcended. The organic community that is thus created resembles all other organic communities and positions the client and therapist in a variety of roles typically held by members of organic communities: friendship, solidarity, mutual care, shared values, the creation of new values and attitudes that arise from the particular relationship—all of these elements make up a strong and highly articulate private language, and the corresponding language game (a particular type of dynamics that characterizes the relationship between the two persons). Such a strong, highly private game is at once therapeutically effective, because the client is under a strong healing influence of the therapist, and vice versa, the therapist is additionally sensitized and enriched by the client. The strong mutual influence, primarily that of the therapist on the client, allows for the achievement of significant personal change and development. However, the boundaries of such a relationship are often blurred in relation to professional standards. Once they step into a community of strong interpersonal empathy and develop their own private language and the flow of a private language game, the client and therapist step out of the ordinary social relationship categories, including the professional one. Everything they do in such a deep organic community, while therapeutically effective, also tends to be normatively controversial from the point of view of professionalism. Love is not the least of such controversial, yet powerful facets of the organic therapeutic community.

Love and Psychotherapy as Foundational Processes in Organic Communities

I have some clients who are career criminals. This has come to me as an unintended part of my counselling practice. First, one client appeared who had been drawn to me through my YouTube channel, where he found some videos that he was able to identify with. He was abroad and in a difficult life situation. Upon returning, he started therapy, demonstrated a high level of psychological vitality, and in time overcame his major existential issues (a failed long-term romantic relationship, joblessness and difficulties in primary family). It turned out that this client, while not a criminal himself, was immersed in a highly criminalized neighborhood, and soon other clients started coming to me from that same subculture who appeared to be real delinquents. I never had any personal safety issues with them, though they tended to be unstable and irregular in attendance. However, at one point, when I asked one of them why he and his friends kept coming to me when none of them appeared to really want to change their way of life, he responded: "this is because you love us".

I don't think that I particularly love criminals, nor am I inclined to even listen to their "problems from the workplace". Most of my work with them is focused on their emotional and family lives, with occasional overtures to the underlying need for them to change their life structure and their "work". However, they fascinate me as human beings, because I have never met a person from that milieu who is slow in thinking, insensitive, or indifferent to their family and close friends. Individuals who engage, long term, in the criminal world seem to possess a misplaced, perverted leadership personality structure, where their talents to inspire others and take risks for their close family members and friends are distorted into all kinds of unacceptable behavior.

It turned out, in time, that some of my other clients, when I asked them similar questions, responded in a similar way, suggesting that they felt that I loved them. This caused me to rethink my practice and the way I relate to the people I work with.

Upon reflection, I decided that my unconscious selection of clients was not exactly "professional". I select clients based on whom I find interesting, who I feel initial empathy for, and I deselect and refer to other colleagues those whom I find boring, dislikeable, or not within the realm of issues that I maintain a personal interest in. Hence, those who I work with are individuals that I feel for and who are dear to me. It turns out that they have precisely pinpointed the simple core of our relationship that was opaque to me: I do "love" those people in a particular way in which I am able to form a relationship with them, regardless of whether I approve or disapprove of what they do. They matter to me.

It is a familiar aspect of psychotherapy that therapists benefit from many therapy sessions on a personal level. We develop as persons and are often able to view our own life issues in a more constructive and explanatory light due to the conversations we have with our clients and thought our clients' experiences that we become aware of through therapy. Our clients, in an important way, help us to become better persons, better parents, lovers, friends, colleagues. Yet, this mutuality is not a betrayal of the professional relationship whereby the client receives a service from the therapist through the therapy process. The service itself is the relationship, and the mutuality of it gradually leads it beyond being a mere professional service. Once the therapeutic relationship becomes an organic community, it takes on characteristics that define various types of organic unions. Not infrequently, the therapeutic relationship is one of human love (agape). We become friends who care for each other, and this friendship, while retaining the professional layer of service through the therapy process and the retention of the roles of therapist and client, in its substance, stretches considerably further than the mere service. We become involved in our clients' lives and they become a part of our lives. Our empathetic relationship carries us further and further from the original professional encounter and navigating that sea of potential directions in which our alliance could lead us becomes one of the major challenges for the therapist. Freud befriended many of his clients. Despite his proclamations that the psychoanalyst must be detached and precise like a surgeon and should never analyze those who are close to him or socialize with them, Freud frequently invited his clients for dinner at his house, travelled with them, and engaged in joint business ventures, where they often supported the psychoanalytic movement with their time, funds, social connections, etc. They left a lasting imprint on Freud's very psychoanalytic thought and, without a doubt, on him as a human being. The same is the case with most other fathers of modern psychotherapy, from whichever tradition they might have come.

The love that characterizes the organic community applies to all kinds of alliances that contain a professional element, but, by their very nature, stretch beyond that relationship. Psychotherapy is perhaps the most intense organic profession, but consider academic mentorship. We start mentoring our PhD students on a professional level. In most cases we do not even know them and agree to offer them our services to build their major work after which they join the guild. However, with some of them, we develop deep friendships that stretch far beyond their PhD defense. We care for them, know many things about their lives that nobody else knows (a common element with the psychotherapeutic relationship), write together with them, travel, go out, visit each other at home, and develop strong interpersonal bonds. Years later, such relationships are no longer a formal supervisorship, but they tend to retain the element of academic mentorship. We are still not the same academically, because one leads the other, but on a human level we are sincere friends. Not so infrequently, academics who die, in the absence of a family, are buried by their former students and now friends, and their estates are managed by their younger colleagues whom they once supervised. I am not sure how frequent this is between psychotherapists and their clients, but the links of organic alliance in both professions are apparent.

In conclusion, let me take this argument one step further. So far, I have argued that a deep psychotherapeutic relationship is an organic community that resembles, in its key features, all other, now largely lost, organic communities, and that venturing deep into such an alliance leaves the professional standards and criteria largely behind the newly emergent quality of a deeply human and decidedly private relationship between the client and therapist. There is, however, a more radical conclusion at hand here. It is not just that any deep therapeutic relationship is an organic community; any organic community is by nature also therapeutic.

Given the earlier argument that we connect deeply only through our vulnerabilities, through an empathetic reaching out to each other through the recognition of the universal pain that marks our lives inescapably, the organic communities that we establish through such deep empathetic interpersonal connections are naturally healing, comforting, and supportive. A large part of the reason therapy is so necessary in modern society is the absence of organic communities and their healing influence. It appears that most of what we do in therapy is re-create and revitalize these same mechanisms of empathy and human love that are the very foundation of human togetherness in an environment of institutional, detached, and rule-driven societies that are no longer communities. Some regular experiences within the psychotherapeutic process reflect this principle, as individuals who have more access to any remnants of organic communities through hobbies, sports, or religious groups tend to be more resilient and progress more and faster through therapy, while those who are completely denied access to organicism, physicality and significant, empathetic others present much more difficult and demanding cases in counselling and therapy. The same applies to individuals with highly articulate languages arising from complex and close language games. Their internal resources, including their ability to articulate and interpret problems, allow them to progress swiftly in addressing issues of self-change, while, on the other hand, those with sparse symbolic and linguistic resources tend to have a harder time articulating and addressing their problems. It appears that the ability to formulate an issue is associated with a particular type of experience of sociality and social emotions that translate into greater personal resources to deal with the social adversity that is associated with most complaints addressed in psychotherapy. The social dimension of our mental life, the intentionality of our minds, and their structural propensity to reach for others (Searle, 1983, 1989) are essential elements of our ability to address psychic pain.

Julian

I first met Julian many years ago. A man in his 70s, active and socially propulsive, Julian had been an active politician and businessman. Julian has a mellow, civil appearance; he is socially intelligent and able to entertain various ideas without prejudice, despite his age. One could say that he is mentally younger than his physical age. However, Julian runs in a pattern of learned behavior that involves the use of half-truths, reneging on explicit agreements, even contracts, and maintaining deliberately very vague and semi-articulated relations with those he sees as inferior, in particular his employees and business associates.

Julian's communication with his staff and colleagues is superficially agreeable, but people who work for him never know whether what he says he has decided will be implemented, when, how, and under what conditions it will be implemented. This generates an atmosphere of perverse fear, in which Julian sits on a throne of power while his numerous subjects, so to say, elbow each other around his throne trying to get his attention, all the while aware that whatever benevolent gesture they might extract from him, Julian might not in the end follow through with his promises.

Using this ambiguity, Julian has managed to portray himself as an enlightened public figure. However, his way of running his business is ruthless.

Now, what is the psychotherapeutic problem with Julian?

Julian operates in a society where names are everything: the way he is perceived in his social circle and society in general determines his profits as a businessman. His entire world is nominalist: it all about his reputation. Human society in general, after all, has historically been based on reputation; however, in organic societies reputation was occasionally checked and confirmed, or validated. One has always had to earn and maintain a reputation by at least a periodic praiseworthy and publicly visible action. In more complex social circumstances, reputation is less genuine; one might build a reputation based on one's public persona without necessarily acting on the values and standards one professes publicly, and one may be able to maintain such a reputation through the mere continuance of public appearance, without ever having to effectively behave in line with the fictitious reputation.

In trying to effectively communicate with Julian, I started by trying to analyze his values. This proved much easier than I expected. The key value was money. The next most important value was respectability. The third in the hierarchy of his values was a sense of personal power over those he believed he could control. Balancing these three values facilitated a manageable relationship with Julian. Next, I tried an experiment in psychotherapy.

My strategy was to avoid any kind of critique of Julian. All the explicit statements I made in conversations with Julian were positive: I told him that I found his actions, even those I disagreed with, attractive on some level, because his ambivalence was amusing to me, and I went out of my way to show an understanding, even empathy, for his desire for profit. I decided to work on making bare both sides of his ambivalence: the need to use and dominate others, and the need to appear conscientious. In most situations, the former desire prevailed, while the latter was a bit of a late starter; however, I was convinced that both sides of him were alive. Ambivalence is a dynamic state that is often underestimated in psychotherapy for its destructive power for the person and for their quality of life, as it grows quickly and can tear the person apart.

Julian was caught between two modal worlds in such an ambivalent structure that this very ambivalence defined him as a person and determined important aspects of his life. To use Gilbert Ryle's distinction, Julian's "inclinations" and "agitations" were so deeply intertwined that they could not always be mutually distinguished (Ryle, 1986, pp. 90–91).

Having said all of the above, what could Julian do to alleviate his anxiety about who he was? I am fairly convinced that he was aware of the nominalist nature of his problem—that all he was concerned with was appearances. However, he was unable to go so far to embrace an extreme epistemic solution, which, in his case, would be phenomenalism: a view that reduces all our experiential reality to mere phenomena (Ayer, 1986, pp. 84–134). On the one hand, Julian appeared almost exclusively concerned with the public appearance of his person and his business; however, he was also deeply and secretly worried about the characters and intentions of those he was involved with, either in business or privately. Appearances were the only thing that mattered to Julian when they concerned his own business and personality in the eyes of others; however, appearances were not sufficient for him when it came to the closer relationships that mattered to him in everyday life. He demanded more from those he associated with—perhaps the most conspicuously, he demanded loyalty. This was more than just the application of double standards by Julian: there was a value tension inside him. He felt secure only when he thought he could "read" or understand the interests of other people that he was involved with, and he tried to manipulate those interests, at least as he saw them, into structures where people would have an interest to be loyal to him. On the other hand, he did everything he could to avoid having to be loyal to others. While, on the one hand, he tried to control others by maintaining what he believed was their perception of their interests in their relationship to him, on the other hand he did everything possible to leave his own options open when loyalty was expected from him. Thus, many of his employees, with whom he was superficially friendly and whose loyalty he counted on in earnest, never knew whether their contracts would be extended at the end of the year, nor what their workload would be. Only those who had managed to establish a more resistant or independent relationship with Julian (those who did not work only for him, and thus had alternatives, or those whom he believed benefited his company by their mere presence, because of their public reputation) were treated somewhat better and more predictably. Most of the employees who did the lion's share of work in his companies faced uncertainty about the content and terms of their job. This detracted from the effectiveness and performance of Julian's business, which could have been far more successful if the structure of the staff was more of a loyal team and less of a group of discrete employees who only pretended to be a harmonious collective; however, Julian was unable to go beyond this inner value tension, this ambivalence between what seemed like a desire for organic human interaction and solidarity, on the one hand, and a deep disbelief in human trustworthiness, on the other.

The structure of the described internal situation of Julian is typical for many clients in therapy, and of many people who find themselves "stuck" in their relationships in general. On the one hand, they desire human connection and a commonality in the pursuit of their group, institutional, or corporate goals, while on the other they seem unable to bring themselves to extend trust to others. A related type of therapeutic issue occurs in romantic relationships, where individuals appear unable to "commit" to an emotional relationship despite their desire for companionship, security, or family. Neither side of the motivational geometry prevails sufficiently, and this creates ambivalences that at first seem trivial and manageable, and later grow into draining, life-degrading dysfunctional dynamics that require therapy.

In my work with Julian, I was saddened to see how such a divided inner world in this man was so resistant to change, when so many alternative modal worlds were available to him, given his intelligence. Julian had many resources to make both his company and his colleagues truly flourish, yet he consistently chose to make them fearful, miserable, and dependent on him. This clearly had something to do with his self-perception and his perceived need to inflict discomfort on others in order to feel important. However, given his high intelligence, I continued to be puzzled at how he appeared unable to see all the compromises to his own happiness and that of the people who surrounded him that he had caused by his rigid need to oppress and maintain a below-the-surface structure of dominance, while showing a superficially mellow, friendly, and equal face in his every-day dealings with others.

On a socially sensitive interpretation, Julian is part of a particular social world. In his social circle, he is surrounded by old friends and allies from the political times when he was an active political decision maker. Although he is generally adaptable, he has failed to adapt to a new society, because his contacts with that society are mediated by the old guard who themselves have not adapted. Hence, mentally, Julian still lives in the world of his more youthful experiences. As far as social relationships are concerned, this world he lives in reflects in his business. All of his allies and confidants are people from the same political ideology. Thirty years later, Julian' psychological organization, his awareness, remains unchanged and fundamentally maladapted.

Julian's contradictions in desires merely reflect the social controversies he lives in. He lives in two worlds: in the world of old habits, where a sense of personal security and importance is derived from (tacit) domination and oppression of the weaker, and at the same time in the competitive world of competence and international propulsion, within which he wishes to publicly portray his public persona and reputation as being progressive. At some level, he is aware that he needs to adapt to this new world; however, his most important inner transactions, his deeply ingrained sensibilities, remain in the past. The two worlds alive in him simultaneously tear him apart. His inner tension is both social and existential.

Our social world integrates our awareness. There is evidence of people who had moved to different cultures and continents with their compatriots and members of close, organic communities, and have managed, over decades, to retain the benefits of their culture—not only psychological, but also those in the realm of physical health (low blood pressure, low cholesterol levels, longevity, etc.) in a new culture where all of these health problems are extremely pronounced. Parallel studies also show that people from the same communities, who had moved to the same countries alone, soon started to suffer from the same ailments, physical and psychic, as most people from the culture they moved to (Chopra, 1993, pp. 51–66). Perhaps this social nature of most of our mental pain can help explain the fact that experience in psychotherapy shows that many generic treatments are adequate for very different diagnoses, even those that appear mutually incompatible in their presentation and internal dynamics ((Van Van Groos, 1989, p. 352)—yet another apparent paradox of psychodiagnostics (Verhaeghe, 2008, p. 75, footnote 28). Namely, if most psychic dysfunctionalities spring from similar causes, which, in their key dimensions, are social, perhaps the generic treatments address the pain and discomfort as a reaction to the social causes, rather than as articulations of medical conditions. This does not mean that there are no psychiatric disorders that are medical in their important aspects; rather, it suggests that the variety of such diagnosis and their symptomatic presentations can be, and in fact are, successfully psychotherapeutically addressed on the level of their social causation, rather than on the phenomenological level of their medical appearance. The social conditioning of disordered presentations of mental states is articulated, among other things, through the language one uses to create one's immediate social world. One interesting aspect of the language game that characterizes Julian's language is common to most power-impregnated worldviews and relationships—it is deliberate ambiguity.

One of the elements in which the language games show character and help shape the style of interpersonal interactions is the use of information. If our relationships are a game that follows certain rules, they take on many characteristics of other games, including the game of negotiation. There is an influential distinction in negotiation theory between the so-called integrative games or integrative negotiations, and distributive games. The former are based on the idea that the interaction's goal is to maximize the distribution of a particular good that, in itself, is infinite, so that all parties to the game profit and leave the game with more of a particular good that the negotiation was about than they entered the game with. Examples of such integrative games include friendship, trust, or any kind of relations where the negotiation over a good that might in itself be limited (victory in sports, success in a business dealing, etc.) and where the immediate negotiation and its immediate goal are treated only as pretext for broader integrative relationships with longer-time reach (conceding victory in sports in the interest of greater cooperation, agreeing to better commercial terms for the other side in business negotiations than one would have to, in order to foster future collaboration, etc.). Integrative games are often described as ones where everybody wins and there are no losers. Distributive negotiations, on the other hand, are ones where a limited good is distributed more or less to one rather than the other side, and the disproportionality of the distribution reflects the decisiveness of the victory (in sports matches, the more goals in football one team scores against the other team, and the less goals the other team scores, the more decisive the victory of the first team is). Distributive games are also called "zero sum games", where one side wins, and the other loses. The two types of games, or negotiations, factor information in radically different ways (Lewicki et al., 2016). In integrative games, information is generously shared because it allows all the participants to pursue the most effective strategies to maximize the (infinite) good, such as trust or solidarity. In distributive games, information is a strongly guarded commodity, whose possession often facilitates a competitive advantage of one party over the other. Thus, deliberate ambiguity as a language game reveals one's perception of the relationship as a distributive game, rather than as an integrative game, even if the superficial articulation of the relationship appears integrative. In fact, most relationships (and most underlying games) are combined integrative and distributive games, where the exact proportion of each game will largely depend on the personalities of the participants (their worldview or character) and to some extent also on the nature of the goods involved in the relationship.

Assuming that relationships are, as Wittgenstein describes them, language games that are integrated into broader patterns of behavior, the structures of meaning articulated through the particular language game gradually create one's social world and impact, increasingly deeply, one's overall sensibility and sense of sociality. That is the game theory equivalent of the concept of "group chemistry": belonging to a group gradually changes the individual's perceptions of reality and aligns them with those of the group. This means that a person who is deeply immersed in predominantly distributive games will likely develop a broader worldview that sees human relationships as distributive negotiations in which deliberate ambiguity is a weapon for fighting for limited resources. This is what Julian's sensibility reveals about his experience and his worldview. Conversely, one's trusting attitude and volunteering of information reveal a likely personal history of playing mainly integrative games, where the base worldview is that of collaboration and joint goals. It is this type of analysis that psychotherapist often apply to childhood experiences and assessing family functionality based on young people's current patterns of relationships and social interactions.

Hopeless Clients

The modal way of thinking generally rules out hopelessness, for if various states of affairs co-exist at the same time, "hovering around" the current modal world or set of circumstances, the modal worlds in the proximity in principle offer opportunities for a change which is more or less immediate and comprehensive; this is the ultimate logical grounding for psychotherapeutic optimism. However, clients can be hopeless in certain cases. The question of hopelessness in psychotherapy is at once epistemic, metapsychological and linguistic.

Logically speaking, our beliefs and attitudes represent more or less affectively charged statements. The content and nature of the modal world can be represented in the logical status of the propositions that describe that modal world. Such statements can be necessarily true (in which case they hold true in all modal worlds, such as the statement that a person is identical to himself), they can be contingently true, or possibly true, in which case they hold true in some modal worlds and false in other modal worlds. They can be possible or impossible, probable or less probable in various modal worlds. It is the statements that are not necessarily true (and thus also do not automatically describe possible and highly probable states of affairs) that are of primary interest to psychotherapy, because we work on making possible things that, in the current modal world, are impossible or hold a low probability of being or becoming true.

For statements which are necessarily true ($\Box A$), namely those that hold regardless of the modal world in which they are made, we have a limited use in counselling and psychotherapy, because such statements are the most general philosophical and mathematical principles, such as the so-called analytic statements (sentences where the predicates merely extrapolate the defining characteristics of the subject), such as A=A. These statements are philosophically relevant for us in a deeper sense, when issues of identity and key decisions which mark our self are concerned, but in most cases, we focus on more informative, synthetic statements (statements where the predicate contains certain ascriptions of properties to a subject which do not automatically follow from the very definition of the subject itself), such as sentence N1 below:

> "Julian is fearful of who he is expected to be and how he will fare in his social world if he abandons his old ways". (N1)

Sentence N1 is not necessarily true. It is true in some possible worlds and untrue in others. In symbolic language: $\Diamond N1$.

Formally,

N1 (P1...Pn), where P1...Pn is a range of possible worlds across which Julian is fearful of who he is expected to be. (Chellas, 1980, p. 4)

In narrative form, N1 is true in a range of modal worlds described by P1 to Pn.

The concept of a model in modal logic relates *all possible worlds* (W) with *those possible worlds which could be specified to define the validity of any sentence* (P). Thus, the logical symbolization of a model takes the form (W, P). Hence, P is contained in W. P stands for an infinite sequence of modal worlds, a subset of W, which, in Julian's case, define the validity of the sentence "Julian is afraid of who he is...", or N1. P is the subset of modal worlds that determine the validity of a sentence or proposition.

For example, the set of all modal worlds (W) includes such modal worlds as Julian's emotional relationships with his children or those that describe Julian's life as that of a passionate angler or hiker. These possible worlds do not determine, in either way, the validity of the proposition that in his career Julian is fearful of who he might be expected to be in his business interactions with his partners. However, at the same time, W contains modal worlds such as that of Julian's view of society, the nature of interpersonal relationships in the society, his view of how personal interests fare in society vis-à-vis human emotions, solidarity, and the mutual identification between people. Such modal worlds are directly relevant to the validity of the statement N1. They constitute the range of possible worlds P that, within W, determine the validity of proposition N1 (or any proposition).

Modal logic sets up the scenery for psychotherapeutic intervention in MIP. The fact in the described case that $\Diamond$N1, and not $\Box$N1, is a principled source of hope in MIP. Julian is *not necessarily* afraid of who he is; he is only "possibly" (and factually, but not necessarily) afraid, thus his situation is *contingent* on a range of circumstances P1...Pn. In some of the relevant modal worlds, which do not happen to be the current modal world, he would *not be afraid* of who he is or who he might become or be seen to become in the public eye. Often the aim of psychotherapy is to move to such a different modal world.

The focus of MIP is not on the analysis of the meaning of N1—the genesis of Julian' situation described in N1—or on interpreting his predicament. In MIP, the focus is on the modal worlds P1...Pn, which determine the validity of statement N1. To change the troubling manifestation of N1 for Julian and other people whom he oppresses, an intervention is required in the modal worlds P1…Pn.

MIP is deeply social and, methodologically, it rests on socialization, or re-socialization, a part of which is choosing one's social circle and those whose affirmations and negations help establish and maintain our core beliefs about our relationships with others.

Consider the implication $A \rightarrow B$. Let us say that it stands for:

A: Julian is capable of re-evaluating his social circle and values.
B: Julian can switch to a modern, transparent and reliable way of conducting his business.

Thus, the statement $A \rightarrow B$ (if A, then B), describes the conditions under which Julian can enter a healthy realm of professional and business relationships.

However, the modal aspect of the implication requires the introduction of another variable, namely ἀ, which stands for a particular modal (possible) world. The implication would then have the form:

$$(A \rightarrow B)\dot{\alpha}.$$

The key problem in psychotherapy is exactly the modal world ἀ. One must first establish what makes up ἀ for Julian, for only if the conditions characteristic of ἀ are obtained will the implication hold, namely only in such a situation will Julian improve.

There are a number of modal worlds in which Julian may operate. Other than his social circle, these include his family, his health, his mood, any external influences, such as those by politicians, the public, students, his colleagues and employees, etc.

If Julian is trapped in a modal world ß, where he is systematically discouraged from "jumping" to a different set of perceptions and values, or, if Julian lingers in a situation where he moves from one modal world to another, where each modal world belongs to the set ἄ…ọ, whereby he can make the "jump" to a different way of acting only in modal world ἄ, and where all the other modal worlds are discouraging for his "switch" to a desirable change, then he is what can be described as a "hopeless client". He is not literally hopeless, because he can still change his disposition if he ends up in ἄ; however, this choice is extremely narrow, with just one set of circumstances allowing for productive change. The result is that the likelihood that either Julian, or his therapist, will successfully maneuver Julian into exactly the one productive modal world, ά, and keep him there long enough for him to make the switch, is very low.

MIP starts with exploring P, namely identifying the range of possible worlds that determine the value of key propositions that determine the client's situation (following the articulation of such propositions, of course). This may seem trivial at first sight; however, determining P is often the critical step in psychotherapy, because it allows the psychotherapeutic process to move deeper into what determines the significance of certain events and statements about life, as well as the person's internal dynamics that define the potential vectors of personal change. Sometimes, the range of possible worlds involves simply moving to a different physical and geographic space, with all the psychological consequences that such a move typically invites. In other cases, P will involve the client's becoming aware of their deep desire to abandon certain relationships in their life that they have hitherto considered crucial to their very identity. Determining P is likely the phase that, to the greatest extent, decides the success of psychotherapy in each case.

Once P is determined, its richness and content tell us much about the person and their resources to achieve considerable improvement. The more productive possible worlds there are, the more realistic and likely it is that the person will "land" in better and more healthy circumstances than one's present circumstances. If more modal worlds in P (w1… wn) allow for the productive change, the more likely such a change is, and the more hopeful the client's situation is. Most of these possible worlds are profoundly social, namely they describe various social situations for the client. The more social opportunities there are, the more hopeful the client's situation will be, and vice versa, the more constricted and closed one's social horizon, the less likely their psychological improvement will be. For example, a depressed person who is a digital nomad will have many more possible worlds in their P range to address their problem, including moving to different places, varying their job and using their skills to gain new contacts, friends, and potentially an entirely new social circle. A factory worker qualified to assemble just one particular part in one particular type of machine, who suffers from the same type of depression as the digital nomad, will have a far sparser P, and will have fewer options to experiment with in dealing with the problem. The level of symbolic resources and flexibility that are available to the person is an important part of P. The greater and richer the P, the more "tools" the person will have at their disposal to disassemble their problem and reassemble some other type of modal world where they would face a different life situation (likely one with different problems, though).[1]

Given that most possible worlds are largely socially defined, they relate to the capacity to adapt, and hopeless clients can, in a sense, be described as socially deprived: they are surrounded by poor, or destructive, life-worlds of social relationships which, instead of helping them to improve, motivate them to socially deteriorate. A change in one's personal values and perceptions of the world presupposes a *change in one's social positioning*, the introduction of new people and new qualities into one's social life, and, more than likely, the removal of some old acquaintances and some inherited habits. Julian lingers in a world of the past: as he ages, his ability to leave that world decreases, and his current (in fact past) life-world's grip on him solidifies, thus further shrinking his P modal range.

In my work with Julian, I discovered that he was troubled by the most productive and lucrative department of his company. Many times, he said to me that he did not understand why this department made so many sales when their actions and the quality of their business were low and unethical. Yet, the profits were so high that they basically kept Julian's company afloat regardless of how his other departments performed. He was tied to the staff of the problem department and forced to follow their views on many issues he personally disagreed with and saw them as ethically controversial.

Logically, there is nothing inevitable in what Julian does. His behavior is not describable as a logical implication.

There is a principle in modal logic that

$$\text{If } \models A, \text{ then } \models \Box A.$$

[1] I use the extremely ugly term "tools" here merely for convenience. Generally, this is a very unhelpful term that is widely used in psychotherapy. The term suggests that problems can be "fixed" with the use of appropriate tools just like a mechanical defect can. Sometimes, psychotherapeutic interventions do involve "tools", such as in the described example, where the range of P is reminiscent of a "toolbox"; however, in most cases, the vocabulary of tools is unhelpful because it obscures the deeply human and empathetic nature of the psychotherapeutic relationship, where the therapist does not use any "tools"; rather it is the client that might use the tools from their P to address their issues. In this context, "tools" are not psychotherapeutic interventions, but the client's personal resources to approach and address their issues.

In other words, if A (a proposition, or sentence) follows from certain premises, then the necessity of A follows from the same premises. Thus, the sentence:

> Julian's most profitable department's staff keep his business afloat ⊨ A (Julian acts the way his departmental staff wish him to)

would only be true if the following implication was also true:

> Julian's most profitable department's staff keep Julian's business afloat ⊨ □ Julian acts the way his departmental staff wish him to.

The above sentence is obviously untrue, as Julian has the liberty to act differently. There is no necessity in his acting the way his staff wish him to act.

The modal reasoning here shows us how, while Julian is, on one level, a hopeless client because he is trapped in the social conditioning of his circle of friends and cronies who do unethical business for him, there is no necessity for him to be so trapped.

Julian can break free at any moment—not only theoretically, but his breaking free might call into reality a different modal world where he might be seen as progressive and modern and might profit even more than he does in his current modality. Julian's business is in education. He could launch an initiative to make his business ethical and develop new practices that would become an ethical brand. At any point, by departing from the current stalemate defined by profit-driven compromises, which Julian knows are short lived, Julian can become an industry leader. His P range is currently socially limited; however, by the power of insight, this intelligent man could decisively shift to one of the P1… Pn modal worlds that are available within this sparse P range and still emerge existentially, socially, and morally victorious. It seems that even in practically hopeless situations, modal logic saves us.

If Julian can be made aware of his "modal freedom", he might be motivated to use that freedom; if that freedom is presented to him with sufficient simplicity and encouragement, it may move him away from his trapped, hopeless condition. It is his insight here that makes the difference. I focused on developing a trusting relationship with Julian to try to encourage him to move in a radically different direction.

In psychotherapy, clients face situations that they see as the inevitable results of their choices, which (choices) they also perceive as dictated by the circumstances that they find themselves in. This is the familiar "circle" in which clients often describe themselves as being "stuck". In modal logical terms, they see their choices as unequivocally arising from the premises shaped by their current circumstances:

$$\models A$$

where A represents decisions, and the implication the following of those decision from whatever is in front of the implication $\models$.

When this simple symbolic representation of any such situation is offered as a logical analysis, the client finds it easier to accept that, logically, there is a possibility that

$$\neg \models A,$$

or the negation of the statement that A follows from the premises that describe the client's situation, because it is not logically necessary that $\models A$.

Once this seemingly trivial logical demonstration is presented, the client can be invited to explore how $\neg \models A$ might be articulated in the narrative about their circumstances, or modal world. The simple $\neg$, or negation, of what one has long seen as the very foundation of one's thinking about one's life world and overall experience, is a frightening prospect. To accept that negation, one first needs to cognitively recognize the logical force that presents the $\neg$ as an equal potential reality as one's current reality. If this logical narrative is followed by a strong therapeutic alliance and the development of an empathetic therapeutic community, MIP creates the conditions for the person to rationally negate key aspects of one's current modal world, within a protective and collaborative relationship with the therapist. There is hardly anything conceptually simpler and at the same time practically more difficult in psychotherapy. The use of modal logical approach in first logically undermining one's current modal world, and then following up by strengthening the client to make the cognitive move and make the appropriate decisions to abandon that world and move to another is a distinguishing methodological feature of MIP.

I am not suggesting here that logic alone is sufficient to obtain results in psychotherapy. People in interpersonal relationships are generally not persuaded by rational argument; they orient themselves through emotions. However, modal logic is used as the first step in MIP to shortcut otherwise highly emotionally and otherwise costly ruminations by clients prior to establishing the key elements of desirable change. Logical analysis sets the stage for the narrative intervention that takes place next. Even the clients who appear hopeless after a long process of traditional therapy can surge into psychological and existential change through a modal range of possibilities when they are presented with the modal logical structure of their situation. It takes a very high degree of irrationality for any person not to recognize the structural logical argument that opens transformational hope by undermining the implications that hold true in their current modal world—ones that are limiting, but deemed valid and necessary by all those who are a part of that modal world, including their loved ones, their peers, their social circle, and their therapists with a non-modal view of "external reality" as something that is outside the traditional reach of psychotherapy.[2]

An illustrative method for modal thinking in MIP is Deep Psychotherapy, described in the next chapter. It is a method where intense change is induced through the immersion of the client in a full-time relationship with the therapeutic group or with the therapist alone, in a setting partly

[2] Some clarification is required here. Traditional psychotherapy focuses on changing the personal reality of the client. This is often described as "changing the client" and is posited as the goal of psychotherapy. A result of such change, when it is successful, is often a change in the client's external circumstances. Thus, traditionally psychotherapy often also results in a change in the client's circumstances, through the client's decisions and actions. However, MIP goes one step further. There are situations where clients cannot achieve personal change in particular directions because it is logically impossible; they are constrained by the external reality, or by their modal world. In most cases, traditional psychotherapy does not venture into the "objective" and logical constraints that make certain beliefs and the overall existential situation of the client necessary. Changing this situation, however, is a precondition for the very possibility of the client's personal change. Rather, traditional psychotherapy does it the other way round, encouraging the client to change only when a personal change is already possible. This is a serious limitation of traditional psychotherapy with many clients, because many arrive for counseling after a long process of trying to resolve their issues in a consistent way on their own, which means that their problems are often impossible to resolve on a level other than their ability to psychologically metabolize their given reality. MIP works with modal worlds, with the circumstances that determine the possibility or impossibility of personal change by exploring, with the client, the grounds on which the situation that limits the possibilities of change can be abandoned and a different reality called into existence. This is both a metaphysical and logical endeavor that goes considerably beyond the purely psychological approach to mental wellness.

separate from the client's everyday reality, where a (temporary) shift in the external circumstances triggers a different sense of possibility and access to alternatives than those allowed by the client's usual vista on life. On a principled level, MIP operates by shaking the ground, or shuffling the client's circumstances in order to disturb the balance of possibilities that consequently initiate a deep reconceptualization of experience and potential avenues for decision-making by the client. Clients in psychotherapy are not irrational or incompetent to draw logical conclusions or to appraise the viability of most of their life situations: a change in the situation, even if temporary, will throw the logical balance within which they are "stuck" and open inroads into previously inaccessible or improbable avenues of thought.

The Therapeutic Narrative

Once the modal logical coordinates of one's decision-making situation are laid out, and the person understands them, the psychotherapeutic intervention takes the form of a conversational narrative. This narrative focuses on *values as place holders of personal identity*. Hence, the understanding of psychotherapeutic intervention hinges on our understanding and use of values.

Any understanding of any kind of phenomena requires a value-ordering of perceptions and representations and giving them a more or less systematic meaning: thus, any process of conveying meaning in the form of interpretation is normative by nature. Such normativity is based on values. The very meanings that we rely on arise from the language games that we play. These language games are based on the respective communities and represent languages that are to various extent private. The rules of the language game, however, spring from the foundational norms of intersubjectivity within any particular community, and these norms are based on values. Thus, ultimately, values are at the core of everything we purport to "understand", interpret, make sense of, and integrate into our worldview. Values are the essence of who we are, and working with values is the key to narrative psychotherapeutic work.

We are now a different community from what we used to be a few decades ago, and what is considered decent and proper has accordingly changed. Our values have changed dramatically, in a very brief period of history. This is the general principle according to which language games are created.

In close relationships, people often address each other by names that others cannot even guess. These include the names of animal species, various concocted words that do not exist in the literal language, and all kinds of expressions that the members of the organic, close community recognize immediately, while they are puzzling to other users of the same general language. However, when an emotional couple becomes estranged, when they break up or divorce, the private language characteristic of their close relationship disappears. The foundational norms where the general rules of meaning used to be bent, because the couple felt that they were so close that the general language was insufficient to reflect the warmth and emotional unity between them, suddenly spring back into effect, as the underlying values dissipate and realign with the more ordinary relations between the members of a particular general linguistic community. In the professions, we develop language games that are often opaque to the broader community, where the rules of ethics, efficiency, and responsibility to the professional community are reflected in the concepts, rituals, and interpretations of actions that those who are not members of the same profession would find it difficult to relate to. Similarly, in therapy, when the therapeutic alliance is particularly strong, new meanings are likely to be developed for general linguistic terms between the therapist and the client that may reflect their unique relationship. Likewise, in the community of psychotherapists, both the norms of professional loyalty and the ethics of relating to and caring for the clients and patients overlap to create a particular, sometimes confusing, language game. Those who offend against the rules of that game are considered either controversial or, depending on the type of their offences, delinquent in the community. The foundational norms of the community have also changed through its history. In the twentieth century, it was possible for some of the most intelligent and creative people in psychotherapy, some of whom are the fathers of the field, to become sexually involved with their patients or clients. To be sure, it was frowned upon, but it was not considered a cardinal delinquency, nor was it clearly sanctioned. In some cases, it remains unclear whether such relations, which, today, in most cases, lead to a fairly direct and immediate termination of one's membership in the appropriate professional communities, actually harmed or benefited the patients or clients.

Consider likely the most notorious example of the change of foundational norms and the corresponding language games within the psychotherapeutic community, namely that of Carl Gustav Jung and his intensely sexual relationship with Sabina Spielrein, who Jung became romantically involved with after she was hospitalized with him as her psychiatrist. After their relationship, Sabina became a psychoanalyst and leader of the psychoanalytic movement in Russia, until her death at the hands of the Nazis. Even today debates are led about whether the relationship with Jung helped or harmed Sabina, especially given that subsequently Jung suffered a nervous break-down and his wife invited nobody else but Sabina, who at the time was married to a different man, to treat him (Lothane & Shpilrain, 2023). Not long after his relationship with Sabina, Jung entered another romantic relationship with two other similar patients, Maria Molzer and Antonia Wolff. Both relationships changed him profoundly, and there are reasons to believe that both patients, and at the same time romantic partners, might have benefited therapeutically from their relationships with Jung (Cohen, 2020; Hannon, 2024). Betsy Cohen describes all three Jung's relationships with his female patients as "emotional, deep, and healing relationships" (Cohen, 2020, p. 44). Sabina Spielrein herself, who at the time of her encounter with Freud was only 19 years of age, later wrote to Freud, who was Jung's friend and psychoanalytic elder, in the most loving terms about her past relationship with Jung, to such an extent that Freud, revolted by the affair and her continued affection for Jung, wrote back to her: "I am sorry to hear that you are still consumed with longing for J. (…) I imagine that you love Dr. J. so deeply still because you have not brought to light the hatred he merits. (…) I can hardly bear to listen when you continue to enthuse about your old love" (Lothane, 2024).

There are those, of course, who argue that Jung was sexually exploitative of his patients and, furthermore, that modern Jungian psychoanalysis allows room for misuse in therapy in the way of sexual exploitation of patients (Jones, 2010). Whatever might be the merit of the case, as Tim Hannon points out, Jung's sexual behavior towards his patients was the most famous case because of Jung's fame, but it was by no means uncommon at the time as boundaries between psychotherapeutic intervention and potential sexual involvement with patients were relatively blurred (Hannon, ibid.).

Norms that, not so long ago, were treated as ambiguous, have since been crystallized into preclusive community norms. In the present psychotherapeutic community, Jung would likely not be allowed to continue working with patients, and in some countries today he would likely be arrested and sentenced to a prison term. Should such a set of values have been clearly established early in the twentieth century, we would probably not have his analytical psychology today. There are benefits and costs associated with all systems of values, just as there are the respective foundational norms for various communities, and the language games that arise from such norms and are played out between the members of such communities. The language games of sexuality and therapy were once intertwined and confusing, giving rise to ethical controversies. While we may have the impression that such flagrant deviations from what seems as a clearly warranted set of professional norms today were a matter of psychotherapy's immaturity as a profession in its early days, such a conclusion might be too rash given the current ethical problems in the profession that are associated with its current confusing language games.

One such issue is the financial motivation by psychotherapists, which in the early days of Freud and Jung would not have been such a major theme, because psychotherapists of the time were well paid doctors who championed a new method of talk therapy among the wealthy European clients, and their main inspiration to develop their psychotherapeutic practice was not to supplement their earnings, but to create new theoretical and clinical paradigms. Today, however, we face language games and value issues in the profession that are associated with financial interests and perception of the psychotherapeutic profession as a private business that ought to create sufficient revenue. The ethical controversies arising from that type of language games are likely graver and more dramatic than those associated with the early porous boundaries between therapy and romance. This brings us to the question of ethical structure that determines both the therapist's professional profile and the context within which the therapist oneself is seen as the object of ethical intervention.

Structure Within and Structure Around Psychotherapy: An Ethical Context

I once faced a situation where I had to deal with a colleague psychotherapist who I was forced to treat almost as a client, although she was not formally a client. In fact, her professional actions, in which I became institutionally involved, and which were disturbing and invited a potential professional and institutional response, highlighted an interesting context for a consideration of linguistic pragmatics in the light of ethics. This case highlighted the issue of communication structure, not only as a part of the therapeutic methodology, but more so as structure around the therapist, one that may impact the ethical quality of the therapist's actions. How does the language we use within and around therapy help shape not just our relationships with our clients, but also our very self-perception vis-a-vis the broader normative communities—those of other professional peers, and the society at large?

Nevena is a woman in her 60s. She is a psychiatrist with academic ambitions that she decided to pursue relatively late in her career, causing her to leave her clinical field and become involved in university teaching that, subsequently, she found did not agree with her personality. While as a therapist she is well liked, as a university teacher she is perceived by students and colleagues as less adept than would be desirable. I became involved with her following several incidents where she acted in court as a forensic expert and exhibited extreme negligence, leading to questions as to whether she should be dismissed from the ranks of court appointed experts. Her field is family systemic psychotherapy, a school of psychotherapy of which I personally don't have a high opinion, given its Marxist ideological basis and what I believe to be its manipulative rhetoric that describes family pathology in terms of capitalist exploitation, using terms such as "scapegoat", "exploitation", "domination", and other similar prejudicial concepts, almost as premises for therapy.

A particular problem with Nevena was concerned with the ethics of profits. Within the academia, she sought a "niche" for herself by focusing on her formerly dominant clinical practice, which was work with child custody cases. While as a psychiatrist in a state hospital Nevena had the reputation of a competent doctor, working with parents and difficult divorces involving child custody proceedings, after she had moved to academia she started fostering a particular alliance with social services and developed a strange system of admitting social workers who were not academically qualified for therapist training into a psychology study program, where the prerequisite for enrolment was a costly "pre-training" with Nevena. Upon examination, this pre-training proved to be academically inadequate, merely a profitable scheme. The consequence was a serious degradation of the psychology program in the university where Nevena worked, and a further consequence was her increasing focus on "family issues" in her teaching that proved increasingly problematic in terms of methodology and quality. In time, Nevena became unstable, made unsettling statements in front of students, started to fail to appear for classes and exams, and generally became a problem for the profession and the institution. Her inner disorganization manifested in her increasingly erratic behavior, including episodes where she apparently told students that "whoever votes for so-and-so political party cannot pass an exam with her" or allowed members of her privileged group from the ranks of social workers to pass psychology exams merely by studying from her Power Point slides, with no reading of any literature whatsoever, and where she appeared in the media to comment on various attention grabbing events in psychologically highly dubious terms. All these problems were met with silence by the professional community. There was a sense that she was a problem, yet she was positioned in a pivotal role where she structurally influenced not only the schooling of psychologists in one of the largest psychology departments in the country, but also the training of numerous psychotherapists. A sequence of scandals ensued in the coming years within the social service, revealing serious issues of incompetence and irresponsibility within the ranks of the social workers, where a large number of those involved turned out to be connected to Nevena and her circle.

Nevena is intelligent and careful. When faced with potential questions about the destructive consequences of her role in the vital aspects of psychology and psychotherapy training, she would respond cryptically and avoid any open discussion. She was careful not to engage with any of her critics, too. Nevena avoided any professional work where her competences would truly be tested among her peers and focused on a mass production of fresh graduates in social work who quickly staffed the social service system that was in dire need of personnel. She took the same persons in as trainees in her family systems psychotherapy program, awarding them not only psychology degrees, but also credentials to work as psychotherapists with children and vulnerable adults. This went so far that she admitted nurses with high school–level qualifications, lawyers, and administrative workers as psychotherapists. The program was lucrative, it was massive, so dismantling it was difficult, and it was notorious among the professional community. Yet Nevena remained untouched by either psychotherapy ethics bodies or by academic peer pressure. I appeared to be chosen by the academic community to sting and would keep her on her heels—a role that, ambivalently, I simultaneously shunned and enjoyed.

Nevena's subjective experience of her career and social strategy most likely reverberates in her personal instability. Her actions, her disturbing statements made in public, her withdrawal from peers, and her tendency to avoid any public discussion of the way in which she does her work reflect her awareness of the moral nature of her actions and a deliberateness that makes the described professional transgressions particularly callous. Clearly in Nevena's case the modal logic argument would be superfluous, because she has made a calculated decision, choosing the modal world she is in. In working with Nevena (and as I mentioned this was not formally the case, but there was a clearly felt expectation that something "should be done" about her), the logical analysis would not be necessary; she knew exactly why she had chosen the modal world she had built and how this modal world militated against the wellbeing of those she should professionally care for. In her case, any narrative intervention would immediately focus on values. Along the MIP approach described earlier in this chapter, Nevena's modal world should be shaken. This would likely produce both a change of perspective for her in the strictly therapeutic sense and the ethical questioning that is so direly needed, specifically a questioning of her view of the world and her profession. There is a professional and social expectation of the observance of certain values by members of the psychiatric and psychotherapeutic professions, and one such set of values concerns integrity vis-à-vis the pursuit of profit. While parts of the psychotherapeutic training community are increasingly characterized by the admission into the profession of increasingly broad layers of candidates, including those whose background education does not appropriately belong to helping or even conversational professions, and obviously profits are a part of the rationale for such low entry standards for psychotherapy, there are recognizable limits to such logic. Nevena was transgressing those limits. Could therapy with Nevena be conducted without addressing these glaring ethical inadequacies in her actions as a professional? It seems to me that Pinel's idea that any psychotherapy is at least to an extent an exercise in moral reformation and moral improvement has merits in this type of contexts (Verhaeghe, 2008, p. 84).

Pinel was the founder of the psychotherapeutic clinic and the initiator of "conversation therapy", as opposed to the harsh treatment of the mentally ill in the psychiatric asylums of his time. His idea was that a value change, leading to behavioral transformation, was what was needed for his patients to become socially accepted and personally valued by other people. Eventually, this would lead to their own psychological improvement. It was the social aspect of mental illness that Pinel saw as key for psychotherapy; the apparent stigma attached to the mentally ill and their inability to relate to others, for Pinel, was a problem *sui generis*. It was not merely a consequence of an independent "medical" condition which his patients suffered from; it was in fact the very complaint, the difficulty which, if resolved, would likely lead to improvement in all other subjective and emotional dimensions of their "mental illness". Thus, for Pinel, making the patient socially acceptable by changing his values was the way forward.

Pinel's "conversation therapy" was a way to achieve a moral reformation through reasoning and the application of all the methods of self-examination and testing of one's assumptions and values—in other words, critical thinking. This is the initial phase of psychotherapy, based on elucidating the modal logic of the interlocutor's situation. Once the modal logical framework is set, the narrative intervention can unfold.

In the case of Nevena, who is not "mentally ill", but has a "warped" social strategy, where she at once appears socially accepted and is also deeply deviant in the way she manipulates and uses this apparent social acceptance, the setting of the modal logical framework can be skipped as a phase of therapy. Nevena knows that her actions are ethically unacceptable, and she is comfortable with their socially and professionally malignant nature. In her case, psychotherapy would require direct recourse to moral reformation through the therapeutic narrative. However, given her life-long "track record" of such unethical behavior that it borders with personal pathology, it is dubious whether any kind of reasonable and benevolent intervention would effect a constructive change in Nevena. Hers is a case for professional committees and an issue for social ethics, as well as for psychotherapeutic evaluation.

At one stage, a colleague informed me that Nevena had been involved, years ago, in a child custody case where she offered an "expert opinion" on a mother with whom she had never spoken, all this resulting in major family drama for the concerned individuals and their children. Apparently, she was asked by a court to offer an opinion on who should be given custody of two under-aged children in a divorce case, and she did this without ever talking to the persons involved; she wrote her recommendations to the court based on a psychometric test administered in the waiting room by a nurse. This shows a long-term pattern of highly unethical professional conduct.

Nevena did not ask for help, but people who were hurt by her did. Due to her place in a fundamentally corrupt network of social services and educational establishment she was able to evade scrutiny systematically. While generally psychotherapeutic help is offered only to persons who suffer and seek such assistance, there are cases where the harm sustained by others from a person who exhibits pathological traits, while not seeking psychotherapy oneself, might also warrant psychotherapeutic evaluation and intervention. After all, many narcissistic individuals pass under the diagnostic radar because they do not seek help and do not register their discomfort in life; however, they inflict major suffering on numerous individuals that they use as sources of "narcissistic supply" (Fatic, 2022). The same considerations might apply to the case of Nevena.

The example of Nevena is one of so problematic values that, if the individual was a client in MIP, the MIP therapist would be forced to cross the conventional boundaries and act in the interest of society to protect the vulnerable from such a person. Such intervention might involve different levels of coercive action, ranging from exerting gradual pressure on Nevena within a particular social group (her department, the university, the psychotherapeutic community) potentially all the way to singling Nevena out publicly and calling her out for her actions in a nominalist, anonymized yet recognizable manner. The level of intervention in this sense is determined by the modal test: whether the particular intervention might change Nevena's and others' modal worlds in a way which challenges her values sufficiently, either by her questioning her own values, triggered by any adverse experiences she might encounter as a result of being called out for her actions, or by others forcing her to act differently or to withdraw from her profession. The formula:

$$(A \rightarrow B)\dot{\alpha}^{n}.$$

might stand for the following sentences:

A: Nevena will feel such discomfort that she will have to explain her actions.

B: Nevena will face her values and the consequences of these values for the vulnerable people she affects adversely,

where $\dot{\alpha}^{n}$ is the modal world called into Nevena's reality by the therapeutic narrative $^{n.}$. $(A \rightarrow B)\ \dot{\alpha}^{n}$.

The above formula describes the structure of a well-set MIP therapeutic situation. From this point on, specific therapeutic goals in terms of the examination of values, identity, preferences, and choices, hopefully leading to value change, can be pursued using a variety of therapeutic techniques. Importantly, in cases solely consisting of ethical pathology, such intervention might unfold without the person affected explicitly seeking help or formally becoming a client in therapy. The MIP methodology can be applied outside the formal therapeutic setting.

The description offered here of the two initial steps which lead to $(A \rightarrow B)\ \dot{\alpha}^n$ illustrates why so much of traditional psychotherapy *loses its effects* with the passage of time: *the two steps are often omitted* and an intervention is initiated on the basis of providing "empathy", "security", and "confidentiality" for the client, etc. All these traditional principles are valid; however, the absence of the first, logical phase where modal facts of the client's situation are established and modal alternatives identified and offered to the client presents a structural failure of therapy. This failure causes therapy to collapse into what Lacan calls "hysterical discourse", namely a discourse that ends up pursuing a "missing object", a desire or something the client is after, in an attempt to "help" the client, and without structurally appraising the situation and the strategic possibilities for the client, without necessarily addressing the missing object, whose potential attainment will inevitably lead to the creation of a different missing object. In some cases, such as the so-called hopeless clients, with grave difficulties in their internal normative structure, such as Nevena, the only hope is the strict adherence to the two phases of therapy where the modal logical phase precedes the intervention phase. In such cases, the intervention narrative may transgress the traditional boundaries of shaking the foundations of the client's current modal world. The principle illustrated by this case is that the absence of structure leads to ineffectiveness of therapy.

Nevena's case illustrates Pinel's view that "moral" (more precisely, value-laden) reformation is the goal of "conversation therapy"; in fact, this view ought to be understood as a *theory of the therapeutic narrative* (Pinel, 2008). Pinel's theory is controversial because a normative, especially moral re-education, potentially involves coercive elements, while the modern culture of psychotherapy rests on the values of voluntariness and offering relief to pain and trauma. Nevena's example illustrates a particular class of cases (at least some of the cases involving narcissism belong to this category) where coercion is a necessary part of shifting the person's modal worlds, where a particular type of personal change must be introduced by more or less coercive actions in the interests of the vulnerable persons who are harmed by the actions of the person who is the object of intervention. This vision of the client changes the rosy perspective of subjecthood in psychotherapy, which assumes that both the therapist and the client are subjects in therapy, and thus none is the object. They collaborate on the same goals. However, with "hopeless clients", especially in ethically highly problematic contexts where these clients function, MIP allows a temporary objectification of the client. Once the modal world where unethical actions are comfortably undertaken is shaken, outside the client's control or contrary to their desires, the very subjectivity of the client shifts; one is forced to orient oneself in a changed modal world. Different things become possible, and the previous choices become impossible or carry a high social cost. In such a changed environment, a client who, in the present modal world, is "hopeless" might acquire a new type of subjecthood and agency and be placed in an architecture of possibilities where a value change might be in sight.

References

Agamben, G. (2013). *Opus Dei: An archaeology of duty*. Stanford University Press.

Ayer, A. (1986). *The problem of knowledge*. Penguin.

Chellas, B. F. (1980). *Modal logic: An introduction*. Cambridge University Press.

Chopra, D. (1993). *Ageless body, timeless mind: A practical alternative to growing old*. Harmony Books.

Cohen, B. (2020). Jung's personal confession. *Jung Journal: Culture and Psyche, 14*, 44–71. https://doi.org/10.1080/19342039.2020.1822119

Fatic, A. (2016). *Virtue as identity: Emotions and the moral personality*. Rowman and Littlefield International.

Fatic, A. (2021). Value identities: Personality as an ecology of values. *СОЦИУМ И ВЛАСТЬ, 2*, 18–35.

Fatic, A. (2022). Narcissism as a moral evil. *Revue Romaine de Philosophie, 66*(2), 371–381.

Hannon, T. (2024). Jung and sexual ethics. Irish Association for Humanistic and Integrative Psychotherapy. Retrieved September 13, 2024, from https://iahip.org/page-1076278

Jones, S. (2010). A survivor's account of sexual exploitation by a Jungian analyst. *The Journal of Analytical Psychology, 55*(5), 650–660. https://doi.org/10.1111/j.1468-5922.2010.01874.x

Lewicki, R. L., Barry, B., & Saunders, D. M. (2016). *Essentials of negotiation*. McGraw-Hill Education.

Lothane, H. Z. (2024). The untold story of Sabina Spielrein. *The American Psychoanalyst, 58*, 1. Online. Retrieved September 13, 2024, from https://tapmagazine.org/allarticles/u9jmx46hm65ah3nutt46n6xuyjebnm

Lothane, H. Z., & Shpilrain, V. (2023). *The untold story of Sabina Spielrein: Unpublished Russian diary and letters*. Unconscious in Translation Publisher.

Pinel, P. (2008). *Medico-philosophical treatise on mental alienation* (G. Hickish, D. Healy, & L. C. Charland, Trans.). Wiley-Blackwell.
Ryle, G. (1986). *The concept of mind*. Penguin Books.
Schopenhauer, A. (1966). *The world as will and representation* (E. F. J. Payne, Trans.). Dover Publications.
Searle, J. (1983). *Intentionality*. Cambridge University Press.
Searle, J. (1989). *Speech acts*. Cambridge University Press.
Slote, M. (2010). *Sentimentalism*. Oxford University Press.
Stewart, J. (2023). Schopenhauer's theory of human suffering and lack of meaning. In J. Steward (Ed.), *A history of nihilism in the 19th century* (pp. 126–148). Cambridge University Press. https://doi.org/10.1017/9781009266734.006
Van Groos, K. (1989). De werkelijkheid achter de feitelijkheid. *Tijdschrift voor Psychiatrie, 31*(6), 351–353.
Verhaeghe, P. (2008). *On being normal and other disorders: A manual for psychodiagnostics*. Karnac.
Wittgenstein, L. (1958). *Philosophical investigations*. Blackwell.
Yalom, I. (1996). *Lying on the couch*. Basic Books.

CHAPTER 6

Interventions in Modal Integrative Psychotherapy

Abstract This chapter introduces characteristic intervention techniques in Modal Integrative Psychotherapy (MIP), including Tasks for Dreaming, Method of Physical Exhaustion, Socratic Dialogue, PEACE Method, and Dilemma Training. The ways in which MIP understands the narrative, its structure, and potential damages to it are also discussed, along with interventions that amend, restructure, or stabilize the narrative as an element of therapeutic interventions.

Keywords Dreams • Dreamlike states • Exhaustion • Dialogue • Rationality • Dilemma • Narrative

The range of interventions in MIP is extremely broad and includes both the traditional psychotherapeutic interventions characteristic of most conventional schools of psychotherapy and the particular philosophical methods. All these methods are informed by deeper philosophical theories and assumptions. I thus present and discuss them here in some detail with reference to the theoretical hypotheses and arguments that they are based on.

The very format and intention of a MIP intervention reaches for an insight that will result in broader change in thinking and behavior, to the extent that one's modal world shifts. This typically requires the person's

A. Fatic, *Modal Integrative Psychotherapy*,
https://doi.org/10.1007/978-3-031-91934-3_6

current modal world to shake and give way in some ways. Subjectively, such a process manifests as instability and crisis. Experiential crisis precipitates deep change, and it is the role of MIP to manage the crisis and control its inevitable aspect of disturbance, even suffering, while leaving for the client a horizon open for the incoming stability that arises from a new modal world. In many cases, the change first manifests in dreams. It is experienced either as a series of experiences, dreams, or ideas that surface in dream-like states, or as a sense of new psychic reality that emerges from dreamlike states and almost envelops one's waking everydayness. Though MIP, one emerges into a new context, interpretation of life, or new layer of reality where, from a new "block" of psychic reality, one is able to carve a new the specifics of one's experience and emotional relationships, while leaving the old layer, like a painting set aside in a studio, intact and preserved for potential future use. This is why the first MIP method I discuss here is "Tasks for Dreaming" (Fatić, 2015).

"Tasks for Dreaming"

Tasks for Dreaming is intended to allow a greater conscious impact of the content which arises while one is dreaming or lingering in a dream-like state (daydreaming) on one's conscious experience. This includes facilitating a greater influence of the bodily sensations and intuition on our daily decision making. The method broadens our ideation by allowing ideas as sparks or projections of the subconscious to arise in the consciousness and shift our way of thinking in ways that would be impossible to achieve strictly rationally. Such changes are always metaphorical, pictorial, and general, like a changed lens on an optical device: they suddenly transform the scenery and offer different and previously unavailable dimensions of perceptions of life and associated planning and decision making. When one looks at a landscape with one type of simple binocular, the details, angles, and lighting one sees allow a certain amount and scope of interpretation and planning of movement, construction of new edifices, or recreation activities; however, no amount of analysis of such a vision will facilitate any activity or decision that requires any details that the picture does not contain or at least suggest. A changed lens, however, might present a very different reality: it may sharpen the picture, or it may impose a filter on the perception that will spark an idea that a new landscaping project might be possible over the current landscape that will change it completely. Likewise, changing one's mental landscape may, and often does, require changing important aspects of one's external reality: pulling out some metaphorical trees, planting new ones, changing some of the soil, or bringing in plants or animals from far away. To be able to change one's modal world in such radical ways, one must trust the new lens and be able to face sufficiently new realities, go to new places and deal with different people, in order to be able to bring novel content to the old and familiar scenery. Once one plants tropical plants in one's garden instead of the old oaks one has grown up with, one's garden is no longer the same. Such a garden will likely attract different birds and invite different outdoor activities, with different friends. One's life will change; however, the old ways associated with the old garden will disappear or at least be buried deep underneath the current garden. It is no wonder that the metaphor of a garden that is nurtured or transformed through creative efforts is such a frequent one in religious prayers and scholarly texts. The garden is our modal world, and the changed lens that presents the garden, or any scenery that determines our lives, in previously invisible shapes, light, colors, and moods, is a new modal world that tends to set in relatively suddenly, almost as the result of a transformative dream. The process is much more like artistic creation than like rational reasoning; it resembles more the process by which an artist dreams up a painting than that by which a scientist devises experiments and speculates about potential discoveries. Tasks for Dreaming is a method intended to play with such potential transformative ideas that occur in dreams or dreamlike states.

This method can be practiced in two ways. The first requires the client to reorganize their daily life within a specified period (a week, possibly even a month), so that their obligations and commitments are reduced to a minimum, workhours are scaled down or one takes a leave of absence from one's job, and the conditions are there for a period of intense introspection and maximizing the quality of sleep. Then the client is instructed to focus on specific issues at hand, previously identified through standard conversation therapy, and to keep careful notes of all ideas that arise in the process, as well as all unusual feelings, bodily or otherwise, which one experiences. The client keeps a notebook or a voice recorder next to their bed while sleeping and is asked to be alert when a dream arises, and he or she awakens in the night not to "let the dream go" and forget it. This takes deliberate effort to act while one is still half asleep and to focus on the content of the dreams. The aim of the process is to reverse the habit we all have of letting the ideas and dreams experienced in our sleep slip away, to isolate the ideas presented by the dream or associated ideation in the sleep and make a record of them as much as possible. Periodically in the process (in some cases daily), the ideation gathered through this process is discussed in conversation therapy. The difference between such conversation therapy and the standard psychotherapy that discusses dreams, as well as other sources of ideation, is that in Tasks for Dreaming dreams are not inculcated as spontaneous content that may or may not arise during psychotherapy: there is actually a task for the client to facilitate dreaming or dreamlike ideation first by changing their daily rhythm to maximize relaxation and sleep, and to focus, during this period, on specific themes, which then, often, reverberate through one's dreams and dreamlike states and the ideas that they give rise to. The ideas and sentiments that surface through dreams often allow the person to substantially change their relationship to the various triggers in everyday life, including inadequate, disappointing, or traumatizing experiences with loved ones: they facilitate a quick change to self-perceptions within specific relationships that are often the cause of prolonged and deep suffering. Such a change happens almost as the imaginative creation of a different self, or interventions and changes in the self: it happens as a reconstitution of the narrative of the self almost as a single act of artistic-like creation, as opposed to the painstaking process of rebuilding the narrative through lengthy conversation therapy in the waking state, where many of the emotional milestones in developing a truly internalized narrative are never achieved, because they are not sufficiently emotionally embedded in one's psychic experience. Conversation therapy is not a sufficiently deep and incisive format for such experiences to shine through one's experience, while dreams and dreamlike states might be.

Having once experienced Tasks for Dreaming as a therapeutic method, individuals may make it a personal resource which they rely on repeatedly in different circumstances, thus tapping the potential of intuition and their body. As the method, once learned, can easily be self-administered, especially in combination with standard conversation therapy.

The described regimen of using the free time, free associations, dreams and daydreaming may seem as a very relaxed way to approach intuitive and somatic cognition; however, it is a difficult task, because it requires a great deal of discipline and willpower, which manifest in the ability to change hardwired patterns that have been operative in the person for a long time, and have many times served the person well, however whose limitations have contributed to the intractability of their current problems. Some people find it very difficult to maintain focus on the method, and some are in too disorganized a condition to even be able to structure the circumstances that allow them to work through the method for any substantial time.

In cases when the first type of application is impracticable, Tasks for Dreaming can be implemented through what we at the Institute for Practical Humanities call "Deep Therapy". Such an approach involves the actual spending of time together by the therapist and client for several days. The session requires considerable preparation and can only be used with familiar clients who have already undergone standard conversation therapy. Not everybody is a candidate for this type of treatment, as staying alone with the therapist, typically outside of the city, away from the crowds, at a more secluded place, carries risks of its own. For example, a person who is prone to decompensation and may not be regularly medicated would not be a candidate for this type of therapy, and neither would those who have a particularly strong transfer with the therapist and may have trouble controlling it in circumstances which might be irregular compared to the typical hour of counseling every week. Similarly, Deep Therapy is not for every therapist, as it requires the development of particular tools and attitudes that will allow the therapist to adequately react in situations when the relationship with the client goes in the wrong direction. This includes the ability to cut the treatment short and, when Deep Therapy takes place outside the place of living of either the therapist or the client, to safely and efficiently move back. The risks involved are proportional to the proximity, mutual dependency of the therapist and the client while spending extended time together, and the lack of alternatives to compensate for any negativity that might emerge within the long session through any activities, conversations, or other moments outside the binary relationship that envelopes the whole treatment.

Deep Therapy typically consists of at least three two-hour-long sessions daily: the morning, afternoon and evening session. Sometimes a midnight awl session is added, depending on the client, the theme and the circumstances, especially when Deep Therapy is conducted with groups, when a late session can be both entertaining and revealing, in a safe and sharing way. The distribution of sessions in the morning and evening allows the therapist to prepare the client(s) for sleep with instructions as to how to focus immediately after waking during the night, or in the morning, how to take notes, how to go back to sleep when appropriate, and in what way to try to remember the specific meanings, connections between dreams, ideas within a dream and their meanings. All of these may shift in interpretation minutes after waking up.

In Deep Therapy, the therapist and the client (or groups) share their full day, they have their morning coffee together, prepare the sessions, cook meals together, do the housekeeping, and take walks together. In this way, within three days, typically, the therapist and the client can become so close that this compresses what would otherwise be at least several months of regular therapy. The shared experience allows them to access a level of personal interchange and interaction that would be impossible to trigger in conventional therapeutic settings. Deep Therapy is an intense, potentially extremely effective, and obviously taxing method for the therapist in terms of the investment of energy, time, and focus. On the other hand, Deep Therapy is very convenient for the client, as it allows them access to a greater range of support by the therapist and facilitates greater opportunities for self-revelation than conventional therapy, due to a broader range of situations where the client might self-disclose.

The preparation for Deep Therapy is critical; however, often a lack of time and opportunity to conventionally meet frequently enough with clients who require urgent in-depth assistance prevent as detailed a preparation as would be ideal. Such situations, for example, might involve clients in a tumultuous romantic relationship who must make abrupt decisions about whether or not to continue the relationship (somebody is moving away, is ill, or someone is pregnant), those who face urgent problems at work and must make strategic choices quickly, or those facing the death of a close person. This places an additional burden on the therapist to impose rules and boundaries with the client practically "as they go" within the process of Deep Therapy.

The theoretical assumption on which Tasks for Dreaming is based is that of fluidity of consciousness and the corresponding fluidity of personal identity. Jung writes that "the wealth of the soul exists in images", that the soul must be "nourished" by cultivating its images and following its spontaneity, otherwise a soul hungry of cultivation and proper images will "bread dragons and devils" into our hearts (Jung, 1989, p. 232). Tasks for Dreaming is a method that focuses on "listening in" on our inner self, on our body, and on our intuitive impulses that reveal themselves through dreams and dreamlike mental states, in a state of relaxation. This method is initially a therapeutic intervention; however, with sufficient practice it becomes a tool for what Jung calls "nourishment of the soul", namely for contemplation and meditation which allow us to give space and time to our body to reveal to us a subconscious content and insights which in our ordinary states of mind we would not be able to access. This method is contrary to the next one described here—the method of physical exhaustion.

Method of Physical Exhaustion

Another way to access the intuitive repository of insights that lies within the body and the subconscious is to reach the stage of exertion of the body where rationality is diminished, and one responds more instinctively and intuitively. Traditionally the method to ingrain skills that are executed subconsciously, without conscious intent, such as combat skills in wartime, has been to train those skills in a state of physical and mental exhaustion, so that the body accesses the knowledge attained through practice on a subconscious level. Military training thus includes combative drills after long marches, sleep deprivation, or intensive physical training. This ensures several benefits. For example, training under such conditions allows only the movements that are actually available to the person under the stress of combat: the loss of control of small muscle groups and of hand-eye coordination, in military drills, makes aiming, for example, a pointless drill for intense combat, for in such combat the physiology is so altered that no precision is possible. Once under such stress, the brain partially shuts down, peripheral vision is lost (a phenomenon known as tunnel vision), much of the auditory sensitivity is also gone, and all one is able to do with one's body are the movements of large muscle groups, the crude movements of the arms and legs. It therefore makes sense to train for such situations under conditions which will leave the soldier with just those movements and skills that one will actually have control of under the real conditions of combat, rather than spending hours and days drilling precision aiming or complex martial movements, all of which require a degree of control of the body which will be automatically lost once the soldier is immersed in the havoc of a battlefield (Molina et al., 2019).

It is often said that in combat, one responds subconsciously according to the way one has trained to respond, however only if the training was appropriate to the actual conditions of the combat. Thus, someone who has trained in competition marksmanship, under perfect conditions, with referees in place, will not be well prepared for combat, where the conditions are dramatically different, and one is likely to die if one relies on the skills acquired in competition marksmanship.

Similar conditions apply to most life situations, especially to the difficult dilemmas which we occasionally face, which cause us to grind to a halt in our decision making and seek assistance through therapy. Just as the deeper bodily and intuitive inclinations and automatisms take over in situations of combat and override all training that was not tailored specifically to the combat conditions as they actually are, the same kind of influences take over in critical life situations and pull us in directions which we would not rationally choose to take. For example, one of the experiences of World War II was the so-called 80–85% non-firing rate, where it became apparent that soldiers, however long their training before the battle might have lasted, ended up failing to fire at the enemy even when their lives were under threat, because of the innate repugnance to killing another human being. Statistically some 80–85% of the soldiers did not fire, fired into the air, or aimed so as to deliberately miss the enemy, especially in situations of close combat, where they could actually face the enemy and where they were aware of the enemy's identity. Most firing and most casualties in most battles occurred *after the battle had already been won* and the enemy forces had been retreating. Such scenarios involved firing from a distance in the backs of the retreating soldiers, where the personal, face-to-face dimension of the encounter was lost (Grossman, 2009, pp. 25–28).

To address the forces that come from the intuitive depth of our identity, one must work with the subconscious. Explaining to the soldiers that they should fire at the enemy because that is the way to win has proven utterly ineffective—it has, of course, been tried many times. In the trenches of World War II, officers often kicked and hit soldiers during battle because they would not fire at the advancing enemy, and no amount of persuasion or threats would do the trick: a normal, healthy human is naturally averse to killing another human unless one has strong specific and personal reasons to do so; this in fact holds for most species in nature. Animals will fight and occasionally kill other members of their species if they fight for females and can't win without killing, or because their alpha male status in the heard is challenged and the defeated contestant does not back down. Humans will kill other humans if they are provoked, but, under ordinary circumstances, an average human being will be reluctant to kill another person simply because they are told to do so. Thus, special forces training for missions such as assassinations requires accessing the soldiers' deep values and attitudes, either by trying to "freeze" them and immobilize the natural responses from the deep of the human psyche, or, more ambitiously, by trying to amend them. The bulk of special forces training does not consist in teaching the skills required to kill a human being: this is not too difficult when weapons are used; rather, the most important training aims to empower the person to kill without remorse and reintegrate the experience in their subsequent supposedly normal social life. There is ample experiential evidence that once the threshold of killing another human being is crossed without specific provocation or personal reason, the personality of the killer is often never the same again. Veterans from various wars often find themselves at the fringes of society, immersed in crime or showing utter disregard for their own life through drug, alcohol, or other addictions, even in situations where they have supportive families and a society that values their contribution. Such consequences of killing in war are regarded as the psychological cost of war, and such individuals are considered "psychiatric casualties of war" (Grossman, 2009, pp. 43–49).

Bringing all these deep inhibitions to the surface under the conditions of exhaustion is a key part of military training. Dave Grossman, a former Army Ranger officer, describes his own exhaustion training in the following way:

> exhaustion (…) caused many of us to have repeated hallucinations. These were incredibly vivid dreams that we would experience while wide-awake. (…) The mind teetered on the brink of madness (…). For weeks after graduation many of us awoke in panic and disorientation in the middle of the night. (Grossman, 2009, p. 67)

Only under the described conditions was it possible to develop an access to skills which would immediately "kick in" when required, in conditions of depletion of the cognitive resources which typically characterize the battlefield experience.

Similar conditions, though not obviously life threatening, exist in critical situations, where some of the most important values are at stake or are being lost, such as a family, children, one's spouse, career, self-respect, or when one faces a profound sense of powerlessness and inability to influence even the basic events in one's life. Ordinary people, who have lived exemplary lives for 40 years, kill multiple individuals when their children are being taken away from them. Some kill when they face judicial injustice that triggers them. Others, equally exemplary and nonviolent members of society, kill when their property is violated; they kill escaping robbers and trespassers. Others, with no history of depression of self-injury, commit suicide when they are powerless to react to situations that destroy what they value the most. Profound life crises cause people to respond intuitively and subconsciously and to both show and overcome their inhibitions, under different conditions and with different triggers. In such altered states, the more one is aware of one's resources and abilities, like a soldier in battle, the more likely one is to make the most of one's capabilities and judgement. Key decisions in life, just like in battle, are almost never made under optimal conditions, in a process that Kant calls "rational deliberation", where one rationally weighs the pros and cons of a particular situation. Rather they are made under exigency, with deficient information and largely on a hunch. Training and therapy alike ought to focus on such realistic scenarios, rather than pretending that we are working on optimal decision making or coping with stress in sterile, optimal conditions. After all, under such conditions there is no stress, nor can stress ever occur under fully controlled circumstances. The merits of the physical exhaustion method arise from this type of logic.

As the name suggests, the physical exhaustion method includes intensive physical training. Obviously, this requires a check-up on any pre-existing physical ailments and issues. The client then chooses the way in which one wishes to pursue the training, either by working out in the gym or by swimming or by exercising at home (e.g. riding a stationary bike) in the presence of the counselor. Once the client reaches the stage of physical exhaustion (they can no longer repeat weights exercises, they experience failure in attempts to continue running or cycling), we focus on a pre-selected topic for counseling. Once the client recovers sufficiently to be able to speak, the therapist explores what the client sees in one's situation, and what one is inclined to decide regarding the pressing dilemmas, in a changed "chemistry of the brain" induced by physical exhaustion. The counseling process in the physical exhaustion approach is the same as conventional counseling; however, it tends to be considerably briefer and with more decisive conclusions by the client. It appears that physical exhaustion makes bare the values and sentiments that allow the client to decide abruptly and to formulate such decisions in quite direct terms. Most often, clients in exhaustion appear to "know" what they want or what they do not want, which is at stark odds with their hesitant attitude when they are rested. They are more able to cut out certain options and adopt a bolder course of action in facing their problems.

Unlike in the Tasks for Dreaming, the moods and insights clients experience and gain through the physical exhaustion counseling linger with them for days: they do not easily forget the experience and they remember the affirmativeness with which they were able to make decisions in a physically exhausted state. Through physical exertion, clients often become familiar with a side of themselves which they had previously been unaware of: they see their strengths and experience emotions which they can later call on when they make real-life decisions: rather than experiencing a sadness at the loss of a dear person or important value in their lives, they recollect the decision and resilience which they had felt when they had made the mock decision to cut off their ties with someone, to go ahead with a divorce or the breakup of a romantic relationship, to quit their current job or sever relations with a life-long friend. Thanks to the subconscious resource that had surfaced because of the weakening of the conscious controls induced by physical exhaustion, clients later know that they can process an experience or decide in a way they would otherwise postpone or avoid. They become more aware of their resilience.

The advantages of physical exhaustion over Tasks for Dreaming are considerable, because it is an experiential method which allows the person to induce a state where they would act and feel differently from what they would do in their ordinary frame of mind. Tasks for Dreaming requires considerable preparation, a lengthy period of full-time focus and dedication to reaching an altered state of mind within which to consider a particular counseling issue from a different perspective, whereas physical exhaustion is simpler, briefer and requires less preparatory work. In a state of exhaustion, the person relies on their most vital, intuitive knowledge, while fully conscious of the process. This allows rational conclusions about one's actual capacity to endure stress and to make decisions directly and with less intrusion from ephemeral concerns, thus empowering the person to be a more effective conscious decision-maker in the future. All this is not necessarily the case with Tasks for Dreaming. The physical exhaustion method requires less focus, less mental discipline (although it requires much more physical discipline and effort), and its lessons are more easily memorized, without a need for additional mnemonic devices, writing the ideas down, recapitulating them, meditating on the experience, etc.

Socratic Dialogue

The modernized Socratic dialogue that is used in MIP involves collective participation in discussions and may have different foci; however, the most customary is the focus on critical thinking and the clarification of key concepts, emotions, and values. Socratic dialogue deals with issues such as consistency or the universal acceptability of beliefs and often brings the discussion to the realm of ethical methodology, including the examination of beliefs and values in the context of their applicability, their subjectivity/objectivity, and the underlying views held by the participants about their relationships to other people, e.g. whether everybody should have the same rights and entitlements in mutual interactions and, if not, what the differences in entitlements should be based on, etc. It is a fundamentally rational and analytic method that, overall, seeks to make implicit assumptions explicit, in a variety of contexts and on various levels. Socratic dialogue is useful in working with relationship issues, where the tacit assumptions of romantic partners are examined and where their views and desires about a relationship are explored to establish grounds for a rational decision on how to proceed. As a method, it has limited applicability with more seriously disturbed clients, whose ideation and composition of the self are heavily influenced by irrational views and ideas.

A particularly frequent issue discussed in Socratic dialogue is the ability of various decisions to withstand the test of universalization. This is closely connected to the key structural feature of therapy: that it is a process based on a firmly normatively organized relationship. Therapy requires the respect of key norms that, when applied in the broader life setting, help increase the quality of the person's life; the breaking of those norms in therapy, conversely, may additionally debilitate the client from living a successful and satisfying life. This parallel between the norms in therapy and those outside therapy often requires a Socratic-type re-examination of the necessity and/or sustainability of norms and principles in terms of their universal validity. For example, the norm that the client should not lie in therapy or outside therapy is often the subject of Socratic questioning. When the client lies despite the agreement, the consequences that the therapist will impose or envision should the lying continue are often discussed in terms of the damage to values and the consequences of the habit of lying in general life. Often the Socratic discussion revolves around the costs and benefits of lying, the apparent usefulness of "white (benevolent) lies" or occasional ordinary lies to avoid immediate harm, embarrassment, or some other type of social consequence of one's actions. This is then contrasted with the status of lying as a habit on the universal scale: whether the moral nature of lying is sustainable in decent human relationships when lying is taken as a potentially universal practice, what would happen if everybody lied, or if someone lied most of the time, or if lies were acceptable to the point where one would no longer have convincing grounds to even assume that others are habitually telling the truth. This type of discussion in Socratic questioning both reveals the normative issues in the client's thought process and serves as a moral educational tool to equip the client to approach their relationships more effectively and with a higher quality of personal engagement.

In many ways, Socratic dialogue, with its emphasis on concepts, reveals the philosophical core of most psychotherapy in general and may well be the philosophical method that, most of all, applies to what Jung meant when he argued that all psychotherapists were necessarily philosophers: "I can hardly draw a veil over the fact that we psychotherapists ought really to be philosophers or philosophic doctors—or rather we already are so, though we are unwilling to admit it" (Raabe, 2014, p. 383).

For the above reason, most psychotherapy should, or perhaps does, include a degree of Socratic dialogue, at least insofar as consistency and clarity of values is considered therapeutically beneficial. The standard questions in psychotherapy which include queries as to how the person feels with regard to the choices one has or has not made in a particular situation, what one thinks about the outcomes and impact of one's actions or inaction, and whether one believes that it would be acceptable for everyone to act in the same way under the same circumstances, are all asked in Socratic dialogue. Thus, Socratic dialogue is in part a paradigmatic case for what psychotherapy in its philosophical dimension almost always is (Jansson, 2015). In fact, one wonders about the reasons Socratic dialogue is isolated as a particular method. It is a philosophical method that appears to be naturally ingrained in any quality psychotherapy to such an extent that without it psychotherapy would be unthinkable.

Knitting the Narrative

The story of the narrative is well known in psychotherapeutic theory, and it need not be repeated here in detail. Some details about the role of narrative in psychotherapy and philosophical practice that is associated with psychotherapy are summarized in a relatively recent book chapter by Anders Lindseth (2015). Basically, the narrative is a life story which can be treated as a thread of one's perceptions, self-perceptions, and evaluations, which provides a linguistic record not only of one's current state of mind, but also of one's personality and identity in the broader sense.

The narrative can be visually presented as a piece of rope, which can be bent, curved, damaged, and tangled in a variety of ways. A narrative that is a simple straight line would be an ideally healthy narrative. Such a narrative would allow the person to transparently and logically account for their values, choices, and actions in the present, past, and future, linking them all mutually in productive and natural ways. Such a perfectly straight narrative is probably just an ideal, whereas the various healthy narratives are reasonably curved, as life seems to inevitably involve difficulties and inconsistencies that cause us to act in ways not easily explainable in a rational and meaningful expose. A relatively healthy, yet realistic narrative would likely be presented as a snaking piece of rope, with bends and occasional irregularities in shape, however, without major knots and easy to handle (although a snake which is easy to handle shape-wise can still inflict a venomous bite, and so can the seemingly "healthy" life narrative of a client).

This type of narrative would, thus, have something of a shape like the following one (Diagram 6.1):

A more difficult narrative would be more seriously twisted and more difficult to straighten. It would likely look like the following shape (Diagram 6.2):

The above narrative would almost necessarily inflict a degree of emotional discomfort to the person, requiring her to seek counseling. It is a narrative of a relatively serious neurosis, where the person's ability to handle her own life story and its energy and dynamics may be questionable, and the person would likely need counseling to deal with such a narrative and the experience that it leads to.

If the narrative is knotted to such a degree that it requires some parts of the narrative to be handled extremely carefully, with the danger that the

Diagram 6.1 A healthy narrative

Diagram 6.2 A neurotic narrative

Diagram 6.3 The psychotic narrative

Diagram 6.4 Severe psychotic narrative with a broken sense of identity

narrative might be compromised or broken, and that the person might thus become decompensated, such a psychotic narrative would likely take a shape like the following one (Diagram 6.3):

If the person is already decompensated, has serious issues with self-perception and her own identity, and cannot grasp reality, if she suffers from a sense of "brokenness" of her life experience such that life frequently seems unbearable, this is a severe psychosis, and the narrative likely looks resembles Diagram 6.3.

The above diagrams suggest what the therapeutic intervention in the context of narrative entails. The therapist handles the narrative, and thus also the identity and experiential reality of the client, either by changing the structure of the narrative or by untangling it, painstakingly and carefully. In radical situations, the therapist and the client mend the narrative by reproducing or creating anew the parts of it that are missing, such as in Diagram 6.4, where the person cannot even survive psychologically, even physically (suicides are common with such a narrative), without developing a sense of continuity and power which comes from a consistent and structurally continuous narrative. This is the familiar Lacanian idea that the psychotic symptom is a compensation of inability to metabolize a particular segment of what Lacan calls "the unbearable Real", where the symptom presents a bearable interpretation of the otherwise unbearable life experience, even if that interpretation is imaginary, such as in paranoid ideation (Redmond, 2013).

The ability to understand the narrative is a prerequisite for successful intervention, and it is here that most difficulties in therapy arise: some narratives are so warped and twisted that one cannot rationally disentangle the actual beginning and end of the narrative, nor can one understand the dynamic forces at work in a personality that have helped make the narrative so difficult and traumatizing. This is, structurally speaking, the reason for misdiagnosis and the frequent uncertainties about the nature and extent of psychosis in apparently non-psychotic disorders such as personality disorders (Redmond, 2014).

Often, in working with borderline personality disorders, one notices a narrative whose ends cannot be found: there is a bunch of cords, so to speak, but the beginning and end of the cord are buried so deep inside the knots of the narrative that it is impossible to start to disentangle the cord. In such situations, the only way seems to be to cut through the knot. Obviously, cutting the cord will bring the demons out, and this is what usually happens in interpersonal relationships with borderline persons: the other person or persons cannot manage the tangled narrative of the borderline, so they try to start from a "clean slate", namely they cut the narrative of the borderline person demanding that a new game is played with transparent rules within their relationships. This brings out the wrath of the borderline, because the pain they feel from the severance of their narrative, which is impossible to handle for the significant other, is intense, and they lash out at the cause of that pain in the other person. There is a marked difference in perceptions here, because the borderline sees herself as fully justified in attacking the interlocutor for the pain inflicted by ignoring or verbally slicing through their narrative, while the interlocutor feels righteous because they believe that nobody should be asked to deal with such convoluted and problematic behavior arising from what seems like an entirely incomprehensible narrative. This is the cause of much conflict between borderlines and their family members, friends, romantic partners, colleagues, etc. (Lis & Bohus, 2013).

Borderline is a particularly interesting disorder for MIP because it reflects many different facets of the normative foundations of psychopathology. This disorder has ranged from being treated as non-manifest schizophrenia (Redmond, 2014)—thus a more or less purely medical condition—to being interpreted as a fundamentally moral, and not clinical disorder, where issues of socialization and internal normative structure are at stake that are basically common to healthy people, as well (Charland, 2006, 2010). These various dimensions of borderline impact the therapeutic narrative.

MIP usually (but not exclusively) treats borderline primarily as a moral normative disturbance, where a degree of reeducation and disciplining is required. The person who is described as borderline often lacks the awareness that their actions produce consequences and that they must face these consequences. They equally frequently lack the awareness that they are not entitled to hurt others, that there is a valid social expectation of them to show tolerance and to act empathetically. All these and other social emotions are often absent in a borderline client, who is entirely preoccupied with their own interests, views, pain, and welfare. Thus, borderline clients in therapy usually focus on the need for others, the community, to understand that their toxic behavior is associated with internal suffering and to approach them with empathy. Almost never does one hear in a conversation with a borderline client that others also deserve empathy or that the borderline client ought to feel empathy for someone. This type of narrative is addressed by being "pulled" straight, partly by the clear normative expectations within a therapeutic process. Once proper therapeutic transfer is developed, the therapist will explicitly tie their relationship to the borderline with the latter's willingness to acknowledge certain social and moral expectations. The problem here is usually with the establishment of the transfer itself, because the borderlines' preoccupation with themselves often makes it difficult for them to even develop a proper transfer with the therapist: they will seek a therapist who approves of their choices and of their normative sensibility, but as soon as the therapist is seen as being critical or even implicitly unapproving of what the borderlines do or believe, what initially seemed like a transfer quickly turns into open animosity. It is common for borderlines to defend their knotted-up narrative of values and actions by focusing on the therapist as the one at fault, typically after initially idealizing them. The dynamic is known as the "black and white" borderline ideation. Dealing with such a narrative is extremely demanding and requires conditions that rarely apply in private counseling, which is likely the main reason many therapists avoid borderline clients. With such clients, therapists often end up not with an ally in therapy, but with a resentful enemy who not only fails to benefit from therapy, but aggressively pursues an even more pathological narrative of self-righteousness at the hands of the unjust world, of which the therapist is often seen as being a protruding part, convenient for enmity. Placing a borderline's moral normative issues or weaknesses under any kind of pressure triggers resentment or rage.

Another important view of borderline in modern psychotherapy is the Lacanian view that borderline is in fact mild schizophrenia. In this interpretation, the narrative of the borderline would be seen as fundamentally psychotic, and the borderline should be treated in structurally the same way as all psychotic patients, namely by developing acceptable symptoms which will compensate the personal disorganization caused by the psychosis (Redmond, 2014, pp. 20–28). The Lacanian psychiatry sees psychosis as fundamentally incurable: the intervention simply temporarily stabilizes the disorganization of the person through the development of a symptom which will act as a proxy for the lost "primary signifier", namely the authority figure that normatively organizes and socializes the person, which Lacan called "Name of the Father".

From the point of view of the narrative intervention, the nature of the disorder is reflected in the complexity and practical difficulty in handling the narrative: the differences in kind are not primarily relevant, and this makes "diagnoses" largely a non-issue in MIP. What matters in the MIP intervention is understanding, interpreting, and manipulating the narrative into a simpler and healthier structure.

A relevant view on this point by a respected colleague, Anders Lindseth, is that what the therapist deals with is the factual story that the client tells the therapist (Lindseth, 2015, pp. 359–361). I disagree with this. The narrative is the whole "life story", both told and untold, implied and suggested, the tale of who the client is and what they think they are. True, the whole of the narrative is grasped from the explicit statements by the client, through the facts that they relate; however, it is our intuition, our sense of the whole, that plays a much greater role in the process than the mere discussion of the facts. In fact, I would tend to believe that "facts" are the least important part of psychotherapy: they can serve as bearers of hidden meanings, as buoys floating on the surface to mark where the real treasures are sunk, or, equally, as decoys for the interlocutor while the client runs from therapy in a different direction. Both the excavation of the hidden treasure and the anticipation of the flight of the client are skills that apply to the interpretation of the client's narrative; however, these skills are intuitive, fleeting, largely unconscious, and by no means tied to the facts of the explicit narrative. To return here to Verhaeghe's point that in psychotherapy the truth is not an epistemic, but ethical category, one must recognise, nevertheless, that it is the truth behind the explicit story that we seek, not the explicit story itself (Verhaeghe, 2008, p. 64). What we seek is the normative truth, the moral orientation, or structure behind the explicit story which allows us to grasp who the person is and what their real values are. This truth is almost never offered in the explicit story and often needs to be carefully pieced together from a variety of exploratory actions, the most important of which is not to take the explicit story as all there is, nor as the most important and reliable thread or inroad through which the therapist is to proceed with the person. To untie the knot of a narrative, or to reconstruct a broken narrative, the real, full narrative, both told and untold, must first be discovered. This is often the most difficult part of the process, more demanding than even the intervention and the "cure" itself.

The PEACE Method

This method of decision making with considerable application in MIP has been developed by Lou Marinoff (2002). The method is predominantly rational and consists of five phases in the following order.

Problem

The first phase, "Problem", includes a definition of the problem to be solved. This seems a trivial task, for without knowing what problem one is solving, no solution is likely to be attempted in the first place; however, in practice it is arguably the most difficult phase. While we often sense that something is wrong, that we are stuck in a life situation, or that, as an organization, we have an issue which must be addressed, we often cannot quite put our finger on the precise problem and we tend to meander around many possible formulations and core issues. The formulation of an appropriate problem to be addressed is a well-known issue in psychotherapy, and most experienced psychotherapists almost assume that when a new client arrives, their initial narrative is unlikely to be the actual formulation of the problem that they will be addressing once the therapy progresses. It appears that seeking help is predicated upon some kind of grasp of one's being stuck and facing functional difficulties; however, it is rarely the conceptualization of the problem that will shed sufficient light on the difficulties to empower the person to resolve them. Another level of the same issue is the emotional relationship to the problem, where the first level problem, which the person may formulate correctly, is so difficult for them to accept that the real existential problem is the person's very reluctance to face the problem. Phase P of PEACE method would, in such cases, lead to the formulation of a meta-problem, namely the person's attitude to the first level problem, as the relevant "Problem" for resolution by the PEACE process.

There are many examples of this difficulty in formulating the problem, and some concern everyday issues, such as dilemmas as to whether and how to proceed with relationships with other people. They are perhaps best understood through well-known, global examples from diplomacy and international relations, where the formulation of an actual problem may quickly lead to effective solutions; however, each of the stake holders harbors their own version of what the "actual" problem is, and the PEACE process, or any other kind of decision making procedure based on a clear vision of the problem, cannot even commence, because the conflict is about the very definition of the problem. Consider the Israel-Palestinian strife (and the current war of Israel against the Palestinians in Gaza and the West Bank and against Lebanon, during the writing of this book in 2024 and 2025), where one side sees the problem as the need to secure (and potentially expand) the national homeland without much regard for either international law or humanitarian concerns, while the other sees the only chance of survival on their ancestral land in a defeat of the adversary and destruction of their homeland. Such views generate a "zero sum game" situation where mass killing of civilians, including children, is an everyday occurrence, while the sides try to come to an agreement about the actual nature of the problem that they can both accept and that can then begin to be addressed. The same kind of dynamics exists in a variety of personal and interpersonal situations: consider the hundreds of thousands of zero-sum games played between divorcing parents over the custody of their children, and the subsequent psychological warfare that many wage on each other at the cost of the children, putatively in the interest of those same children, because the sides cannot agree on the actual nature of the problem between them. The latter case is perhaps more easily understood in therapy when the various underlying problems surface, such as someone's inability to accept an emotional break-up, a sense of threatened self-worth resulting in the urge to punish the partner who has abandoned the person, etc. However, the dynamics in the two types of cases appear to be sufficiently similar to illustrate just how crucial the formulation of the problem is, not only as a logical precondition for even starting the process of resolution, but also as a key practical contribution to the very resolution and its applicability once it is reached. The parents in conflict may reach a formal resolution through a court verdict; however, unless the problem that is thus addressed, which is likely psychological, is adequately formulated and dealt with quite separately from the legal outcome, the verdict itself may do very little to help them, or may even militate against what might be an optimal solution for their children. Similar considerations apply to the Israeli wars in their vicinity: any potential ceasefire or peace agreement reached under international pressure would be (and, as history shows, has been) only temporary unless deeper issues of fear of others, self-aggrandizement, and a sense of being "chosen" to act above the level of the norms and laws that ordinarily regulate states' behavior are addressed. Obviously, addressing such psychological problems on a collective level is much more demanding than doing so with couples in conflict or individuals facing difficulties in formulating their personal problems. If the articulation of a problem is not conducted with utmost care and sincerity, so that the actual, core problem is addressed in the subsequent phases, rather than dealing with what seems like the "obvious" problem, when it is in fact merely a conceptual façade for the core issue, the whole process may easily be compromised.

Emotions/Elaboration

The second phase of the method, "Emotions", refers to the articulation of emotions which we feel regarding the problem that we have defined in the first phase of the process. Sometimes emotions pass under the radar of our consciousness: we are often unaware of just how the exact problem at hand makes us feel and, given that our emotions are the fuel for our decisions and actions, this means that we are also unaware of the exact reasons we make certain decisions and take specific courses of action to address the problem. Thus, contemplation and a focused analysis of our emotional reactions are required before we can proceed with the process of decision making, because the outcome of the process ought to balance our emotions, as well as reach an optimum rational solution for the problem (the last phase, "Equilibrium").

In my adaptation of the method for organizational decision making, phase E is switched to "Elaboration", rather than involving the articulation of emotions, so that various aspects of the problem defined under P are specifically elaborated: in complex organizations, phase P will often lead to several conceptualizations of the problem, and after one is chosen to proceed with, under phase E the organization gets the chance to develop specific facets of this problem, which might satisfy various stakeholders within the organization. For example, the problem of poor standards at a university, which may be defined as a problem for corporate decision making, might be more specifically divided into several aspects under my version of the method in phase E (Elaboration), so that it involves, for example, the unwillingness of academic staff to be seen as difficult and to set standards higher than their colleagues do, because that would make them less popular with students, habits developed by students to expect everything to be offered "on a plate", such as study materials, so they don't need to even go to the library, or their expectations that lecturers would be there to assist them in anything they might need to pass the exams, including assisting with their problems with learning and their potential lack of study habits, etc. The more aspects are developed under this version of PEACE in phase E, the more precise the further organizational solutions are likely to be.

Alternatives

The third phase of PEACE involves a process of decision making whereby several alternative solutions to the problem are identified. The important facet of this phase is that all the solutions must actually solve the problem in various ways. In the adaptation for organizations, where E stands for Elaboration, the various solutions might, and often do, correspond to the various facets of the problem, where then, the selection of one of the alternatives involves the actual giving of preference to one dimension of the problem. This is an integral part of the very concept of decision making, where a solution to the problem is acquired by means of a process (in this case a rational one); however, this also means that the other possibilities are abandoned. Choosing always includes both embracing a choice and at the same time leaving behind the other potential choices. It is this aspect of decision making that makes some people agonizingly reluctant decision-makers.

Further on in the PEACE process, in phase A, one of the alternatives is *tentatively* chosen as the best solution and is subjected to further consideration through the remaining two phases. Assuming that, in the example with Israel-Arab conflict, a particular dimension of the problem, such as Israel's fear of potential terrorist attacks in the future, is isolated as key (and it has been voiced as such), a tentative solution might be to set up a security corridor along Israel's borders with Palestine where nobody would reside and which would be easy to oversee, and then establish the so-called two state solution, namely have the state of Palestine, formally recognized by Israel, along with subjecting all of those who have engaged in necropolitics (creation of subhuman conditions of life for large sections of the Palestinian population as a strategy to drive them out of their lands) to the mechanisms of criminal justice nationally or internationally. This solution might then be tested further in the decision making process through phases C and E. In the example with feuding parents, a tentative solution might be to impose an equal and shared custody of children, where any parent who transgresses the equal rights granted to both in raising the children (equal time spent with the children included) would agree to be stripped of custody. This solution might then further be tested through phases C and E. Importantly, however, whichever solution is identified within phase E, it must have the potential to really solve the problem; it cannot be a feeble attempt to come up with some remotely plausible theoretical alternatives.

Contemplation

In the phase of "Contemplation", or phase C of PEACE, the decision-maker allows some time to pass and thinks about the solution one is inclined to accept, not least to check what kind of emotions this solution brings up. Sometimes, rationally, after identifying several alternative solutions to a problem under phase A, we can relatively easily identify the rationally best solution. However, after a period of contemplation, all kinds of emotions become "churned up" inside us, and we see that this solution would not be so good after all, because it would go against our deeply held values that give rise to our emotions. It is through emotions that we identify our values. For example, Israel might decide that, having elaborated a potential solution described above, it cannot, after all, live with a Palestinian state and with permanently giving up its ambitions to expand into the West Bank and Gaza, and it might reject this solution and return to war, or seek a different solution. The parents in conflict might feel that their animosity to the other parent is so pronounced that one or both cannot emotionally accept a shared custody, and they may resume their legal battle. These outcomes, though unfortunate, are legitimate within the PEACE process. If such an outcome transpires, the process moves back by one phase, and if, on the other hand, the identified potential outcome is perceived, in phase C, as acceptable, the process moves to the final phase E (Equilibrium).

Equilibrium

The final phase checks whether "everything is in its place" within us with the proposed solutions. Here we are still able to change our choice of a solution if we see that our cognition, our emotions, and our subconscious reactions, often manifested through the body, are not "in sync" regarding what we have chosen to do. If there is a problem, a disequilibrium here, we go back one or two steps in the PEACE process and do the work again, until we come up with a solution that, in the end, will generate an equilibrium: a solution that both optimally solves the problem, and one that we can live with, given who we are: our values, our sensibility, and, in the case of organizations, our collective identity and mutual relationships, which we will need to preserve and nourish for our further decisions and collaborations.

PEACE method highlights an important aspect of decision making, namely that what we take away from the process is far more important than the actual value of the decisions that we are able to make. This means that a good process will solidify our identity, clarify our values, and serve a therapeutic purpose for us. In the ultimate consequences, such a process will cause us to feel better, both as persons and as collectives, if PEACE is applied for organizational decision making, while at the same time hopefully increasing the efficiency of our decision making (thus making us less reluctant to make decisions and, by virtue of that fact alone, already better decision-makers). PEACE will also likely increase the quality and effectiveness of the decisions we make.

Even if it were possible to gain a better decision through a process that would compromise our relationships with others, with whom we share a part of our life through work, or our relationship with ourselves, by obscuring our sense of identity and our values, that process would be less adequate than a process such as the PEACE method, whereby our important positions, emotions, values and reasons are given an equal place in the decision.

PEACE method is fundamentally rational in the sense that the identification of alternative solutions and the choice of a final solution are rational; however, this rationality is tempered by the space it gives to emotions in the last two phases, Contemplation and Equilibrium, where emotions and intuition are allowed to check the decisions previously made rationally and perform, in a sense, the ultimate verification of the sustainability and correctness of all decisions.

Dilemma Training

Dilemma training is a complex, seven-step method designed for organizational decision making with an ethical emphasis. Its aim is to balance the instrumental quality of the decisions with their ethical soundness, thus facilitating a degree of monitoring of ethical decision making in complex organizations. Thus, the very existence of Dilemma Training as a method of choice in corporate decision making to some extent guarantees the ability of the organization to follow and verify the ethical soundness of the important decisions made by its various groups.

The steps of decision making in Dilemma Training include the following:

1. *Formulate the basic moral question in a corporate dilemma*

To accomplish this task, the group starts by articulating several moral questions which could compete for the fundamental question. These questions capture different moral aspects of the issue at hand in decision making and should be formulated in one or both of the following two formats:

(a) "Is it morally acceptable to do x?", and
(b) "Is it morally necessary to do x?"

The two formulations capture two fundamental aspects of moral thinking, namely whether there is a duty to make a particular choice, whatever other considerations might lead us to decide otherwise (format b), and whether, all circumstances considered, it is morally acceptable to do something that is otherwise in line with our goals.

Examples of the two types of moral dilemmas abound, such as the question of whether it is morally acceptable to raise the prices of a fundamental good (such as food) in a specific market, and some of the considerations involved in deciding would likely involve issues of the standard of living in the community, the company's reasons for raising the prices, etc. On the other hand, the same dilemma might have a different format, namely whether it is morally necessary for a company to provide food to the community regardless of the policy's financial viability in a specific period, for example, at times of natural disasters, political or military crises, etc. In such circumstances, a failure to stock shops with food could have catastrophic consequences for the people. Such are fairly simple and clear-cut examples, but they generally illustrate why the two types of moral questions are asked in the first step of Dilemma Training.

The second part of the first step of the process requires the decision-makers to choose one of the questions with which they will proceed, while leaving the others aside. This is a methodologically important move because it allows all the participants in the decision making team (Dilemma Training is primarily suited to group decision making) to become aware that the decision making process includes leaving some of the questions unanswered, and some of the problems unsolved. In this reasoning, the group decides which of the previously identified problems can be left unsolved without impacting the key decision, or group interest, or value, in a major way. It is a practical aspect which helps group members become better decision-makers generally, by learning how to choose what not to decide about in order to be able to decide on more important matters.

For example, a group of political decision makers at a time of political turmoil and public unrest over a change in the constitution might identify several moral issues which might be relevant for their decision. They might, for instance, be tasked with deciding on whether to proceed with a set of proposed constitutional changes which lower the threshold for the success of referenda by abolishing the minimum requirement of 50% of voters who actually vote in order for the referendum to succeed. If such changes occur in the midst of difficult national decision making, which concerns sovereignty, citizen rights to property (land ownership and state expropriation of private land), etc., the decision making process might spark public unrest.

Suppose that the government, or the country's president, who must sign the law after it is voted for in the parliament, have created a team to make a decision, and this team has identified several related moral dilemmas, including the following:

Is it morally acceptable to change the constitution in a situation where most citizens will see this as a maneuver to pave the way to make controversial political moves?

Is it morally acceptable to push through the proposed amendments to the constitution despite public anger given that so much political capital has already been invested in bringing the process this far?
Is it morally acceptable to make decisions on key national issues, which are decided through referenda, with less than half of the registered voters having their say on the matter?
Is there a moral necessity to have as broad a consensus as possible on key national decisions, regardless of the specific circumstances at hand?
Is it morally necessary to listen to those who voice their dissatisfaction in an organized way in a democracy, regardless of what we, as political decision makers, might think about it in terms of the merits of the demands or popular objections?
Is it morally necessary to show humility before the public and at least delay the signing of a controversial act when people protest against it in the street and threaten a more serious and widespread public upheaval?

All of these questions are relevant in this case, and their solutions could contribute to dissolving the crisis, however depending on which question the political decision making group chooses to proceed with, the rest of the process will likely yield different conclusions. For example, choosing the question of whether it is morally acceptable to push through the constitutional amendments given the amount of work and political capital invested would likely generate quite different answers than if the group chose the last question, whether it is a moral necessity for democratic governments to abandon the decisions they have intended to make if the public strongly protests, and at least reconsider and show some degree of caution.

Obviously, as in the PEACE method, in choosing which of the several relevant questions are the most important to us we show who we are, in fact we decide who we are, either as individuals or corporate subjects, or as political decision-makers. The choice of the question tells about our character, our values, and our priorities.

2. *Identify all of the stakeholders in the decision*

Imagine that the political decision makers in the described example have chosen as the most important the second last listed question in the previous subsection:

Is it morally necessary to listen to those who voice their dissatisfaction in an organized way in a democracy, regardless of what we, as political decision makers, might think about it in terms of the merits of the demands or public objections?

In this dilemma, there is a wide array of stakeholders, and it is important to list them all. They would include all those who would be affected by the proposed constitutional changes, those who have invested their social capital, their reputation, time and energy in organizing public protests, and who, if defeated, would be dissatisfied with the decision. The stakeholders also include citizens at large, who observe how the government behaves with regard to their rights and with regard to those who oppose the government's decisions. Political parties who have a stake in one or another decision are also stakeholders, as are foreign companies who expect this legislation to happen in order to make their capital investments easier and more secure, etc. All the interests involved must be clearly laid out and assessed compared to all other interests.

3. *Who must make the decision?*

The third step consists of three sub-steps.

First, it requires us to remind ourselves *whose responsibility it is to make the decision*. Discussions about the moral aspects of a particular decision tend to be spread between several people and often between several groups who collaborate on the decision, but the primary responsibility lies with those who are factually entitled and due to make the decision. In the described example, for example, if the legislation has already passed the parliament before public protests erupted, it is for the president, in most modern political systems, to decide whether to sign the constitutional amendments or to refuse and return them to the parliament to reconsider, potentially change them, and vote again. Thus, the formal responsibility for signing the constitutional changes into law belongs to the president.

However, a *second* related question is also asked, namely *who is factually responsible for this decision*, who are the individuals, advisers, committees, and others who consider the decision and offer a recommendation to the president to sign the decision?

Related to the second question is the *third* question of *who can reasonably be expected to feel at least partially responsible for the decision*, or who has had an opportunity to influence the decision (even if factually these individuals claim that they do not feel that they are responsible)?

In the above example, there are an array of people who are factually responsible for the president's decision, at least as much as the president himself is responsible. They are the ones who make the decision, and he is the one who endorses it. Thus, they have a factual, although not formal responsibility for the outcome of the signing of the constitutional amendments.

Apart from those who are factually responsible, there are those who would have influenced the decision, such as publicly exposed academics, lawyers, public rights activists, leaders of political parties, the media, and those whose opinion is sought informally, and in many decisions such individuals are fairly numerous. All of them, in an ethically sound process, must sense a degree of moral responsibility and must be reminded that they are responsible for the outcome, proportional to their involvement and the actual influence their views have had on the decision.

4. *What additional information is necessary to make a sound decision on the particular matter?*

Step 4 of Dilemma Training requires that an assessment be made of the following three options:

The existing information is sufficient for a sound decision to be made;
Additional information would be useful; however, strictly speaking, it is not necessary for the particular decision;
More information is required for the decision. It cannot be made as things stand.

The above example would, for example, likely fit in one of the first two options, as the fact that people are protesting what seems like at least a controversial set of constitutional amendments should be enough to move on with a political decision, at least with a view of allowing additional time to reconsider the matter. However, if additional information was available and it suggested, for example, that the interests of foreign investors, articulated in a corrupt way through individual politicians, stood behind the whole process of constitutional amendments, such information would obviously be useful for decision making. All kinds of considerations could apply here, and, depending on the circumstances, the decision-makers might choose to see additional information, which they do not yet have, and which could play different roles in their decision making: from being entirely unnecessary (they know enough) to being potentially beneficial but not imperatively required, to being crucial for the decision. This is a matter of judgement; however, that judgement is likely to later be reviewed and adjudicated on its own merits, should a problem arise with the decision which results from this process.

5. *What arguments are there for and against a proposed solution to the dilemma?*

This phase of the process requires a listing of the arguments in the familiar way of "putting on paper" the pros and cons, however, they are considered from two separate ethical perspectives, namely from the *deontological* and the *consequentialist* perspective.

The deontic model of ethical reasoning is based on the so-called absolute moral norms, which apply as principles across a range of circumstances and are fundamentally independent of circumstantial considerations. Perhaps the best-known example of deontic principles are the Ten Christian Commandments. A more philosophical way to understand deontological morality is by reference to the most famous deontologist Immanuel Kant, who formulated several different articulations of what he called "the categorical imperative", namely a structure of moral thinking which is designed to help us decide what is morally right to do in any circumstances. One of the formulations reads: "Always act so that you may wish that the maxim of your choice may become a general principle". This suggests that we always choose that course of action which, if we take ourselves to be rational beings, we would rationally (not just accidentally, selfishly) be able to desire as a general principle, namely we should always act according to the same principles that we could wish everybody else to adopt, including when they act in ways which influence us and our interests. A simple folk formulation of this type of categorical imperative, although philosophically imprecise, is "always act in a way in which you would wish others to act towards you"; however, this is not entirely a deontic principle, because it omits the element of "being able to wish" (as a rational being). Namely, I can decide to rig a public procurement in order to benefit a friend, thinking that I would also wish my friend to do the same to benefit me; however, this has little to do with the categorical imperative of deontic morality: it merely reciprocates between two actors. In order to apply the categorical imperative, I would have to be able, as a rational, intelligent human being, to actually wish that everybody should steal from public funds and rig public procurement procedures. Kant would say that, as a rational being, I could not really wish that, because should everybody rig public procurements, the state would go bankrupt, public procurements would become meaningless, and we would revert to a state of disorder in which my interests, as well as the legitimate interests of the other members of the political community, would suffer. Thus, the deontic morality would imply: "never rig public procurement procedures", even in situations when it would seem to inflict little damage, and your friend might benefit immensely, because if this type of behavior were to become universal, an important aspect of economic life in the society would collapse.

Similar considerations apply to the Biblical commandment "never to desire another man's wife". If infidelity were to become universal practice, then marriage and family would become obsolete, would not be able to survive, nobody would know who their parents are, and we would descend into a very dark moral chaos. Thus, even if there appear to exist extenuating circumstances which justify such actions, "do not desire your brother's wife". End of discussion. This is the type of deontic reasoning which applies as bottom-line morality in many social contexts, marking those "boundaries" which, if crossed, bring the society into disarray.

Consequentialist thinking, on the other hand, justifies actions based on the foreseeable consequences. The best-known form of ethical consequentialism is utilitarianism, which implies that an action is morally justified if, in the ultimate sum of its predictable consequences, it benefits the most stakeholders. This means that actions for which it is assumed that they will generate the most "utility" for the most people should be considered morally preferable to alternatives.

In the above example, one would, for example, consider the consequences of going ahead with the constitutional amendments in terms of the unrest which this could spark, and thus proceed along the lines of a consequentialist argument. Alternatively, one could take the position that if every decision by the parliament, which is reached within proper procedure, could be stalled because some people decided to demonstrate against it, then hardly any law would be able to be enacted, and this would be a consequentialist argument in favor of ignoring the public protests and signing the constitutional amendments into effect. On a deontic level, one could ask whether one could potentially rationally wish that governments do whatever they manage to get through parliament regardless of protests by parts of the public, even if this concerned, adversely, their own interests. Would one rationally wish the government to lower the threshold for the success of referenda on key national issues so that however many people vote, the referendum succeeds? This would mean that one could wish, for example, that the government could organize a referendum to abolish the parents' rights to bring up their children, and however many people vote, even if it is just 10 percent of the registered voters, this would then become law. Could one wish such behavior to become "a general principle"? Or could one, rationally, wish the government to be circumspect of the sentiments of its citizens, and to be very careful not to offend important citizen groups and interests, even when it has the majority needed to "bulldoze through" its intended solutions? These are the sorts of concerns that need to be listed carefully in Step 5 of Dilemma Training.

The typical values that deontic norms protect include honesty, privacy, loyalty, and justice. On the other hand, the most typical considerations in consequentialist moral thinking in Dilemma Training involve influence on the environment, profits, company reputation, workplace relationships, a sense of community, etc.

In measuring the arguments identified in Step 5 against each other, Dilemma Training envisages the use of a "rule of thumb":

Whenever there is a conflict of considerations based on principles (deontic arguments) and those based on consequences, deontic arguments have the priority. The only exceptions are situations where there are strong rational arguments that the consequences, in the particular case, are obviously more important than principles.

For example, when there is a conflict between the consequentialist argument that if the constitutional amendments are finalized and made effective, there would be unrest with serious violence, bordering on a revolution, and the deontic argument that the constitutional amendments have been the result of an impeccable legal process, which otherwise characterizes all government and parliamentary decisions in a perfect rule of law, normally the deontic argument would methodologically be given priority, however, in this particular case, given that loss of life would be imminent, and the consequences of unrest would obviously far exceed the mere procedural priority of the deontic principle of implementing what has been reached as a conclusion in a previously agreed upon, legally unassailable way, priority would have to be given to consequentialist considerations and the amendments would have to be withdrawn in some way.

6. *Conclusion*

Once all the arguments listed in the previous phase of the process, both deontic and consequentialist, are assessed against each other, after it has been clearly delineated which arguments are deontic and which are consequentialist, where the rule of thumb is applied and how and where there are justified exemptions from the rule of thumb, a conclusion is formulated which must answer the key moral question. For example: "we will now give up on these constitutional amendments?"

The conclusion is followed by a sequence of actions consistent with the conclusion: for example, given that the constitutional amendments have already passed the parliament, now the president will not sign them and will send them back to parliament. The process is that the parliament can either revise the proposal and adopt it, after which course of action the president can no longer refuse to sign the amendments into law, or the parliament, or the government, which proposed the amendments in the first place, can decide to abandon the initiative and refrain from resubmitting the amendments for reconsideration. Given that our described situation borders on civil war and is very dangerous, as a large number of citizens consider such amendments unacceptable to the point of being willing to challenge the government's authority by violence, the likely solution would be for the government to withdraw the proposal from parliament once the president sends it back, and that would close the matter in the safest possible way.

In making these decisions, the so-called moral reserve or moral reminder is called into action, where the decision, in this case, to withdraw the constitutional changes, is again reconsidered from the point of view of deontic and consequentialist criteria, just to make sure that something important has not "slipped by" in the decision making so far and that everybody involved in the decision can agree that this is ethically the best decision.

7. *How do we feel after the decision?*

The seventh and final step of Dilemma Training is listening in on our conscience, and asking ourselves questions like the following:

Am I prepared to publicly announce my position on the matter, and to argue in favor of it with the various stakeholders in the case?

Would I decide in the same way in similar future situations?

Both of these questions and many similar ones test our sense of being at peace with the decision we have made, and whether we can continue in our roles, convinced that we have done a reasonably good job with this decision and prepared to act principally in the same way in any similar situations in the future. It is obviously a very similar phase to that of "Equilibrium" and partially of "Contemplation" in PEACE method (Dubbink & Smith, 2011).

Both PEACE method and Dilemma Training are technologies for decision making: they make sure that complex decisions, made by a group of individuals acting on behalf of an organization, are made in a way that can be traced back and reassessed afterwards, thus affording the organization a degree of control over the integrity of the decisions made. PEACE method, unlike Dilemma Training, was initially designed for individual decision making: it is thus more suited for use in private life, while it can easily be adapted for organizational applications. Dilemma Training, on the other hand, due to its complexity and reliance on differing views and interests held by various stakeholders, is primarily an organizational decision making tool.

References

Charland, L. (2006). The moral nature of the DSM IV cluster B personality disorders. *Journal of Personality Disorders, 20*(2), 116–125. https://doi.org/10.1521/pedi.2006.20.2.116

Charland, L. (2010). Science and morals in the affective psychopathology of Philippe Pinel. *History of Psychiatry, 21*(10), 38–53. https://doi.org/10.1177/0957154x09338334

Dubbink, W., & Smith, J. (2011). A political account of corporate moral responsibility. *Ethical Theory and Moral Practice, 14*, 223–246. https://doi.org/10.1007/s10677-010-9235-x

Fatić, A. (2015). Tasks for dreaming: The somatic cognition of emotions in moral judgement. In M. N. Weiss (Ed.), *The Socratic handbook* (pp. 67–82). Lit Publishers.

Grossman, D. (2009). *On killing: The psychological cost of killing in war and society.* Little, Broown and Co.

Jansson, T. (2015). Identity — A dialogue problematizing who we are. Theory and practical tips on how to philosophise in groups. In M. Weiss (Ed.), *Socratic handbook* (pp. 293–302). Lit Publishers.

Jung, C. G. (1989). *The red book: Liber Novus* (M. Kyburz, J. Peck, & S. Shamdasan, Trans. & S. Shamsandani, Ed. & Introduction). Norton.

Lindseth, A. (2015). Being ill as an inevitable life topic. Possibilities of philosophical practice in health care and psychotherapy. In M. Weiss (Ed.), *Socratic handbook*. Lit Publishers.

Lis, S., & Bohus, M. (2013). Social interaction in borderline personality disorder. *Current Psychiatry Reports, 15*(2), 338. https://doi.org/10.1007/s11920-012-0338-z

Marinoff, L. (2002). *Philosophical practice*. Academic Press.

Molina, J. S., Robles-Pérez, J. J., & Clemente-Suárez, V. J. (2019). Psychophysiological and fine motor skill differences of elite and non-elite soldiers in an urban combat simulation. *Military Psychology*. https://doi.org/10.1080/08995605.2019.1654293

Raabe, P. (2014). *Philosophy's role in counseling and psychotherapy*. Rowman and Littlefield.

Redmond, J. (2013). Contemporary perspectives on Lacanian theories of psychosis. *Frontiers in Psychology, 4*, online. https://doi.org/10.3389/fpsyg.2013.00350

Redmond, J. (2014). *Ordinary psychosis and the body. A contemporary Lacanian approach*. Palgrave Macmillan.

Verhaeghe, P. (2008). *On being normal and other disorders: A manual for psychodiagnostics*. Karnac.

CHAPTER 7

Modal Integrative Psychotherapy and the Culture of Trauma

Abstract This chapter discusses the role of trauma in both modern psychotherapy and modern culture, relating the emphasis on trauma to the prospects of developing the attributes of sound mental health, including resilience. While trauma is an undeniable experience of many, the culture of trauma in psychotherapy presents trauma not merely as an experience coupled with a particular perception and interpretation that leaves a long-term mark on the person, but also as a normative element in psychodiagnostics and therapy. In this perspective, trauma is increasingly seen not only as an event and its reception by the person, but as a hypothesis, a potential explanation, and a prerequisite for treatment, so that trauma is sought as a potential explanation of difficulties that do not initially present as traumatic. The chapter introduces two methods of responding to trauma, the Flow Model and the Concert Model, and elaborates on the role of organic relationships and micro-communities in addressing trauma.

Keywords Organicism • Anxiety • Fear • Worry • Sense of solidarity

Trauma is likely one of the most pervasive psychological alibis of our time: ascribing a person's dysfunctionality, immaturity, or narcissistic traits to the consequences of a trauma almost absolves the individual of any personal responsibility for the value choices one makes. This abuse of trauma

A. Fatic, *Modal Integrative Psychotherapy*,
https://doi.org/10.1007/978-3-031-91934-3_7

leads to situations where the prospect of living a philosophically good life, as the ultimate aim of any kind of discourse therapy, is seen as conditional upon the absence of trauma, or at least the successful, usually protracted, and demanding processes of "reliving" trauma and resolving issues engendered by trauma.

While, in this chapter, I by no means suggest that trauma is to be neglected as a source of difficulties, I discuss some of the main aspects of it in the therapeutic field (specifically the related phenomena of anxiety and fear) and develop an account of trauma, which, in its methodology, is Lacanian, and in its symbolic therapeutic prospects is integrative and philosophical. It seems to me that trauma has become the subject of political correctness and is now part and parcel of various ideological toolboxes where the pain encountered through trauma is used to advance various political agendas in psychotherapy, be it feminist, socialist, or Marxist. The last is the case in the so-called systemic family psychotherapy. In fact, this type of therapy directly takes over the Marxist theory of the family, whose pitfalls are methodologically extremely serious as it assumes value determinations that a psychotherapeutic theory and practice ought to be very cautious of, and should seek to validate or invalidate them in practice, such as the assumption of "exploitation" (Russell, 1976).

Trauma is a generic concept and a universal human experience. There is hardly a person who has not experienced a trauma, and this fact alone makes using trauma as an ideological weapon highly inappropriate and both psychologically and socially damaging. My argument here is that trauma presents us with the challenges of waning organicism in our social lives, and that a reaffirmation and return of organic links automatically mellows down the traumatic potential of our social structures by reinvigorating our authentic sociality, care, and emotional directedness toward others. Thus, trauma and the responses to it are paradigmatic for the healing role of community and the human connection that is at the heart of how MIP sees the psychotherapeutic process. For MIP, the catalytic role of that process is reflected in the person's ability to think modally about what has traditionally been seen as a "given" reality, where only personal responses and interpretations were seen as able to be amended through traditional psychotherapy. Trauma also elucidates the key feature of modal integrative psychotherapy, namely that it addresses not just personal experience, but also the epistemic connection between the person and the person's life world, where the identification of various modal possibilities is key to changing the world, rather than merely changing the client. The assumption here is that certain events and experiences, including those that present true trauma to the person, influence one's psychological metabolism of experience to such an extent that the fundamental quality of one's life or interpretation of events cannot shift sufficiently substantially in order to offer significant improvements in one's view of reality, values, relationships, and one's overall satisfaction. This brings us to Marx's old criticism of philosophers that they tend to interpret the world, while the whole point of philosophy is to change the world, which, while controversial given the history of Marxist political movements inspired by such philosophy, is highly relevant for psychotherapy. Rather than merely containing itself to seeking a reinterpretation, re-evaluation, and reconfiguration of experience, MIP seeks a change in the modal worlds, where modal worlds are not just the personal vistas of clients, but actual living contexts.[1] The role of trauma, both as a relevant experience for psychotherapeutic theory and practice, and as a culture that determines what is considered correct or incorrect in the various psychotherapeutic approaches, is thus elucidative of key methodological facets of MIP and of its subversive approach to the current modality or established "givens" of one's personal history or cultural identity. To address trauma in this context, I proceed with a sequence of phenomena that either arise from trauma or are closely associated with it, including the phenomenon of anxiety as culturally foundational for various schools of psychotherapy, including, perhaps most challengingly, for Lacanian psychoanalysis, which is methodologically close to MIP and which is returning as a dominant conceptual paradigm into what could be considered psychotherapeutic mainstream.

Political Correctness in a Culture of Anxiety

One fundamental phenomenological presentation of trauma, which encapsulates both its symbolism and its existential pain, is anxiety. Trauma is not just generally followed by prolonged anxiety; it also reveals, on the very surface of the sufferer's behavior, the other psychoanalytically important aspects of anxiety, namely, phantasy, expectation, concern ("care" in Lacan's terms, or "worry"—*Sorge*, in Heidegger's terms), and inhibition.

[1] Marx articulates the criticism in the infamous 11th Thesis on Feuerbach. The *Theses on Feuerbach* were initially written as a draft structure for the first chapter of his book, co-authored with Friedrich Engels, entitled *German Ideology* (Marx & Engels, 1946–1947).

Trauma is thus a trigger for a deeper articulation of anxiety that reflects features of the person's identity and character that articulate themselves in desire, joy, and a particular structure of frustration, or sense of personal insufficiency and "lack" (Lacan, 2014, p. 4).

One of the questions Lacan asks at the very beginning of his seminar on anxiety is whether the anxiety of the client, the analysand, is the same as the anxiety of the analyst, or therapist. Is anxiety a state, a diagnosis, a description of a more or less universal experience which we can identify with to various degrees? Is the client's anxiety essentially the same anxiety that we all, in a sense, "subscribe to"? Is my anxiety the same as your anxiety? Or do we have different, phenomenologically and experientially unique, anxieties, which we can only guess about in another person, while the only real knowledge we can have about anxiety is about our own anxiety?

Importantly, this is not a question of epistemic solipsism, which entails that all we can truly know are our own experiences. The above proposition, that our anxieties are only our own, does not preclude a belief that, generally, various mental states, held by others, as well, can be of such a degree of generality that we can variously identify with them and consider them "the same" in kind as what we feel when we are in that particular mental state. However, anxiety is special, in that it is the intersection of various intentional states, which Lacan throws together, or tries to "tie down together on the ground", in his own words—an idea which he largely takes over from Heidegger. Anxiety is at the same time a phenomenon of fear, expectation, frustration or inhibition, worry, or care, "seriousness" (or awareness of the gravity of the circumstances) and other emotionally charged mental states which fundamentally describe our existence as that of a finite, vulnerable being that is concerned about the future.

The expectation of a future, which Lacan puts forward as an element of anxiety, is linked with care about the future. He takes over Heidegger's idea that we are intrinsically concerned about the future and thus incapable of focusing fully on our present, because we see the present both as striving towards the future and as bearing fruits in the future.

For us, *the present is part of the future*. Our present is hence not only the factual description of a situation we are in and of the mental states we experience with regard to the facts of our here-and-now; it is also our projection of the future, of our expectations which, if fulfilled, lead to a peace of mind, and if unfulfilled, cause anxiety.

Assuming that the present is foundationally about the future, anxiety in the present concerns our view of the future. Thus the Stoic prescription to reduce expectations and learn to live with little positive satisfaction and resources, so that expectations of the future might be reduced, resulting in the reduction of anxiety in the present. However, anxiety is particularly deep-seated when the format of our present, the institutional, social, and other relational factors not under our control, predispose us to *expect a particular outcome* in the future.

Much of our expectations of the future in modern society are couched in our institutional life and the role of institutions in the community. We are taught by dominant political and social discourses in our societies that institutions are there to secure a degree of predictability in our communal lives. This leads us to expect greater predictability than is realistic, given human nature and the subconscious dynamics of much of our interactions, where even our desires and motives are not always known to us, let alone to others. The increasing inability by the majority in institutionalized societies to deal with unpredictability, and the even more uniform set of expectations of what things "ought to be like", gradually grow into a normative structure where, if things do not occur the way we imagine that they should, or must, we see this as a form of social and institutional deviation.

The more we are immersed in institutional processes, the more anxiety we are predisposed to. Such processes disallow us to step aside from a present that derives its quality almost entirely from expectations from the future. A psychological result of this dependency on institutional predictability is that the quality of our present is diminished. The experience of a full-fledged present moment is depleted through anticipation of the future moment, where the very meaning, as well as the fruits, of our present efforts, or even perceptions, are expected to materialize. Hence, institutional influences on our psychological processes that are about the present moment detract from the value of the present and thus from the fullness of our life experience, which is always primarily that of the present. This may well be one of the reasons for the epidemics of depression which plague the most industrialized, and consequently, the least organic societies—an epidemic which Marinoff has described in his *Plato not Prozac* (Marinoff, 2000).

The ways in which institutional life superimposes itself on our organic existence in the here-and-now are innumerable. If one is involved a judicial process, one must participate in the proceedings and must fight for a desired outcome, or risk losing the most important values in life. It is interesting to consider how litigation laws in modern democracies have changed over the past decades, with the onus of gathering evidence in court steadily shifting toward the parties, primarily in civil proceedings, but also in criminal ones. Where once the court, and the institutions involved in judicial processes, such as the executive government and various public services associated with the government, used to be obligated to establish certain facts and check others, regardless of whether the parties in litigation asked for such checks or introduced them formally in court, in the more recent revisions of litigation laws this "official conscientiousness" type of clause has largely been abolished. This means that individuals immersed in litigation are left with an even greater responsibility for the outcome, while the responsibility of the institutions is systematically and progressively reduced (Stuntz, 1993).

If one has a job which requires them to fight for specific future outcomes, for achieving a particular threshold of performance, one's present will be marked by anxiety because of the expectations which cannot be bracketed out from one's experience of the here-and-now. The "status-anxiety", as Alain de Botton calls it, arises from the ever-increasing expectations of the individual that are justified by reference to technological progress, where in fact the level of expectations dwarfs the actual increase of capacity that is facilitated by technology (Botton, 2004).

Similar considerations apply to institutionalized private life. Marriage is an institutionalization of privacy whereby the most intimate human relationships are regulated by law. This is why marital relationships have a tendency to change so abruptly and to transform from the tenderest and most private interchanges between two people and their children into the most vicious conflicts. Today's institutional obsession, greater in some societies than in others, with family violence, and the resultant breaks put on the traditional liberal safeguards of privacy in favor of facilitating a greater institutional, repressive involvement in such conflicts, is largely the result of institutionalization of intimate relationships. Intimacy, if it is protected from the public eye, involves the normal range of emotions and relationships that characterize any type of human interchange, including that which is not necessarily pretty or desirable. Marital and informal emotional partnerships involve not just warmth and mutual support, but also conflict, betrayal, disappointment and all kinds of disruptions. To keep this type of relationship as organic as possible, the state, in the liberal tradition, used to shun becoming directly involved in resolving issues such as family violence outside the more systemic regulation of violence *sui generis*. Without special regulations on family violence, there was no normativity lost on the social and legal unacceptability of family violence, because it fell within the realm of violence in general and was sanctioned as such. However, with the introduction of special legislation on family violence, new procedural, operational norms were introduced where the traditional liberal realm of the person's home and their organic, family relationships were no longer privileged. This meant not only that in particular women were systematically encouraged to bring their intimate conflicts out into the open and involve the institutions in their private lives, but also that the institutions could act of their own accord and intervene in one's private realm on the grounds of an exceptionally pronounced public value, such as protection of women from family violence. This went as far as granting the police powers to de facto suspend the constitutional guarantees of enjoying one's property and order suspected perpetrators of family violence to leave their own homes, which they legally owned (Zimring, 1987; Cocker, 2001).

There is, of course, something aesthetically particularly abhorrent in family violence that seems to warrant changes in the traditional constitutional guarantees of property and privacy of the family. However, such changes, as any systemic changes, while addressing some issues, generate others, including a sense of legal insecurity and unpredictability on legal fronts seemingly distant from the ugly reality of family violence. A particular aspect of this unpredictability is associated with the role of the state, which, as the Lacanian Big Other, sits on the very edge of the register of the Real (which, for Lacan is unbearable without a symbolic interpretation). According to Lacan, the Big Other (the threatening presence lurking in the Real) is reflected, in the register of the Symbolic, in the Primary Signifier, Name of the Father, which allows the symbolic metabolization of the Big Other. For Name of the Father to make the Big Other sufficiently benign for the person to integrate the Big Other in one's healthy experience, Name of the Father must be caring and restrained in its exercise of power. It is obvious that the state, especially in highly institutionalized societies, plays this role of the Big Other, where any unpredictability and willingness to change the legal encapsulation of its exercise of power on the individuals generates an additional collective anxiety that spreads throughout one's social experience (Hook, 2008).

Trauma

The traditional understanding of trauma as a psychological scar inflicted on a person by an extreme experience (physical violence, rape, war, etc.) is highly reductionist: in fact, trauma is a part of our upbringing as human beings, without which no socialization would be possible. Our parents, teachers, and later other significant others in our lives all inflict traumas on us in order to direct us to develop in certain directions and to avoid others. Such traumas range from microtraumas (denial of certain satisfactions that are important to us and leave us wanting) to major trauma (physical or emotional violence). We even deliberately inflict trauma on ourselves in order to effect certain types of self-development: we associate experiences of pain, sometimes even of deprivation, with certain life choices and conversely, we associate experiences of pleasure with other choices, and we work to actually produce pain and pleasure accordingly. The principle of conditioning, one of the oldest and most fundamental mechanisms of learning known to psychology, requires exactly this: the satisfaction of desire as a result of desirable choices, and the infliction of trauma of various degrees of severity in order to discourage other choices. Unlike the actual conditioning, where "reward" and punishment are actually administered to distinguish between the desirable and undesirable courses of action, the modern coaching technique of "neuro-associative conditioning" suggests that, rather than actually inflicting trauma and offering reward, it is sufficient to focus on a feeling that typically follows reward and, correspondingly, to one that typically accompanies punishment, in order to alter motivation (Walther et al., 2005). In both cases, trauma, most often microtrauma, plays a key role. In other words, trauma is not in principle an undesirable, and much less an unacceptable tool in influencing human behavior; it is a necessary part of our socialization and of our very social existence.

The nature of trauma, however, is highly dependent on context. In different communities, seemingly very similar forms of traumatization might have different consequences for those who are traumatized. While in constructive and peaceful communities the traumatic experiences (e.g., trauma inflicted by punishments) can be highly reformatory and reintegrative, in inorganic, highly institutional societies, where even punishments are remote from one's sense of identity, where they tend to be faceless and "sterile", removed from our important relationships with significant others, inflicted by anonymous institutions, trauma is associated with anxiety and can be highly destructive (Fatic, 1995).

In a high-anxiety, inorganic society, life in general is destructively traumatizing. We are traumatized by decisions made by others and by the influence these decisions exert on our own choices, because we cannot relate to those others, who, hidden between their various institutional roles, are far removed from the realities of our personal existence. This makes them a threat, rather than a source of clear and personally acceptable social norms to us.

Sometimes we make decisions whereby we traumatize ourselves because we are separately traumatized by circumstances. This makes understanding and treating trauma more difficult than it might seem at first sight, just as anxiety is not simply a "complaint" or a troubling mental state that we try to deal with by therapy: it is an aspect of our existence that we must make sense of and use in a particular strategy of life. We must harness the dynamic potential of trauma, and of anxiety, in such a way as to increase our well-being.

Describing trauma as an extreme experience which requires some acute "interventions" is the same as conceptualizing the "ordinary" life as trauma-free. This is a misconception that arises in psychotherapy and in all kinds of destructive political ideologies, which present collective trauma as a justification, or strategic reason, to inflict mass suffering on others, or to lead one's own community's social life into self-depriving and limiting collective ways. Trauma is an aspect of our existence, of our life, a part of who we are, and it cannot be written off or explained away entirely by reference to extreme cases of trauma. Dealing with trauma requires substantial tolerance, but at the same time it requires a deeper understanding of how trauma works.

The Flow Model and the Concert Model of Responding to Trauma

Trauma has a way of moving us forward, or inhibiting us, depending on what kind of trauma it is and how our environment encourages us to process it. Some of the seemingly most debilitating traumatizing experiences inflicted on individuals have caused them to fight back even more strongly, eventually overcoming adversity. Consider the adversity and violent trauma inflicted routinely on the inhabitants of the Brazilian favelas, plagued by poverty, drug abuse, and all kinds of crime. Some of the most decorated and now wealthiest athletes came from the favelas—not just a few, but large numbers. There is even a school in Mixed Martial Arts which gathers specifically martial artists from Brazil, most of whom share a troubled, traumatizing early life of poverty and victimization by crime. These are individuals who compete in the world's top sporting organizations, maintain functional families in highly industrial, rich societies, and generate an income that would be inconceivable to most of their compatriots. They are not some kind of violent outcasts who have found their niche in the fighting arts; they are highly professional, disciplined, top athletes who live by a strict regimen of exercise, diet, and behavior to maintain their status in their organizations, while at the same time raising families. Most can be described as examples of exceptional resilience and perseverance that, according to their own testimonies, would not have been possible without their early trauma. For all of the above reasons, I discuss trauma here as an opportunity for the development of leadership qualities, rather than as a merely debilitating and pathologizing experience, which must somehow be "cured". Working through trauma does not mean getting rid of trauma, but rather learning how to use the potential of trauma to better address present and future challenges.

The conclusions one draws from trauma, and the habits one forms because of, or based on, the experience of trauma, may be constructive or destructive, benign or socially malignant, depending on how the individual chooses to use one's trauma and the energy which it exerts on one's personality.

When Joachim Guzman, known as "El Chapo", one of the most important Latin American drug lords of our time, was captured in 2019 and sentenced to life imprisonment, it became a front-page story in most western media (CNN, 2019). However, the media focused on the criminal exploits of El Chapo, who, among other things, had become famous for prison breaks, including one time when his accomplices had dug a tunnel underneath the prison all the way to his cell, complete with lighting and flooring, left a motorcycle inside, and El Chapo absconded underground by riding the motorbike through the tunnel. What most media reports failed to mention, however, were the critical features of Chapo's personality that he had exhibited throughout his rise in the drug world, starting as the son of a simple coca farmer, all the way to becoming the head of one of the most influential narcotics trafficking organizations worldwide. While his role in society has been destructive, his leadership skills within the underworld have been studied as fundamentally similar to those required to run any organization, compared to the management skills required in legitimate organizations (Catoira & Bratton, 2018).

Chapo was born into a life of depravity. His boyhood conflicts with his father were about the money made from coca rubber or paste and about reasserting his ambitions to become a significant figure in the drug world. The dynamics of these conflicts show a traumatic element of socialization that structurally, through criminality, mirrors the ordinary processes of socialization through a boy's relationship with his father. Where some other boy's aspirations, in different circumstances, might have been to surpass his father in business or in playing a piano, or being an academic, Chapo had the aspirations to surpass his father as a member of the drug cartel. Having embarked on this road, Chapo capitalized on his early trauma of deprivation. His poverty drove him to immerse himself deeply in the circle of violence that surrounded drug trade. The depravity in his early life was a catalyst for his rise in the criminal world.

Chapo advanced to positions of authority because of his relentless quest for weak points in his opponents: wherever he was, he sought to buy information which would expose the vulnerabilities of the institutions, the police, the prosecution, and their individual members. If he could bribe his way to freedom and political connections, he would pursue "friendships" with politicians, police officers, and leaders of competing criminal organizations. His repeated incarcerations and the betrayals he had suffered from competitors in the criminal world, as well as from members of the legitimate society, would have broken most individuals in his place. He was tortured in prison, subjected to long-term sleep deprivation, to beatings, months of isolation at a time. Many times, he was forced to offer the last of his money as bribes for his freedom and had to start from afresh, using only his skills, connections, and resilience to survive and come back on top of his circumstances.

According to his own statements, Chapo's trauma was his most precious tool for success in his world. However deviant this world might be to us ordinary folks, we must respect the fact that Chapo had overcome dramatic adversity to rise to a position of leadership which required many of the same skills as legitimate forms of leadership, such as political or business prowess. He had built his entire leadership style around *resilience*—an obvious reaction formation to his youth marked by adversity. His value system was founded on affluence as his main life goal—not simply as a desired life style, but also as an early marker of his manliness, social worth, and identity. In the culture where he lived as a young adult, Chapo was considered a valuable son, husband, father, member of his group, only if he could provide for those he loved, regardless of the way he did so. Without his early trauma and the resilience and values which he had developed in response to that trauma Chapo would likely not have been able to withstand the years of imprisonment, numerous disappointments and betrayals by associates and friends, or the tortuous encounters with the Mexican police and military. It was trauma, Chapo's trauma, that made him a leader and allowed him to become the person he wanted to become. Yet in the modern culture of trauma it is almost indecent to suggest that trauma might serve as a necessary engine for building personal resilience, even though we see examples of this principle everywhere, including in global affairs. With the war Israel waged on Lebanon in 2004, one of the most often cited "qualities" of the Lebanese people was resilience, which was attributed to the decades of having been subjected to invasions and destruction. Many Lebanese pride themselves on their society's ability to sustain a relatively pleasant and humane way of life while living under aggression. The Lebanese have not become monsters because their country has been a battleground for the opposing forces around them, causing their cities to be repeatedly destroyed and their community members to be killed and maimed. On the contrary, they became a shining example in the Middle East of humanity and a functional civil society. The same applies to survivors of many wars: those on the losing side, having been severely traumatized, often emerged as healers and helpers. Consider just the personal story of the founder of logotherapy, Victor Frankl, who lost his parents, wife, and unborn child to the Nazis, only to survive concentration camp and found one of the most influential methods of psychotherapy. In Bosnia, survivors of the genocide committed by Serbian forces against the Bosniak (Muslim) population, during the civil war of 1991–1995 that culminated with the tragedy of Srebrenica, do not seek vengeance, but reconciliation. They have not become monsters; visiting their part of Bosnia reveals a culture of sociality that makes one wonder whether these trauma survivors are the only normal people left in Bosnia. The aggressors, on the other hand, show numerous symptoms of identity and community disorders. One can, of course, construe trauma in all kinds of ways, including that which would attribute trauma to the executioners, as well as to the victims, but that would be a cynical and hypocritical approach to trauma. Even the extreme, criminal trauma such as that of genocide does not necessarily create abnormality and monstrosity in the survivors; it is thus unjustified to assume, as a cultural norm in psychotherapy, that trauma on other, ordinary levels (loss of great love, neglect or being hurt by one's parents, being victimized by society or by individual people) is more or less uniformly a predictor of pathology. There is something to be said for the lack of at least microtrauma as a predictor of personality disorders, where the lack of personal resilience and ability to handle stress and frustration leads to the development of manipulative and abusive interpersonal and social strategies that have caused many urban populations to remain on the therapy couch for much of their adult lives (Fatic, 2018).

Similar circumstances are widely present in the personal histories of many successful people. People who have suffered personal uncertainties and problematic early relationships often become psychologists and psychotherapists. This can be a double-edged sword. Such people can be extremely damaging to their clients, if through their profession they try to cater to their own psychological wounds. Unfortunately, such situations are very common. However, on the other hand, they can also be extremely valuable if they are able to put their own personal experiences to use as means to assist others.

Just as Chapo could have been crushed by his deprivation and could have led a life of poverty, drinking, and wife-beating in his village, instead of using his trauma to rise to the top of his world, people who undergo mental difficulties and later become psychotherapists can become mentally compromised self-help seekers instead of helpers to others, who bring the entire profession into disrepute. Alternatively, they may become leaders in the field and break new horizons in theory and practice, based on insights gained through their trauma. The principle is the same in all cases: we choose whether to make our trauma a resource, or an inhibition to our own development. In fact, psychotherapeutic practice shows that clients often prefer therapists who have had a personal experience of similar trauma as they have undergone, because they believe that having lived through such trauma uniquely qualifies someone to help others. The modern Dutch practice where psychiatric patients are routinely assigned a three-member team of carers, consisting of a psychiatrist, a psychologist, and an "expert by experience", where the last one plays the leading role in therapy, is an example of this principle. The model acknowledges that having experienced a problem and having successfully negotiated a way out of it uniquely qualifies the person to help others above the level of formal qualifications bestowed by institutions on those who have not had a personal experience of the same type of problem. It is my belief that in psychotherapy one should avoid working with issues that one has not been able to grapple with successfully in one's own life, and this is the reason I often tell clients who come for marriage counseling that I may not be the right therapist for them, because I myself have not succeeded in what they seek to achieve through marriage therapy. However, almost always, they insist on a belief that someone who has experienced divorce can better understand the road to divorce than someone who has avoided, or never had to face the prospect of divorce. The same principle may well apply to many other topics in therapy. Obviously, we cannot experience everything and will work with clients whose experience does not resemble our own; however, when there are similarities, they can either powerfully enhance our capacity as therapists or lead us to a complete distortion and failure of therapy, depending on how we use the trauma, or some other adverse experience, which we share with the clients.

On a surface view, it seems that the constructive use of trauma in developing our identity can take at least two forms: (i) that of a person's ability to "let oneself be in the flow" (the Flow Model), or (ii) that of a sequence of events and personal decisions that, ultimately, "fall into place" and thus create a symbolic structure where trauma is an important signifier, or bearer of meaning and source of motivation (the Concert Model).

(i) A state of flow is that where one is able to emotionally accept whatever comes one's way, seeking to interpret the sequence of events and experiences as signs of directions to take in future decision-making. When trauma is concerned, being in the state of flow implies seeing trauma as a direction and a determination about where to turn next. When microtraumas are at stake, this is the sort of everyday decision-making which typically orients the person away from the source of trauma, whether it is related to work, personal relationships, or other aspects or outcomes of life which one might have desired prior to experiencing the trauma. In this context, trauma is seen as a cognitively significant event which, in a sense, "makes decisions for us". However, when one experiences major trauma, then the meaning of it as part of the flow is more complex, because the emotional effects of such stress on the person's integrity are interpreted as signposts pointing to a person's change in the future. Just as microtrauma can be seen as pointing to small changes, macrotrauma points to large transitions, to comprehensive personal change, which may be required to merely psychologically survive the aftershocks of the trauma, or which may be the best way forward given the changed circumstances generated by the trauma. Macrotrauma is like an earthquake that opens new chasms within the person, while at the same time closing some old ones. The potential outcomes of such trauma thus vary: new wounds are opened while perhaps old ones are erased; healing new wounds may require a different methodology from healing the old ones, and this might lead to different personal styles and deep personal changes that have constructive life-changing effects. Cancer survivors often develop a different personality after the illness, as do heart attack victims. Their values change: they heal different wounds than they used to care for before and can overcome personal challenges that, before their cancer or heart attack, were the problems that defined their priorities and indeed their personalities. Such a transcendence of previous problems and vulnerabilities comes at a price; yet undeniably it is a transcendence whose nature, on balance, is constructive and improves one's persona and quality of life.

Having experienced arrest, divorce, or major illness, to name but a few relatively common major traumas, the person who adopts the Flow Model will approach the trauma by re-examining their values which become articulated in these traumatizing experiences, and depending on one's sensibility and the circumstances of the trauma, one might radically change one's values. In such a case, the person will emerge changed after the trauma. The direction of this change is still the person's prerogative, however one which depends much more on their emotional fiber than on any strictly rational reasoning. Some people emerged from the trauma of political imprisonment with far greater conviction and became completely uncompromising opponents of the ideologies, governments, or ruling structures which had imprisoned them. Others emerged changed in the sense that they had given up politics or had switched sides. Arresting or threatening one public activist will turn that person into a major problem for the repressive political regime, while arresting or threatening another will neutralize the activist permanently. It is the emotional and moral material that one is made of that decides what kind of change a trauma will trigger. The flow of attitudes is there, however its direction depends on the individual.

(ii) The above discussion clearly suggests that residing in the flow is the opposite to the model of constructive response to trauma that might be called the Concert Model, where one actively seeks a structure where trauma and the other associated formative experiences would somehow "click into place" within a broader cognition of the meaning of one's life and become part of a broader harmony. The former perspective is open and indeterminate: the person is ready to accept whatever happens and build one's new reality around the new events and facts that one encounters, while the latter is a matter of careful design, which seeks to integrate the anticipations of future events and their consequences into one complex picture, whose all parts fit together. If broad analogies with philosophy could be drawn between the Flow Model and the Concert Model of constructively metabolizing trauma, the former would likely fit into a Nietzschean type of philosophy, while the latter is reminiscent of Confucianism. Nietzschean thinking would suggest that trauma undermines most of the current reality and that the whole paradigm of our interactions with others and our social existence ought to be brought down and leave space for a new, solid structure to be built in its place. This is modal thinking in a radical form, encapsulated in his principle: "If something is falling, one should also give it a push!" (Nietzsche, 2006, p. 168). The latter, Confucian type of philosophical approach would seek to restore, rebuild, and reorder what has been shaken by trauma: to recontextualize, but preserve, and create added value through transforming the damage, the dent into an ornament, or a scar into a personal and social skill (Cheng, 2009). Let me re-emphasize that both general approaches to trauma are constructive, yet fundamentally different, as they reflect different values and sensibilities of character. While the two approaches described here are extremes, clinical practice and everyday interactions reveal much more nuanced articulations of the two sensibilities.

Individuals who adopt the Flow Model approach to trauma, disappointment, or general frustration often appear to observers to easily abandon their life situations and to be highly adaptable to major change, and this sometimes meets with moral reproach. They are individuals who, in psychotherapy, sometimes give away the first impression of a lack of depth and capacity to fully experience pain or tragedy, and this may lead to false diagnoses of personality disorders. In such cases, closer observation and therapeutic work often reveal a deep structure of values and life strategies that is based on the described sensibility of flow, where one tends to opt for a major paradigm shift in response to trauma, rather than to patching up the wounds inflicted by the traumatic experience. On the other hand, the persons who adopt the Concert Model approach to life (seeking to make things "click together") often appear on first therapeutic encounter as highly focused, with exceptional attention to detail, as individuals who are prone to meticulous planning.

The Flow and Concert in a Comprehensive Perspective of Reactivity to Trauma

Despite their sharp differences as personal styles of responding to trauma, early trauma often reveals how both Flow and Concert can be parts of the same process, where the capacities which one develops by living through trauma play a key part.

Working through trauma is a character-building process, which shapes our personalities in ways that may turn out differently. For example, overcoming early adversity by developing exceptional communication and negotiation skills is one outcome. Working through the same traumatic experiences by developing a distrust of people in general and a threatening, intimidating manner of communication is another. Ultimately, it is for each person and community to decide about the most acceptable and effective models of expressing fear, frustration, or suffering. It seems that one of the most general consequences of trauma is prolonged fear and distrust of situations that are surprising or resemble the traumatic experience, even in very superficial ways. Thus, fear seems a good candidate among unpleasant emotions and the associated attitudes that might elucidate the way in which the Flow and Concert models might be seen as complementary paradigms in the management of such emotions.

How does fear "fall into place" within a greater tapestry of life sentiments and experiences, and how does it become part of the "flow", whereby we accept whatever comes our way, try to see meaning in it, and derive potential directions for future action and choices? Essentially, both happen in similar ways: by our deciding to *"give up"* fear.

Lacan writes that one of the phenomenological features of neurosis is that "a neurotic won't give up his anxiety" (Lacan, 2014, p. 52).

Contrariwise, while anxiety is a constitutive element of our life experience and our very identity, in its various shapes and contexts, the healthy, effective way of dealing with fear and anxiety is simply "giving it up".

The above does not mean that anxiety can be reduced to something else—that it can, or should, be rationalized, sublimated, or converted into some other type of emotional and experiential currency. Anxiety and fear as its underlying emotion are there to stay as existential dimensions of our life experience as a whole, and recognizing them for what they are is a prerequisite for accepting those parts of our identity that make us more effective and more adept at life. However, the art of diverting focus, or giving up on obsessive thoughts about our own experiences and anxieties, is the non-neurotic way of handling anxiety. This is typically achieved in one of two ways: by seeking to see how our life experiences "fall together", and how anxiety as an underlying current of those experiences "falls in" within the whole picture. In other words, the way for fear and anxiety to "click in" with the rest of our life experience is exactly by submitting ourselves to the flow of events, where we seek to use specific events and emergent trends to our advantage. In other words, allowing events to shift the entire paradigms of large swaths of our overall experience, values, and approach to reality can reshuffle the complex picture of our worldview and cause various segments of what remains of our identity to fall into place in a coherent way after the trauma. Being radical or "pushing those things that are falling" may in fact be the best way of clearing up the picture and preserving what ought to be reintegrated into a more solid psychological structure. There appears to exist a convergence there, rather than merely a superficial contradiction. Shaking the kaleidoscope through the paradigm shift in the Nietzschean type of thinking facilitates the emergence of a composition that is harmonious, stable, and pleasing. There is no guarantee that the former will lead to the latter, but then neither is there any guarantee that seeking a reconstruction in the Confucian philosophy style of approaching trauma will result in a harmonious structure of values and experiences.

The two perspectives are two extreme paradigms which define how we interpret, or process events in our lives generally, including traumatic experiences. Thus, the psychotherapeutic interventions based on either will differ both technically and strategically. The Flow model exemplifies a vision of dismantling rules and structures as the space for freedom and personal re-invention post trauma, while the Concert model reflects a view of order and composition as the ideal of wellness. One way in which the two worldviews exemplify themselves in history is in military strategy, which can often be used as the blueprint for a variety of life contexts. Consider the following historical example of two such strategies being employed at the same time and in the same military engagements.

In the nineteenth century, naval battles raged between the powerful Spanish fleets and pirates, who stalked Spanish commercial ships packed with valuable cargo along the shores of the Spanish colonies in the Carribbean and the Pacific. The strategies employed by the Spaniards and the pirates, respectively, exemplify the paradigms of Flow and Concert.

The well-organized, strictly disciplined, powerful Spanish navy used heavily fortified and armed warships, equipped with devastating firepower, designed to maintain distance from the adversary, inflict maximum structural damage on the enemy ships from as far away as possible, and then crush the crew of a crippled vessel by boarding it and over-running the defenders in close combat, with Spanish soldiers advancing in tight formation across the enemy ships' decks. This strategy was clearly reflected in the Spanish formations, the type of vessels, and the training of seamen. The whole strategy consisted of various complex elements of tactics that were in precise concert or harmony: the timing of the attack, the strict sequence of the phases, from the cannon salvos to the disciplined and machine-like close-range attack, to assuming control of the vessel. The process could almost be drawn as a mathematical diagram and the likely casualties, even the time the battle would roughly take, could be calculated given the relative strengths of the two ships, the weather conditions, the number of sailors on each ship and the number of cannons and their range. The strategy was an example of how Concert style thinking operates in military strategy.

The pirate captains, on the other hand, used a very different strategy, aimed to undermine the strict structure of the Spanish approach to battle. Their ships were typically smaller, faster, but well-armed. They were built for speed and resistance to collision, with sharp, protruding, reinforced bows. The strategy was not to execute a well-planned and calculated attack, but to induce fear and chaos, "reshuffle the kaleidoscope", and establish dominance by shifting the paradigm of what is happening, where the Spanish sailors would not even be aware that the battle has begun and would suddenly find themselves in an unknown situation, where they had to do one thing they were never trained for—improvise. This was an example of Flow thinking.

The pirate strategy was to approach the Spanish frigates under the cover of night, in silence and with lights out, speeding towards them from a side to ram the sharp, hard bow of the pirate ship into the Spanish warship so as to either literally cut it in half and sail through it, or, if the ship is reinforced, to puncture its hull and jam the pirate ship into it, while the enemy vessel is taking water. The pirates would then deliberately tangle the sails with those of the Spanish ship. Their vessels always had two heavy cannons positioned just behind the bow, at the front deck. They would fire those cannons at point blank range into the Spanish ship's deck immediately after tangling the sails. The attack, when successful, would cause utter panic among the Spanish crew, who were forced to quickly adapt and improvise as circumstances around them developed quickly and in unpredictable ways, while they were taking casualties at each stage of the pirate assault. The pirates would then descend on the victim ship in full force, boarding it and seeking to kill the captain and the officers first, to leave the sailors leaderless.

In situations where the initial ramming of the Spanish ship was unsuccessful (the other ship would see the attack before it was completed and sometimes the frigates would manage to maneuver themselves to avoid the full impact), the pirate ship would speed past the enemy vessel, typically at an angle which minimizes the impact of the Spanish broadside cannons on the pirate vessel, while the buccaneers, the pirate "snipers", with long rifles, would fire from the sides of the pirate ship, decimating the Spanish mariners onboard their vessel.

The two strategies show two different paradigms of thinking: one based on the assumption of structure as the foundation of a strategy to control entropy (and the described situations were impregnated with intense fear by the combatants, resulting in a devastating psychological and organizational entropy for the side taking the assault), and one based on the destruction of structure, or use of flow to debilitate the opponent.

Similar situations are used in conflicts between people that are marked by pronounced fear. In therapeutic experience, it is often apparent that even conflicts where anger and rage seem to be the dominant emotions usually masque anxiety and fear. Some individuals prefer to respond to anxiety-laden, challenging conflicts by trying to stabilize them, either through predictable, conciliatory, or defensive actions, or through institutionalization (through lawsuits, reports to the police, or other legal means). Others approach conflicts by attempting to maximize fear in the other party, by destabilizing the opponent and making them more vulnerable from as many angles as possible. The latter respond to destabilization caused by the conflict by shaking the boat further, by causing the disorder to further increase, and then finding ways to respond in such a churned-up environment.

In facing everyday anxiety in life, likewise, some people try to stabilize themselves by surrounding themselves with supportive others, increasing their work loads and structuring their day more strictly so that they have "less time to think" about the anxiety. Others respond by reducing their commitments, resting more and allowing themselves more *unstructured* time to process their feelings and allow ideas about strategy to address the situation to rise in their minds.

Adopting either of the two described strategies presupposes a psychological moment that Lacan speaks of as "giving up on" anxiety, fear, or any other debilitating emotion. Giving up on anxiety does not necessarily mean ceasing to feel anxiety. The latter is not entirely up to us. Instead, giving up implies letting the anxiety run its course, while not attaching too much importance to it, moving past it intentionally and developing strategies that are designed to succeed despite the anxiety and fear. Both going with the flow and seeking a complete rationally understandable "meaning" where the various elements of our lives "click together" are such strategies of dealing with anxiety and fear. They are the opposite approaches that can be integrated in a more complex strategy of addressing trauma and adverse life experiences in general. The two ways of handling adversity allow the person to work through the trauma by implementing an approach that is intended to address chaos and be effective in disorderly circumstances. The frame of mind implicitly involved in this type of thinking involves moving "past" the trauma, danger or fear: one looks "through and beyond" the trauma, seeking a goal that lies in the background. In this process, one seems to temporarily let go of, or give up on, anxiety. This does not require "confronting" anxiety; giving up on anxiety is simply allowing anxiety to exist while moving past it. Both the Concert and Flow strategies inculcate this moment of deflecting, rather than facing anxiety, in order to focus on a way to overcome adversity.

Dealing with fear and anxiety always includes "giving up on anxiety" in one of the two described ways.

Fear and Loss

There is a prominent view in psychoanalysis, engendered by Freud himself, that anxiety is triggered by loss. Freud offers his characteristic explanation of this loss originating in infancy, where "the absence of a mother's breast" causes the child to be anxious. Lacan strongly opposes this idea and argues that, rather than resulting from a lack or loss, anxiety in childhood is triggered by "imminence": the imminence of breast-feeding, the imminence of controlling and disciplining the child—the imminence of "whipping the child's back" (Lacan, 2014, p. 54). Similarly, anxiety later in life is set in motion by the imminence of some kind of experience, rather than the absence of experience.

Consider a common situation in counseling, where individuals often report anxiety immediately prior to meeting a potential romantic partner, on all levels of contact, ranging from the first meeting after an initial online contact to having sex within an already developing relationship. They don't feel anxiety about the meeting long before the date, while they are separate, where they would logically experience a lack. Rather they feel heightened anxiety when a meeting, a moving out of one's comfort zone, is imminent. Similarly, anxiety in people who await surgery is triggered by the imminence of surgery. Hardly anyone sleeps well the night prior to the surgery; however, most people sleep much better on the nights while the surgery is still some time away, lurking in the future. When students undergo exams, anxiety surges just before or during the exam, or at times when the student portrays the exam to themselves mentally so vividly that it replaces the actual imminence of the exam with an imagined imminence. In each case, it appears that the dominant scenario where anxiety sets in is imminence, rather than lack, which is not to underestimate the destructive psychological effects of lack. When anxiety is triggered by a loss, it is the imminence of loss that triggers it, not the mere absence of something. This imminence, the experience of immediate prospect of an event, contracts together anxiety and fear. For example, loss of life in battle for a soldier is a possibility that is part of the military profession. When individuals choose this profession, they must become reconciled, to some extent at least, with the possibility that they might lose their life while doing what they are professionally required to do. They know that the likelihood that they will die from violence is considerably higher than that for most other members of their community. The same applies to police officers, who, in a sense, sign up for situations where they know that they will be exposed to violence and face far higher odds of dying from it than the other members of their community. Thus, there is a moral paradox in the legislative provisions of most countries where the killing of a police officer is considered an aggravated form of the crime, not because of the nature of the act, but because of the identity of the victim. Yet, a police officer victim has chosen to be there, to face the danger with full awareness of the risks. Police officers are armed and trained to engage in violence, unlike ordinary citizens. Thus, morally, it would be a more cardinal crime to kill an ordinary citizen than to kill an armed police officer who engages the attacker, however, in practice, legally, it is the other way round, for different reasons, obviously. The prospect of loss of life does not ordinarily cause major anxiety to soldiers or police officers until such a possibility becomes imminent. Professional soldiers are typically not too anxious while they deploy to a war theater with clear prospect of engaging the enemy. They are often seen smiling, waving, and cracking jokes while they board planes or ships to go to a distant battlefield. However, just before the battle or mission (it is questionable whether in modern military conflicts there are still "battles" in the traditional sense), nobody cracks jokes, at least not authentically. Nobody has a good night's sleep just before a mission close to or behind enemy lines, where they know that they will likely have to kill someone and face the possibility of being killed.

The relationship between an imminent event and fear is particularly visible in group psychotherapy, when certain life experiences which cause anxiety to group members are relived through group dynamics, although they do not actually occur in the group members' real lives outside the counseling room. The dramatized imminence of these events in a group setting causes the levels of anxiety to rise. This, after all, is how therapeutic groups achieve improvement: their members use them as "laboratories" of real-life experiences where they practice their choices, behavior and develop their personal changes under controlled circumstances. In group psychotherapy, many of the mechanisms of real-life validation and invalidation are active; however, the most debilitating consequences of the bad choices are neutralized. A psychotherapeutic group is like a theater: it contains all the events that occur in real life, however without the real consequences that these events cause when they transpire outside the theater. The actors who are abandoned in theater return to their loved ones in real life; those who are slain on stage rise, and those who are lost emerge after the show. Likewise in group therapy: where for certain choices and actions the social consequences would be debilitating, in therapy the same actions and choices are limited to validation or invalidation. They do not include exclusion, grudges, or break-ups. Still, the emotional reactions of therapy group members to the acting out of others are the same or very similar to those they would experience, and those who act out would encounter, in real-life situations. For example, a person who has lost an important relationship in a way which has traumatized her may fear betrayal in the future and be inhibited from developing the trust that is required to initiate a romantic partnership. Such a person will express this fear while reliving the initial experience of loss in group therapy. Others who relate to the experience in the same therapy session may recollect their own emotions, which will likely differ. They may involve loss of self-respect or self-value, of the sense of legitimacy of their claim to emotional security, etc. While the fears triggered by trauma can be damaging for future life and may need to be addressed by therapy, that does not make them irrational. In fact, fear is rarely irrational. Fear is a regulator of actions or choices that is associated with our values, and that alone makes it comprehensible. We interpret people's fear as healthy or unhealthy depending on how it relates to their values, and how those values correspond to the general societal values that we as therapists can understand. If we see fear as irrational, whether groundless or exaggerated, we tend to label it as phobia. Fear of open space is an example of fear that most people perceive as groundless. An inhibitory fear of insects exemplifies that which most observers see as exaggerated. Both can thus qualify as phobias. The reason is simple: most people do not recognize any danger in open spaces as such, and regard insects as generally harmless, granted certain dangerous and relatively rare exceptions. We would not consider a panic response to observing a shark swimming underneath a person to be pathological, but we would consider the same response to encountering a fly questionable, to say the least. Most of us consider sharks inherently dangerous and flies inherently harmless, and we count on this view being shared in our community.

Consider, on the other hand, a fear of spirits. We do not know, in the positivist sense of "knowing" that our civilization favors, whether spirits exist. There is a sort of consensus among most people that spirits probably do not exist, as there is insufficient evidence for the opposite view. We cannot prove that they do not exist, and there is some evidence that they might exist. Today, we take synchronicities as an empirical fact. Hardly anyone denies the existence of synchronicities or argues that there is no causal connection between certain events that occur synchronically, simply because the occurrence of synchronicities is not so rare that it would be plausible to argue that they are all simply random coincidences. However, we do not have a consensus on the causality between events that cannot be rationally proven, just as we lack a consensus that there are spirits because some people claim to have seen them. The entire western civilization is based on a book that affirms the existence of spirits; our entire morality and social structure ultimately rest on biblical precepts. We have all been raised with fairytales and mythical stories involving spirits, and we raise our children in the same way. We create art depicting spirits and synchronicities. Yet, when a person fears spirits or synchronicities, they run a very serious risk of being labelled as psychotic. We regard that fear that our civilization has recognized from its inception as a mental illness, unlike the fear of sharks, which we consider rational and acceptable.

In various historical periods, the view of seeing or fearing spirits was very different. European armies waged or refrained from waring wars, and raiding parties decided on whether to undertake sea voyages, depending on messages received from spirits in the seers' dreams (or, for that matter, in anyone's particularly vivid or convincing dreams). Leaders conversed with spirits in forests in much the same way as people pray today. Nobody considered them psychotic for relating a conversation with spirits in their dreams or expressing a fear of spirits who haunted them. They did not satisfy the other criteria of psychosis: they were functional, controlled their affect, reacted emotionally consistently to various experiences, etc. Today, however, the same individuals would likely be hospitalized after a repeated insistence that spirits are haunting them. Our fear is seen and validated or invalidated by our community, not depending on the nature of the fear, but depending on the values and beliefs that are involved in the fear, and the respective values and beliefs by the community. For a Danish Viking who fell into the sea while on a voyage to raid Britain it would have been shameful to panic that a shark might attack him (or her, by the way), while for the same warrior to panic on the boat because a spirit or a god told him in a vision or dream that the mission would fail disastrously would have been reason for the rest of the company to seriously consider turning the ship back. For today's Danes the opposite would be the case, just as it would be for the rest of the European culture. One wonders which fear is more rational, that of spirits, or that of sharks, given the overall balance of experience that we face with inexplicable phenomena on the one hand, and with shark attacks, on the other (Agassi & Jarvie, 1987; Fatic, 2023).

It appears that regarding spirits at least we have accepted what Nietzsche calls "the spirit of gravity", where those who do not recognize the empirically provable and rationally easily understandable truths as the only legitimate knowledge are considered "fools", however in religious history and the history of civilization fools have been known to be privileged royal advisors and prophets. Nietzsche thus exclaims: "The human being is hard to discover and hardest still for himself; often the spirit lies about the soul" (Nietzsche, 2006, p. 155). He describes those who seek their own soul as fools, yet fools who have discovered truths that are inaccessible to the rational man (Nietzsche, 2006, p. 154). The quest of drawing a credible distinction between those who are truly mad and those who merely protest the spirit of gravity in the Nietzschean sense has been a long-standing struggle for psychiatry and psychodiagnostics. This, however, does not help us to evaluate the fear of spirits, or of gods, where we act with utmost inconsistency: in places of worship, we admire (or belong to) those who fear the spirits; in psychiatric offices, we hospitalize them. It seems that for some types of fear, and anxiety associated with that fear, we have no response other than a collective, civilizational neurosis that helps stabilize us, even when that neurosis manifests in incongruent and contradictory practices, such as that concerning the fear of spirits.

While anxiety is associated with the imminence of something one fears, trauma as a particular unpleasant experience is different from anxiety. Fear cannot eliminate anxiety, in fact the two seem to belong to the same type of emotions; however, trauma may cancel both fear and anxiety. In this sense, trauma seems to be a threshold experience: it can either inhibit or disinhibit action, decision making, and one's active relationship to the world; it can either give rise to the penultimate fears or cancel the fears and the concomitant anxiety altogether. The latter type of situation is obvious in severe illness: when someone faces a humiliating death from disease, one often overcomes one's most deep-seated fears, and if one survives, one behaves differently. Heart surgery patients are known to change their behavior after the surgery, either becoming more active, even reckless in their choices, or by changing their personality in their relationships. A previously highly tolerant person thus often becomes quite conflictual, and vice versa, people who used to be "highly flammable" before the heart surgery often emerge from hospital being much "wiser" and taking their time to react to triggering experiences. The reason is likely that a close encounter with death, as the ultimate loss, releases inhibitions, or helps articulate insights about life, previously held in check by fear or prejudice.

I have known cancer patients who, while still ill, claimed that their cancer was "the best thing that happened to them", because it liberated them from fear that had stifled them beforehand: after all, few things are worse than cancer, and little is left for a cancer patient to fear having once gotten the ultimate disease. The diagnosis, I was told repeatedly, was a shock, a trauma; however, the subsequent disappearance of all fears was notable and relatively quick. Nobody wants to liberate oneself from fear by becoming a cancer patient, just as nobody wishes to be traumatized; however, lesser traumas, ones that do not come close to cancer, may and should be interpreted and used as transformative experiences that do not necessarily involve or generate fear or anxiety afterward.

One way to approach trauma is to consider it as a small death, the death of a part of the person's experiential world. Just as a cancer patient, having once received the diagnosis, feels as though they have already partially died, many of the more ephemeral concerns and worries in the patient truly die. If we assume that trauma is a sort of the ultimate experience, rather than merely any unpleasantness, then its being the ultimate in a sense cancels out an entire range of concerns and worries that relate to those unpleasant experiences that might occur, and that are less than the ultimate. People who face death tend to be more honest, less calculating, and less afraid of the consequences of what they say or do. Similarly, someone who has experienced violence as a type of trauma tends to see it differently from everybody else, to understand it differently, and while doing everything to avoid it, one does not react to it, once it happens, the same way as everybody else. Survivors of wartime violence do not see war in the same way as politicians or the public; veterans diverge in their view of a justified war from most other people and tend to be less accepting of war, yet in case of warfare they would be more apt at handling it than the general citizenry. Trauma changes the person just like any significant experience does, but trauma, being the ultimate negative experience of a particular sort, also transforms one's fears. While fear is the emotional relationship to a possible or likely unpleasant event and anxiety is the emotion associated with the imminent occurrence of that event, trauma appears to escape the definition in terms of fear: it seems to be something farther and greater than fear.

One way to add some clarity to the concept of trauma is that advocated by Gabor Mate, who argues that trauma is in fact not an experience, or an emotion relating to an experience, but rather a meaning that is attached to an experience—in Mate's own words, our interpretation of the experience

(Mate & Mate, 2022). This view of trauma may explain why the same events may be traumatizing to some people, while being less traumatizing to others; why the same experiences might be seen as more or less traumatizing in various cultures. It is the meaning that we attach to experience that makes it traumatic, rather than merely unpleasant. Many people in modern culture see it as traumatic when somebody genuinely wishes to hurt them, or when they discover that others genuinely dislike them and wish them something bad. The same is the case with many physical confrontations: people who are attacked physically often take considerable time to even understand what is happening to them and to overcome the shock of “why is this happening”. They are so unused to open and direct malevolence by others that facing such malevolence personally traumatizes and inhibits them. Such is especially the case in highly institutionalized societies that stigmatize almost any type of human aggression, as in most western societies today.

While being physically assaulted is invariably unpleasant and painful, wherever one might find oneself culturally or value-wise, whether it will be traumatizing or not depends more on the values and the context than on the content of the actual experience. A couple of decades ago boys fighting in school was so normal that it was almost expected: if a boy never fought with the other boys, the adults worried about his health and emotional development. Today, boys fighting at school is called peer violence, regarded as deviance and responded to by all kinds of institutional mechanisms, school teams, social services, the police, the courts, etc. At both points, when boys fighting was considered normal and now, when it is considered impermissible and deviant, boys feared being beaten up by other boys and were anxious immediately before an altercation. The fear and anxiety associated with physical pain and possible injury involved in a physical confrontation have not changed; however, in most cases, at the time when boys fighting was considered normal, such altercations, including the pain and injury associated with them, were not considered, or interpreted, as trauma, and thus, they were not traumatizing. Boys and young men did not usually remember their fighting at school as traumatizing experiences; to the contrary, many were proud of their ability to stand up for themselves, and thousands recount those experience from childhood with fondness. Today, however, any kind of physical violence in school is considered scandalous, and it does traumatize children: they do not remember it with any degree of humor, but carry them with themselves as unwanted emotional baggage that inhibits and bitters their future relationships, reduces their self-confidence and their ability to enjoy life. Trauma appears to be at least in part a rational construct, which, once in place as a normative skeleton for certain types of experiences, generates the emotional consequences that we associate with post-traumatic difficulties. While provisions here must be made for great traumas, such as mass killings in war or major crimes, which do inflict a debilitating effect on most of their victims, regardless of the cultural context, most traumas that are of a more ordinary nature conform to Mate's model of a semantic, rather than merely experiential or psychological category. Of course, once a semantic structure is set in society, it will then generate its own psychological and experiential qualities and experiences based on the same "raw" events that one encounters.

Fear and trauma manifest in somewhat special ways within the psychotherapeutic process.

In psychotherapy, fear often manifests as an anticipation of potential loss of the therapist's esteem of the client, as the result of some kind of revelation by the client to the therapist.

The client gains certain benefits in psychotherapy. A key is the gain of a therapist as a new person in one's life. In many cases, the therapist relatively quickly becomes the most important person to the client. The therapist's presence in the client's life changes the very "chemistry" of that life and of the client's life experience. Hence, the therapist is not only a participant and leader in the therapeutic process; they are also a benefit to the client; to some extent, they are a desirable life outcome for the client.

The therapist's influence on the client lingers on a long time after the conclusion of therapy. The client achieves a new perspective and a reinterpretation of ordinary reality through the presence and role of the therapist. The client's fear of imminent loss of the therapist is thus common. The client experiences this fear as anxiety about the upcoming change, of facing life without the support of the therapist, or of implementing the personal changes developed through therapy in real-life settings. However, typically, what the client really fears are not these fairly general changes; rather it is the specific loss that is imminent—the loss of a person one has established a strong emotional connection to. Anxiety is merely a surface sign of the deeper-seated fear, which tends to be more specific than anxiety. The difference between fear and anxiety is more on the level of what the subject can *recognize* and locate as the focus of one's affect (fear), than in the actual causation of the anxiety and fear, respectively. Fear relates the person emotionally to the content of the possible future experience; anxiety anticipates the immediacy of that experience.

Why is this relevant for therapy? Because viewing anxiety, as a widely present phenomenon in so many complaints in counseling, as fear, or as generically the same as fear, with some of the differences in scope and focus acknowledged, allows for a more appropriate intervention. Addressing fear as a generic, wide-encompassing problem in counseling is a methodology in itself, and dealing with anxiety is only one part of dealing with fear. A therapy for anxiety, if it is to have lasting effects, must be therapy for generic fear. This is not always the case in conventional psychotherapy.

The main reason the connectedness between anxiety and fear, namely the rootedness of anxiety in fear as the more generic emotion, is relevant to MIP as a philosophically structured method of psychotherapy is the role of fear as an existential condition, as a dimension of our everyday being-in-the-world, which is largely irreducible to various rationalizations, and which we must somehow deal with.

We fear the world to the extent that fear causes or threatens to cause us loss, and it does so every day. The generic fear of loss that is inherent in our very primary experience of the world, from the loss of protection through separation from the mother's body at birth to death is a constant of life experience that is sometimes mitigated by pleasant experiences or forgotten in the intoxicating vapors of phantasy or ambition (Schopenhauer, 1966, pp. 151–155). Hence, given the ultimate nature of the threat of loss of life itself and the main attributes of it (health, community, basic satisfaction), the generic fear with which we approach life, and which has been the main rationale for Stoic philosophy (which is now making a powerful return through Stoic counseling and Stoic communities within the megacities of today's technological, postindustrial society), qualifies as the overarching trauma of all other traumas that we may experience, or acquire as our emotional baggage, through life. In this sense, life itself is a generic trauma. This has perhaps most directly been expressed in Lacanian psychoanalysis, which sees the Real, the immediately present reality of life, as unbearable, while it sees the only way in which we are able to overcome the immediate effects of such trauma as our capacity for symbolization (Babich, 1996). The way to deal with life, in a sense, is the same as the way to address trauma: it is to overcome it by integrating it into one's experience through symbolization. That is the aim of all trauma therapy and at the same time the way to understand the generic nature of trauma as a part of our existence that is increasingly exceptionless as the threshold of what qualifies as trauma through social interpretation is progressively lowered.

Mate himself, as the author of perhaps the most useful understanding of the concept of trauma as a meaning attached to experience, rather than the experience itself, is one of the leaders of the current trauma culture, namely of the progressive lowering of the threshold of the meaning of trauma to the point where Mate openly states that we are all profoundly and systematically traumatized by the very toxicity of the social relationships we are forced to live in, meaning that trauma is a part of the very core of our social existence in modern society (Mate & Mate, 2022).

One of the logical corollaries of this view espoused by Mate is that, given that almost every significantly unpleasant experience qualifies as trauma in modern society, and more so in Mate's own championed trauma culture in psychiatry and psychotherapy, the very meaning of trauma has shifted so that it no longer has the significance that it used to have in the past. If trauma is seen as something exceptional and transformative, then this exceptionality warrants a special theory and treatment. However, if trauma is common and attached as a meaning to any significantly unpleasant event in life, then it is no longer exceptional and does not deserve a special theory and methodology, because it is ordinary. One cannot have trauma both ways: as the penultimate experience of pain and loss after which one can claim that nothing for them is the same as before, and as an ordinary experience that occurs every day for most people in the "toxic society". The culture of trauma led by Mate has in fact degraded and trivialized trauma and equated the interventions to address trauma with the counseling aimed to address quality of life in general.

Mate's culture of trauma is not the same as Lacan's understanding of reality as unbearable and life as threatening. The former reduces trauma to everything that might have caused a suboptimal pattern of thought and action or scarred the person in some way. The latter points to the ethical dimension of the reality of life in general: that it is the register of our existence that foreseeably cancels itself, both through death and through the promise of innumerable experiences of suffering. In this sense, external reality is trauma in the generic sense. To say along the Lacanian lines that life is a major trauma is different from saying, following Mate, that we are all trapped in a traumatizing society where any mental disorder originates in society and only reflects on us, because society's way of relating to us is that of constantly traumatizing us. The latter view is attractive, but philosophically shallow: it really comes down to a generalized ascription of fault for suffering to society. The former view is philosophically sounder: it suggests that trauma is the substance of life, while symbolization, creation, aesthetics, sophisticated satisfactions and joy are moments of respite. Both ways of generalizing trauma may offer relief in counseling, because they shift the onus of being traumatized individually away from the particular condition and choices made by the individual. It is more palatable for most of us to suffer the pain that we know everybody suffers than that which we believe is exclusively our own. However, the redemption offered by the two approaches is of different quality. While Mate's therapeutic culture of trauma relieves and numbs the senses by drowning the personal pain in the generality of a collective experience (again, this is effective), Lacan's and Schopenhauer's understanding of generic trauma of life encourages creative strategies to carve out ways out of the given labyrinth of life's trauma without blaming the society or hoping for a key to unlock trauma based on social critique or societal emancipation.

The difference in slant between the two views of the universality of trauma tends to produce very different attitudes to trauma and adversity. The former is consistent with a high value being attached to resilience; the latter is not. If life in general is a trauma, and any respite from it is the result of developing a high level of symbolic capacity, then the strategic focus of approaching life experience is through developing resilience. On the other hand, if trauma is the mistreatment we receive at the hands of the toxic society, then the focus is on criticizing and changing that society, while acknowledging, registering, and developing the personal interpretation and meaning of trauma. At the surface of it the difference between the two views of universal trauma seems slight, but their consequences in the practical realm are colossal; they translate into two types of psychotherapeutic cultures and thinking: the culture of resilience and the culture of trauma.

One way to understand how MIP understands and adopts the culture of resilience is exemplified, at the extreme, of course, in the way some types of military training are conceived. The parallels between the military and wars, on the one hand, and living one's ordinary life, on the other, have their methodological merits.

In military training for special operations and intelligence, a strategy to resist and overcome torture is widely taught: the key is to focus not on the pain suffered during the torture, but on the meaning and purpose of that pain, namely on one's most important values, including the lives of civilians, one's comrades, one's family, compatriots, etc. By symbolically reshaping the physical trauma in the described way, one increases the limits of one's very physical and psychological endurance. If one focuses on a greater value, one gives meaning to one's trauma, and at the same time mobilizes one's resilience to overcome the trauma. This principle has an important consequence for dealing with trauma therapeutically: giving trauma a meaning will most often result in the person overcoming the trauma. The meaning may be personal, unseen by others, or it may be intersubjective and social, as is often manifested in social activism by trauma survivors.

The ancient way of overcoming the trauma of violent loss of a loved one in many societies has been vendetta. By punishing those responsible for the loss of a family member, one does not bring that family member back, nor does one's sorrow diminish. However, one gives meaning (justice, in the sense of proportionality) to one's reactions to the loss of a loved one by killing the perpetrator or someone close to them. One may cite many arguments against the practice of vendetta and I will not spend time here on discussing them; however, we should not underestimate the fact that vendetta serves personal and group therapeutic purposes much more than it is there to serve general social justice or regulate behavior. Vendetta provides an opportunity for what is sometimes called "closure". Its primary aim is not social control or prevention of future crimes; rather it is psychotherapeutic, however bizarre this might superficially seem. The same psychological value can be attached to the modern death penalty; however, the institutional infliction of such penalties gives rise to many other social, psychological, and existential issues, some of which are connected with the complete lack of proportionality in means and of an identity relationship between the individual who is punished and the state that inflicts that punishment, none of which applies to traditional vendetta (Fatic, 1995).

There is a lesson for modern psychotherapy to be learned from vendetta. Working to strengthen an important value, such as justice, or to punish those responsible for an unjust loss, is a legitimate therapeutic tool to give meaning to one's loss. A person who reacts to a loss by withdrawing and relinquishing all power will be in a much more difficult personal situation than a person who reacts by mobilizing with close others and inflicting a vendetta.

An example of the above principle is the way in which individuals in various cultures and groups react to social, political, and judicial injustices. In such cases the trauma of institutional violence can translate either into submission or, alternatively, into active resistance and a quest of public punishment for those responsible. Revolutions have been triggered by judicial and institutional injustices, sometimes committed against only one man or woman. The therapeutic intervention in trauma thus involves the activation of the person's symbolic resources to give meaning to the trauma in as active a way as possible, including social and political activism, rather than falling into a self-destructive passivity that leads to loss of self-esteem and of personal conviction.

Therapy in the situations of institutional victimization of individuals faces particularly difficult questions, because the trauma inflicted through a loss caused by institutions cannot be addressed effectively on a strictly private level. Such an intervention often requires a degree of publicity, and thus involves palpable risks for the trauma sufferer. It seems that a therapeutic intervention aimed at unleashing the person's capacity to fight in the public is the most effective tool to remedy the consequences of trauma induced by institutional injustice. This is why sufferers of institutionally inflicted trauma often express a desire to appear in the media and to address the public.

Structural Loss

A key question left to be addressed here is what kind of loss we have in mind when we discuss loss as the cause of anxiety and fear. I would say that the simplest way to answer this question is that *we fear the loss of another*, including the appreciation, satisfaction, and affection of another person or persons. It is thus *structural loss* in the psychoanalytic sense that is at stake in our basic predisposition for fear and anxiety.

On 5 December 1962, Lacan gave a lecture on anxiety which ended with his idea that the structure of anxiety outside therapy consisted of two elements: the Other's jouissance and the Other's demand. However, within therapy, anxiety receives a third element, namely a particular desire by the subject that is triggered by the interpretations developed with the therapist, or analyst (Lacan, 2014, p. 54). In other words, Lacan sees anxiety as a phenomenon at the crossroads of three kinds of efforts by the person: to *satisfy* the desires of important others, to meet the *formalized demands* by others (social expectations, institutional norms, the community's most pronounced projections of virtue, etc.), and, in therapy, to *please* or satisfy the therapist. Anxiety, in this context, is positioned between the various directions of *social dependency*. It is founded on the fear of loss of recognition or affection by the important figures in our lives.

The loss involved in anxiety is symbolic; this is the reason it can be overcome by symbolic satisfactions: we need to satisfy others, to meet social expectations, and to make the master figures in our lives proud of the way we are. If we suffer or are traumatized doing so, we will find ways to overcome our trauma most of the time. Similarly, if we are traumatized or in any way victimized, and subsequently receive support and recognition by our peers, this will largely remedy the trauma. Let me illustrate this by a personal example.

On 28 April 2021, I wrote a piece for a daily paper concerning the abuse of children by social services, a topic of particular interest to me in my capacity as a professor of psychology at the time. The article was provocative and was followed by an open letter to the US Ambassador, which I wrote to point out serious issues in the abuse of children and parental rights of the opponents of the political regime in my country.

Just two days after that open letter, a "rejoinder" to my paper on the abuse of children appeared in the same daily, without a personal signature. That "reaction" by an obscure association of social workers, written in an anonymous form, however, cited what seemed like the wrong title of my newspaper article. It was a title different from that which had appeared in the paper. In fact, this was the working title under which the paper had been written, which had never left my computer: the title was subsequently changed and sent under that changed title, so the only way for someone to know or access the first version of the article with the original title would have been to hack into my computer. To make things even more interesting, once I had sent the article to the editor, the editors changed the title again, so eventually it appeared under a third title. The second title could have been discovered if someone had gained access to the editorial office and their (or my) email correspondence; however, the actual first title was never mailed, so finding it out required breaking into my computer. It was thus unclear how a group of social service organizations could have hacked into my home computer and cited the article which had never left the computer. Clearly the security services had become involved and reacted to what they perceived as my unwelcome writing to foreign diplomats, sending me a message that they had me under control and surveillance. Only a day after the "rejoinder" appeared, a special unit of crime police for organized crime knocked on my door. To make things funny, one of the two inspectors turned out to be my former student. This made their visit relatively friendly in manner, but they asked me to come to their headquarters the next day so that they could "help me investigate" what I had written about. They did not neglect to leave me a written order to appear. The same afternoon, my paper disappeared from the newspaper's internet portal.

Angered by this brutality, I wrote another article, describing what had been done with my private file, and I sent it to a news portal. I was anxious that such invasions of privacy were so blatant and that nobody seemed to react to them. The article, however, soon started to be taken over by various news portals representing groups which I held in high esteem. It was published by several pro-democracy media, offering strong support. My anxiety subsided. When I attended the police office the next day, I was already in a proactive frame of mind. This helped turn the tables, in a sense: the morning ended up being spent in "collaborative" discussions with the police officers, some of whom shared their own experiences with child abuse by the social services, however, it was clear that they were told to startle me and nip the public discussion in the bud, removing it from the media by threatening the editors. The feeling was bitter. I felt violated, cheated, and that my efforts were futile given the government's ability to so easily remove any content from the media. However, upon receiving support from civil society, I was able to overcome the feeling easily. Although I was warned by my solicitor to be careful about where I go and what I said to various people, and although she kept pointing it out to me that "legally, it is not good when special crime police turn up at your door and call you in for questioning", I gave the event no further thought and in fact increased my activism. Just a few days later, my car was vandalized in front of the building where I lived, at a car park which was covered by cameras. The recording showed the face of the offender and the whole process of vandalizing the car, yet the police never reacted to my report. The warning had to be complete and clear.

The effects of this episode traumatized my family and friends. However, they did not traumatize me, because I had received support and could attach a clear meaning to everything that had happened. The microtrauma never stuck to me. In fact, my activism increased, not because I am particularly brave, but because the behavior of the repressive apparatus was so transparent, and I could make sense of it as suggesting that they could not think of anything better to do than to try to frighten me through the police and to vandalize my car. This allowed me to process the experience and integrate it easily into my short-term experience.

Why did my internal tension go down so quickly? Because I felt that the people whose opinion mattered to me supported my cause: I felt, at the same time, that those who shared many of the same values with me were satisfied with my reaction, that I had answered what both they and I perceived as a moral duty to resist. Those who mattered had responded.

It seems that the same principle applies to macrotraumas generally. If people can make sense of having been imprisoned, they overcome the experience seemingly without lasting psychological difficulties. People who experience divorce because the husband or wife had found another person and went away with them, often metabolize the divorce much more effectively than people who divorced out of "character differences" the real grasp and meaning of which were not entirely palpable and easily articulated. Making sense of trauma appears to heal the trauma substantially. It is the lack of meaning, the apparent pointlessness of trauma, that causes the greatest difficulties in integrating the trauma into one's overall record of experience, while retaining a full psychological and social functionality and capacity for satisfaction in life.

The described principle suggests an avenue to the effective treatment of fear, anxiety, bereavement, and similar conditions: the therapists ought to consolidate a relationship of approval and validation with the interlocutor and seek, through interpretation, to develop a meaning of the experience. Facing one's fear, anxiety, and loss as a symbolic condition allows us to remedy the suffering by providing a *symbolic compensation* by conferring value on the client's choices, reactions, and emotions. In the above example with the theft of my article prior to it being published, I felt violated in my privacy and personal dignity by an intrusion of criminalized institutions into the confidentiality of my (digital) home. This violation caused me a degree of anxiety. However, the approval and symbolic validation which arrived after I had shared my story publicly, from those whom I considered relevant and important, conferred validation on my concern. Objectively, I remained a victim of criminality by the institutions, but I no longer *felt* like a victim: rather I sensed a regained social recognition as a person who, on a microlevel, rightfully resisted institutional criminality. The therapeutic effect of recognition kicked in for me immediately.

The above-described effect of the action and its communal recognition is associated with activism. However, the activism that remedies trauma is not associated with regulating the proverbial "fight or flight" mechanisms of evolutionary psychology; it has little to do with physiological release and everything to do with symbolism and the acquisition of the meaning of trauma. Namely, the trauma with a clear meaning to the traumatized person is no longer the trauma one initially went through as a raw experience. The same applies to loss. Losing one's limb or a close family member to clearly unnecessary everyday circumstances is trauma which leaves a lasting imprint. However, losing a limb or a relative to a revolution or another meaningful struggle is a different thing, and the loss is experienced differently. This difference teaches us a valuable lesson for therapy: rather than "relaxing" or removing our focus from trauma, it is enriching one's trauma with meaning that really heals. Negations of trauma might provide temporary relief, but eventually the trauma will come back, and the suffering will further increase. We tend to be able to successfully process the experiences that are rich in symbols and meaning; conversely, everything that is meaningless or devoid of symbolism represents the Lacanian "unbearable Real", which brings us to the very brink of psychosis.

Another aspect of curing trauma is closely associated with recognition and acceptance: it is *communication*. The ability to communicate our trauma to another and to receive some kind of cognitive or emotional feedback heals the trauma. When trauma is communicated, other concerned people, members of our organic communities (families, groups of friends and relatives, etc.) can relate to various aspects of it and are able to communicate back a validation of our experience and its interpretation, and even their own self-recognition in some aspects of our experience. This generates a sense of strong symbolic community, whereby the trauma ceases to be only our experience, and becomes a *collective psychological property* of various people who have either suffered similarly, or who can closely relate to the specific trauma that we have experienced. This is the psychology behind support groups: cancer survivors, people who have been victims of violent crime, or who have lost children or relatives to similar calamities join peer groups to share their trauma and overcome it by joint efforts. That is also the reason self-revelation, when used economically and with the right timing, can be so powerful a catalyst of change in individual psychotherapy; when the therapist responds to the client's narrative by relating their own personal experience that validates the client's interpretation of their experience, the empowering and healing effects can be very potent (Vinogradov & Yalom, 1990).

By becoming the property of several—or many—individuals, the trauma becomes a *mark of comm*onality rather than merely a scar on the identity of an individual. Some groups, and even some societies, cultivate the collective memory of their traumas as a defining feature of their very communal identity. The same principle applies to individuals and small groups: if my friends can relate to the fact that I have been victimized by a political system, or an institution, and if some of them have also been victimized in similar ways, or if they can show strong empathy with me, thus self-identifying with my victimization, my trauma is shared with them. They take a co-ownership of my experience alongside me. Thus, I have helpers carrying my burden, in addition to the burden being additionally endowed with meaning. This alone makes my trauma less malignant.

Community and communication are organic remedies for most traumas. It is thus not surprising that there are communities where the destructive consequences of traumatization are far less pronounced than in the western world. Without exception, these are more organic communities, with less formalized inter-subjective relationships, less emphasis on privacy, and a greater propensity for sharing personal experiences. By participating more in the intimate and private experiences of others, members of such communities share more in the ownership of those experiences that, when owned by just one individual, might be debilitating for their whole life. Traditionally, in many European countries, when somebody dies, that is, when someone loses a loved one, it has been customary for all the friends and relatives to gather at the home of the grieving person to share in the grief and take on a part of the burden. It is very rare that anybody is left alone, even when they ask for it. In Montenegro and Albania, there is a practice of collective crying. Each village has women ("narikače"), who can bring themselves to cry loudly in grief for a deceased person. They would attend all funerals and would cry instead of the bereaved family members. The organic practice was intended to relieve the trauma of loss for the individual by expressing a collective ownership of the loss, by at least appearing to share in the trauma that has befallen a community member.

Generally, organicism tends to help in psychotherapy: the closer and less formal the relationship between the therapist and the client, the more likely the success of the therapy. However, organicism as a feature of therapy is not easily achieved, primarily because it requires a great amount of dedication by the therapist and the client, and the crossing of some traditional boundaries of professionalism that often limit our effectiveness in counseling and therapy. To foster an organic relationship with the client, the therapist must be willing to go deep into the client's world. He must be able to give up much of his own time, privacy, and personal pursuits in order to dedicate a part of his life to his clients. This is only possible where the therapist has a great love for the client and a great desire to help. It is this type of organicism that has been built into therapeutic communities, which we know from Antiquity as various philosophical "schools", in fact early monastic communities, and which are now resurfacing in various forms, both as therapeutic communities and as more traditional micro-societies of the like-minded individuals.

Therapeutic Micro-communities

The format of deep counseling, which was described in Chap. 6, allows the participants to move from the traditional roles of "client" and "therapist" to a relationship that resembles that of student and teacher or of a group of disciples who work toward achieving common virtue, a common understanding, or simply toward alleviating pain, without always clearly distinguishing the specific roles of leadership as it belongs to various members of the group.

In ancient times, the members of an organic philosophical community lived together. They shared all their time in what later became a fundamentally monastic model of life: in an early form of practice of confession, members of the school confided all they considered important to the leader. This person offered general guidance and was responsible for the organization of the school. The leader typically sets the school's philosophical and value orientation. The communities thus established subsequently grew in various directions and gave rise to new leaders, who, typically, developed different interpretations of the principles and desires that had brought the community together.

Deep Therapy allows an organic context in which the "complaint" is shared with the therapist or with the members of a therapeutic group. We spend time together in the countryside, outside the bustle of city life, prepare food, share meals, participate in sessions three times a day, conduct Socratic walks, and, depending on the weather and size of the group, go swimming in a lake. The discourse thus envelopes all the ordinary activities in a close-knit community. This adds an organic dimension of counseling.

As organic therapy, Deep Therapy shares a key feature with all therapeutic and peer communities that exert a considerable healing, cohesive influence on its members, namely a strong parallel between the identity of such small communities and that of individual people. Truly therapeutic communities are perceived by their members almost as another person—they acquire a semblance of personhood, although they are groups of individuals. The aim of the community is to establish such relationships with its members that closely remember those relationships that the members establish between themselves as individuals. The community seeks to become friends with each member: the individuals gathered in the community see the group as their ally and perceive the culture of the group as a character trait shared between all members. They thus partake in the collective character of the group, almost like the various parts of a personality make up the personality as a complex structure. They become a part of the group's personality and identity to such an extent that, with the departure of any member, the group's very core suffers from an identity crisis. For those individuals, the group is one of them, and they feel loyalty to the group as a whole in much the same way as they are loyal to one another within the group. The group becomes an addition to the sum of its members. Consequently, the group's members expect from the community as a compact entity to care about them during their personal trials. In political theory, the concept has been articulated as that of "friendship with the society", or even "friendship with the state", and is contrasted with the role of the state as a regulator and policeman—roles that can be described as fundamentally predatory, because in such roles, the state appears as an antagonist to its members. In discussions of corporate culture, the idea has been discussed as that of "friendship with the company" and involves questions such as whether the company should serve the needs of its employees that are otherwise the province of the state or society. Examples here include the large informatics companies such as Google or Facebook, which, on their campuses, offer the employees child care, long leisure hours, sometimes accommodation, and a variety of services which would normally be based in a well-functioning society. The success of such practice has been so pronounced that legitimate questions are asked in political theory about whether many of the traditionally social policies ought to be contracted out to successful companies, because the private sector appears so much better in offering these services than the state (Fatic, 2017).

The same features of organic community, however, to an even greater extent, apply to the therapeutic community. The more organic the union between the therapist and the client, or between the participants in group therapy, the more enhanced their collective identity is likely to be. In other words, to have a well-defined organic community, people must share important values and must foster a degree of positive, *affirmative sensibility* toward each other. They must tend to "like" each other more than they would normally feel affection for individuals who are not members of their communities. Where there is dislike or disapproval in organic communities, there is also a principle of focusing on aspects of mutual appreciation and respect, rather than on aspects of difference and disagreement. All of these dynamic features of organic communities are only possible on the assumption of a *substantive ground* which they share in terms of values: only if people can agree on a set of values, and on a high importance these values play in their individual value systems, can they enter a truly organic, highly functional and relatively homogeneous community, which is capable of weathering any mishaps or contingencies that are sure to challenge its integrity in the course of time.

The described principle of organicism poses issues of its own for the therapeutic relationship: when the therapist meets a client, typically they are strangers to one another. The therapist is faced with their own uncertainties and a desire to reach into the client's world, however in a manner which will not fracture the client's sense of control and composure. The client, on the other hand, is typically keen to reveal the most painful psychic content to the therapist, but most often, they are not aware of what that content is.

Most clients approach therapy with a narrative prepared in advance. When they prepare for therapy, they know that an introductory exposition of the issues at hand is inevitable, and they usually come to the first session with ready answers to most typical questions. However, this narrative is rarely what truly drives their difficulties, and it is this difference between the appearance (the complaint the client is aware of) and the actual issues (the hidden narrative, which runs underneath the conscious one) that is the first subject of analysis for the therapist. Thus, the therapist typically listens to the client's conscious narrative and at the same time "listens in" to the undercurrent of potential hidden narratives. There is a variety of techniques which help detect the hidden narrative and guide the client to understanding the potential hidden meanings; however, they are not the main subject of this discussion. The point to make here is that at the beginning of counseling, or therapy, we (the client and the therapist) "feel", in the sense of exploring the ground, for each other: we try to guess where the key points of leverage lie so that we can use the time and energy of therapy to address what really matters, rather than meandering endlessly around epiphenomenal realities which, while hurting the client, may not be the "buttons to push" to effect change. This initial uncertainty is the environment in which both the therapist's and client's skill of communication and analysis are tested and articulated. At the same time, it is this process that clears the ground for the establishment of an organic therapeutic community.

Not every therapist can or should work with every client, and vice versa. The reason for this well-tested principle lies in the substance of values at stake between the therapist and the client. For the two to enter into an organic therapeutic community, *the key values must be shared*, and this is often not the case. Deep Therapy serves to quickly and effectively establish whether such values are obtainable between the therapist and the client and whether the two can form an organic bond.

A good example of this problem is a value dilemma that is quite pervasive both in therapy and in society today: the dilemma about the rights of the family and the rights to form and maintain a family in modern society. I now turn to exploring, to some extent, the principled dimensions of this dilemma and at the same time elucidating how Deep Therapy works in this case.

The Family, Trauma and the Therapeutic Community

The problem of the family and its crisis in modern society embodies the controversies of organicism and the rights and interests of organic commonness that typically manifest themselves in therapy. Traditionally speaking, the family is the organic foundation, or building block, of the entire society, and much of the practical thinking about functional society or healthy membership in it refers back to the family as the micro-model of organic social relationships. A society with a strong family is thus believed to be a strong society, permeated with good and productive mutual interrelationships between its members, who share in the society's identity. Such a society replicates the organicism that keeps the family together across its other forms of organization and thus provides much more support and has much more "personality" in its relations to its members than a detached, institutionalized society where the family is socially marginalized as an almost outdated form of social organization.

The problem with the family as a value in counseling has both a practical and one principled dimension. The practical dimension lies in the fact that a large number (the majority) of clients in any type of counseling or psychotherapy, regardless of the type of intervention concerned, come for counseling with partnership, parenting, or family issues. Hence, the values associated with family relationships are a prominent theme on the agenda of any counselor or therapist. The principled dimension, on the other hand, concerns the individual rights and interests regarding family life, on the one hand, and the rights of the family as a building block of society, on the other. If the family is a subject of certain bioethical rights, arising from the right to life and an appropriate quality of life, then the first right of the family that would have to be recognized is the right of the family to exist and to be protected when it is faced with what appears as individual interests, and often whims, of its members. Family members, of course, are at the same time constituents of a liberal or post-liberal, individualistic political culture.

If indeed the family is an organic community that is the very foundation of broader organic communities, then it would have to be granted a considerable degree of *protection from dissolution* or adverse tendencies and actions, either by society or by the family's own members. In short, the right to divorce would have to be considered a problematic right bioethically speaking, and would have to be granted only in very exceptional circumstances, such as violence, or a major betrayal of organic family bonds and legitimate expectations.

One of the reasons people get into trouble in their romantic relationships, especially when they have families (and this reverberates through counseling when the sailing becomes particularly rough in family life), is that we are conditioned to believe that our individual human rights are somehow superimposed, morally and legally, upon the collective rights of the organic communities we participate in, primarily the rights of the family. In modern liberal societies the rights of the family thus get trampled all the time in favor of the rights of the individuals, which we are taught to see as primary human rights. This has very real practical repercussions for the relationship between the counselor and the client.

When we see clients whose families are dissolving, or those who are facing a serious crisis, these individuals are typically in a highly agitated or seriously depressed state, with a dramatically lowered quality of life. If their human rights relate to their quality of life and personal quest of satisfaction, then, paradoxically, the pursuit of those stipulated individual rights at the cost of the family, at least in cases that end up in counseling, often directly militate against the very satisfaction and quality of life that these putative individual "human rights" are supposed to advance. This is only a seeming paradox. Our personal happiness and sense of pleasure are inextricably linked to our participation in important organic communities. We need deep and meaningful unions with other individuals, and, with rare exceptions, we cannot be happy, or have a good quality of everyday life, if we are isolated and lonely. Hence, the rights of the family as the key organic community are not opposed to, but converge with, individual human rights if they are seen as bioethically relevant, that is, as rights to the advancement of the interests of life and personal wellness. By these lights, protecting and advancing the rights of the family would be the same as protecting and enhancing the bioethical human rights of all members of the community. This is an example of a principle on which the client and the therapist might agree, when dealing with issues of family dissolution, divorce, betrayal, or dilemmas about the quality and perspectives of romantic partnerships.

The above perspective on values is rare among clients. Most believe in a number of potentially highly damaging and self-defeating, superficial mantras: that "a good divorce is better than a bad marriage", that "their primary duty is to themselves, to pursue their dreams and happiness", that "it is not their fault if love has died in the marriage", that "it is not in the interest of the children for parents to stay together if they no longer love each other", and the like. All these values and beliefs arise from the perception that we all have certain individual, undeniable human rights, namely the right to pursue our vision of happiness or pleasure, and that our belonging to our organic community does not pose normative constraints on our pursuit of pleasure elsewhere, once we decide that the satisfaction that we have within our familiy is no longer sufficient. The problem with such a perspective, which is quite common, is that, while the majority of modern societies agree on the tilting of rights toward the individual's personal pursuits vis-a-vis the rights of the family, the therapeutic communities based on such values, which typically result in beliefs such as those cited above, rarely last, and even more rarely lead to any truly desired personal outcomes.

A large number of individuals who subscribe to the above described, liberal principles have emerged from their attempts to resolve their relationship difficulties, feeling deprived and incapable of fostering deep organic connections with other people, including their own former family members, especially with their children. In other words, they arrive for therapy as sad, disenchanted, unhappy, and deeply damaged individuals who have been harmed by liberal value-informed psychotherapy based on the ideas that "a good divorce is better than a bad marriage", that "one has the right to be happy regardless of one's family", and similar modern mantras of couples and family counseling.

If the rights of the family are seen as bioethical rights that are closely associated with individual welfare, then the curtailing of individual rights that are seen as "human rights", which potentially militate against those of the family, would, seemingly paradoxically, *be in the best interest of individual welfare*. Let us consider this apparent paradox in more detail.

The problem with the above conclusion is only superficially and apparently related to human rights. There are those like Yuval Noah Harari, the author of the bestseller *Sapiens: A Brief History of Mankind*, who believe that human rights, just like the assumptions of human equality, are a fiction, that we have all evolved different, with different qualities, capacities, and thus with different rights, which cannot be uniformly described as human rights (Harari, 2011, p. 123). However, Harari has a more interesting and at the same time less easily contestable point, namely that any kind of community, to be effective in what it does, requires a critical number of "true believers" (Harari, 2011, pp. 124–126). Even in the most hierarchic and organized communities, such as the military community, violence, punishments, and discipline are not sufficient to maintain the community: there must exist individuals who *believe in the founding values* of that community, be it honor, courage, patriotism, or whatever else, who will carry the army forward.

The above is also the case with any organic community, and this means that the family in the context described here, as the subject of certain bioethical rights, in order to hold rights associated with the individual welfare of its members, *must be an organic family*.

Not every family is an organic community. The difference between an organic and inorganic family is in the existence of true believers: whether the family members believe in the values on which the family is based: "in sickness and in health (…) till death do us part", or not. This belief is largely conditioned by culture, which means that, as with any other values in society, we are taught to believe and taught to disbelieve.

In liberal societies, *and in liberal psychotherapy*, people are taught that "a good divorce is better than a bad marriage", rather than the idea that "a bad marriage should be turned into a good marriage". They are taught that they "have the right to be happy, even if that means dissolving the family", instead of that they "have the right and duty to enhance their own and the happiness of their family members", etc. All these statements are parts of *various language games* of which I said more in Chap. 5 on linguistic pragmatics, that are either enhanced or degraded, by social norms or by the messages we receive from our societies as to what to believe and what to disbelieve.

Our psychotherapists are our socializers. They are bearers of messages which help socialize and de-socialize us: if they sufficiently strongly and uniformly tell us that our individual happiness and satisfaction lie somewhere outside the "constraints" of the family, this is what we will believe, and vice versa, if the therapeutic community between the counselor and the client fosters the idea that developing the organic communities, first of all our families, is the same as developing our own satisfaction and life quality, that is what we will believe (Fatic, 2016).

Deep Therapy is about socialization and the clarification and enhancement of values, with a primary focus on bioethical values, namely the values which are in the interest of life: our own and the lives of those close to us.

The organic therapeutic community is one governed by what Giorgio Agamben elaborates as his theory of "effectivity". Agamben describes how "special actions" characteristic of various communities define our membership in these communities, and at the same time affirm our acceptance of their defining values, in turn determining our individual identities (Agamben, 2013). Such a community is characterized by mutual closeness among its members, a high degree of informality in their relationships, and a similarly high level of mutual trust (Uslaner, 2010), and a sense of joint quest of values and insights, rather than what Lacan calls "master discourse", or the division of roles between the therapist, who educates, and the client, who is educated through therapy. In a truly organic therapeutic community, both the therapist and the client exhibit a degree of uncertainty, of wonder and insecurity, and seek to stabilize their value-positions by feeling for common ground, with the therapist leading only slightly.

In Deep Therapy, described in Chap. 6, the counselor and client share several days together at a time: they resemble a family, because they attend to daily duties, typically in a countryside setting, without the usual urban distractions, and organize their time to eat together, read and discuss, rest, wake at compatible hours, and attend to housekeeping. These are family-like activities which allow the deep therapeutic community to develop organic characteristics within a short time span. In other words, to set up an effective therapeutic relationship, one sets up a family-like format where people naturally enter organic relationships. This peels off the layers that typically separate us in conventional therapy: formalism, the need to present ourselves in a tidier and more "desirable" light than who we really are, initial hesitation to reveal our real thoughts, facts about ourselves, our preferences, etc. However, the precondition for being able to "jump" into the family-like structure of counseling is that some substantive value commonalities must first be established: we must value organicism together, and we must believe that the family is a better environment to help each other than a sterile, removed professional relationship. Fundamentally, we must be reasonably like-minded people who share certain basic philosophical views of life. This alone is an illiberal principle that is not always easy to satisfy.

The way we position ourselves vis-à-vis the organic communities is usually reflected in the views we have about the family. One of the reasons so many traumas in modern counseling are associated with intimate and family relationships is that we have learned to see the family and the demands of organicism that are inherent in the mutual expectations among members of the same family as traumatizing, rather than as potential sources of enhanced personal wellbeing. That is also the reason why the state and its institutions have become progressively, and aggressively, involved in our family affairs, taking active roles in destroying so many families. Such policies, as I mentioned earlier, have led to a growing culture of individualism and a certain wariness of organic communities by members of the public. A consequence of such attitudes is that we see an increasing number of our social relationships as threatening. This does not mean that there are no threatening or exceptionally toxic families, just as there are threatening and toxic workplaces, societies, and relationships in general. What it does mean is that the family is not generally a place of danger or repression of individuality, as it is increasingly presented in therapy and society. The family remains the primary therapeutic community, whose capacity to exemplify the organicism required to remedy both a person's specific traumas and the general trauma of life are irreducible to institutionally or professionally mediated relationships.

Organicism as a Cure for Trauma

Organicism is a theory of human relationships that cure trauma. Life in organic communities tends to be of much higher quality, even in circumstances of financial and infrastructural scarcity, than life in highly institutionalized and formal communities that are technologically prosperous and materially opulent. Counseling is a semblance of the organic community that is articulated in circumstances where organicism as a theory of reality is not prevalent, and where trauma is pervasive. The trauma of loneliness, of lack of emotional exchange, of fear, of dependency on the forces one cannot influence, of anonymity in large cities, of extreme workloads, limited rest and leisure time, of technological domination, taxes our attention spans and ability to concentrate and gives rise to myriad of other traumas that, as a matter of general consensus, tend to populate our everyday experiences in large industrial societies.

A key concept that defines organic communities is the accumulation of what is sometimes called "social capital". There are different definitions of social capital, one of the most influential being that by Francis Fukuyama, who defines it as "an instantiated informal norm that promotes cooperation between two or more individuals" (Fukuyama, 1999). In his sociological view of social capital, Fukuyama focuses on its normative character: he thus argues that the various normative mechanisms that facilitate cooperation, such as reciprocity, lie dormant in all our dispositions and actions toward other people, but they "wake up" and actualize through certain structures, such as ideologies, philosophical doctrines, or systems of relationships. In a broader sense, social capital includes emotions, as well. Mutual affinity is a form of social capital, as is love. Moral emotions in particular constitute social capital, given their propensity to trigger morally charged action. Such emotions include, for example, solidarity, loyalty, empathy, and the relationships that bear the same names and rest upon such emotions (Fatic, 2016). The emotional dispositions, and the exercise of actual emotions, are not only the dynamic factors that propel people toward others; they are the foundation of organic communities as communities that do not need institutional mediation in order to exist or function. Conversely, it is the lack of moral emotions and the related lack of social capital that necessitate the institutionalism and procedurality in a community. Counseling and therapy are those windows into organic human relationship, that are permeated with social capital and moral emotions. Such relationships can be priceless in the barren landscape of procedures, institutions, and a liberal culture of personal rights, principles of anonymity, privacy, non-infringement, etc. In counseling we sacrifice a degree of our privacy in exchange for the love and support of another, skillful human being intent on fostering a loving and supportive relationship with us. Such exchanges are "crystals of humanity" (Dimitrije Ljotić, 2003, pp. 146–147) that are picked, kept, and enhanced through therapy so that the quality of the client's life increases. However, to pick the crystals of humanity in a relationship, all the participants in that relationship must make their humanity bear and their vulnerabilities increasingly accessible, which is a separate and difficult topic for the methodology of psychotherapy.

All the mentioned features of the psychotherapeutic community make it one of the most organic communities available, meaning that it resembles the family in many of its crucial aspects, including a high level of tolerance for the breaking of norms and rules and an equally high level of mutual affective connection between its members. The most organic and emotionally effective (productive of moral emotions that generate cohesion and cooperation) communities are those whose membership threshold is high—a concept developed by Robert Putnam (Putnam, 1993, pp. 6–7; Siisiainen, 2000).

The therapeutic community is one with a very high threshold of membership. Various "special actions" (Agamben, 2013) constitutive of that community are required of both or all the participants, that not everybody in society is willing to undertake. The moralistic, a priori trust (Uslaner, 2010), the willingness to reveal one's vulnerabilities and a desire to espouse and share one's values in a direct way, unmitigated by procedures and institutions, are among the salient such special actions. Once the therapeutic community takes hold, and the mutual affection between its members develops, the crystals of humanity that Ljotić mentions become visible and accessible to be picked within the format and vista on life that the therapeutic community facilitates. Such a tight alliance and philosophical friendship between the therapist and the client(s) in themselves inoculate the participants, to some extent at least, from the most debilitating effects of most ordinary traumas.

One particularly illiberal aspect of the therapeutic community is that the rights and entitlements within that community are not the same for all members. There are general principles, particularly in group therapy, which help maintain and organize the therapeutic group until it develops its own self-regulatory mechanisms (Yalom believed that the climax of success of a therapeutic group was the point when the therapist no longer needed to even be present, the group was able to maintain itself, govern itself, and exert healing on its own. He thus used to deliberately miss group meetings, and subsequently, he would tape a greeting that one of the group members would play at the beginning of the session and the group would work without him. In fact, an experiment consisting of two groups responding to taped instructions about how to proceed instead of a live therapist being present showed notably different therapy outcomes depending on the group's attitude to the tape and the absence of the therapist—Yalom & Leszcz, 2005, p. 271). In line with the principles that define organic communities, the therapeutic effectiveness of psychotherapy groups has been shown to consistently reflect the cohesion of the group in values and a sense of collective identity (Yalom & Leszcz, 2005, p. 60). In therapy groups, like in close-knit organic communities, the members are familiar with each other's character, and they make the rules, assign roles, entitlements, and privileges through their communication, where neither is everybody equal in every respect, nor does everybody enjoy the same kind of rights. An example of this inequality in rights is the group's varied tolerance and patience with different members: some are consistently awarded more time and attention by the group than others. Furthermore, Yalom described the extreme of this situation where highly effective groups decided to exclude individual members (Yalom & Leszcz, 2005, pp. 197–198).

One of the key aspects of organicism that manifest in counseling is that our rights and interests arise from who we are as individuals, not only from our status as group members. This means that we don't necessarily have the same prerogatives and entitlements in therapy as others. The ideas that "every client deserves empathy" or "empowerment" vis-a-vis the important others in their lives or to have the counselor "on their side", etc., are not only invalid: they are potentially dangerous. As an organic process, any counseling sees every client differently, and consequently, not every client should be empathized with, supported, strengthened, etc. There are clients who must be confronted, there are those whose close ones should be supported to resist the toxic influences the client exerts on them, there are clients who should be structurally re-educated and brought within certain boundaries which they habitually transgress, just as there are clients who should be given more rights than other people, who deserve more support than most, etc. *Not everybody has the same rights, and this is particularly true in organic relationships.* This principle is at sharp odds with the liberal culture, which assumes that everybody with roughly the same formal status is entitled to the same level of rights (e.g. citizenship or formal qualifications as sources of relatively uniform rights and entitlements).

Typically, groups react with greater compassion to members who are traumatized than to others (although this primarily refers to microtrauma, there is hardly anyone who has not been more substantially traumatized by harming influences at various levels). Organic groups—and all organic communities—extend generosity and an additionally accepting and empowering treatment to trauma victims. Many groups see traumatized individuals as prima facie more noble, more deserving of help, and sometimes, as more able to reach out and understand other close people precisely because of their experience of traumatization. Trauma is hence a potential connection with others, a wound that connects and unifies when placed in an organic context. Thus, the mere placement of a traumatized person in an organic setting is a generic type of treatment of trauma. Such a community, or a transition to it (by definition, trauma occurs in a community or set of relationships that are not healing, but harming) is a shift in modal worlds. Though a simple strategy, it is often not seen as a possibility for treatment. Often, people who are traumatized are kept in the settings where the trauma has occurred, various interventions and debriefings are attempted, and there is even a school of thought that stipulates that, in order to overcome the trauma, the victim should be placed, as soon as possible, in the "regular" situation of one's life where the trauma occurred in the first place, in order to "face" the circumstances that surrounded their traumatization and be able to overcome them (Burton et al., 2015).

The above "state of the art" methodology was applied in a situation that I happened to be a direct witness of, when in 2023, in Belgrade, a 13-year-old boy gunned down a dozen of his school mates, killing 9 children and a school guard and seriously wounding 2. I can attest to this event not only as a professional observer, but also as a direct participant, as my daughter attended that school and was in the school during the shooting, subsequently managing to escape from the scene with her class, but she lost close friends in the tragedy. After the event, which was the gravest tragedy in the history of schooling in the country, the group of select psychologists and psychotherapists appointed by the government, drawing on the doctrine of "enhancing natural resilience", decided to return the children to the same building to continue the school year just a week after the bloodshed, while their friends were still being buried. This was justified as a view held by "the profession" that was based on accepted standards in trauma treatment. The result was a disaster: many children changed school because they could not bear to go back to the "place of execution" of their friends, as they described it. The decision to "enhance the resilience" of trauma victims led to divisions among the parents, where the parents of the murdered children demanded that the school be closed and the school year ended immediately, while the majority, whose children were not directly affected, were of the view that the school should continue normally and that the victims should "overcome" what had happened to them. The issue escalated into major public protests, and the subsequent activism by parents of the victims resulted in a partial closure of the school, namely the school building where the tragedy had occurred, and plans to establish a Memorial Centre for the victims.

Trauma victims have a degree of natural resilience, and Burton and his coauthors rightly point this out. However, this natural resilience, as its name suggests, needs to manifest naturally and spontaneously: its existence does not mean that society is entitled to return the victims to the circumstances of their victimization to allow them to "enhance their natural resilience", any more than one's ability to naturally withstand a degree of cold entitles the institutions to expose them to freezing temperatures in order to enhance this natural resilience. In fact, the idea espoused here is terrible for trauma victims, who, rather than being additionally victimized by the testing of their "natural resilience", need to be placed in a different, caring and supportive, organic modal world, which, at least for a time, will be very different from the circumstances of their victimization and traumatization, regardless of any "natural resilience" that they may have. In the case described, it was conceptually and methodologically easy to establish such a different, healing modal world. Apart from offering the children and their parents individual counseling (which was done), the school should have been closed immediately, the school year in the whole country ended early (this was also done, but with a month's delay, under public protests), and the rest of the school year for the students from the school that was the scene of the tragedy should have been spent in informal settings where they would socialize, spend time together, talk to each other, possibly with very discrete and highly attentive contributions by group therapists, much along the lines of the methodology of group therapy described by Yalom. What happened was that the children were asked to return to school after a week to "enhance their natural resilience", but they spontaneously, instinctively, did everything that the society and the state should have done to help them. They were constantly outside together, hanging out in parks, talking and healing each other. They established an organic community outside the school and the institutions, against the decisions made by "the profession" and the authorities, and they overcame the trauma by shifting the ordinary modal world to that of an organic community. It is within this organic community that their natural healing powers were able to be exercised. I was able to observe those children while they were attending funerals of their murdered friends, and to be directly involved in the parents' groups after the event. The children were far superior to the adults, to the parents, and to the professional helpers in offering each other what they needed. The adults failed miserably, including the psychological and psychotherapeutic professions. The dogma of "enhancing natural resilience", as far as I am concerned, has since been decisively rebutted, because the kaleidoscope of modality which the children were able to offer each other eventually defeated both the traumatization inflicted by the initial event and the re-traumatization inflicted by the authorities and the helpers' decisions after the initial event. The children, with their unmatched capacity for imagination, were able to see the modalities and potential for exercising organicism and healing within their community that the adults could not see, although they were right in front of our very eyes.

While not every trauma concerns killing, displacement, or major loss of close persons in some other way, there are pointers in the organic remedies to macrotrauma that I just illustrated that elucidate key aspects of the structure of more ordinary trauma. In fact, I would go as far as to say that one of the *sources of more ordinary traumas* is the stifling of organicism in normal everyday relationships and the turning of our lives into institutionally mediated processes.

A part of many ordinary traumas of everyday existence in an alienated society, including the traumas of rejection, loneliness, and invalidation, arise from the institutionality and procedurality of our everyday interactions. This is best witnessed by the modern legislation and policy which regulate many hitherto intimate relationships. In many jurisdictions, offering a compliment to someone in the street could get one in trouble with the law, if that person turns out to be obnoxious and declares the compliment to have been "unwanted" or an intrusion into their privacy. Touching another person's child in public, even in affection, could lead to the same type of consequences. In organic communities, such restrictions do not apply. A churchgoer will meet with the approval of the congregation if they show that they notice and like the others' children running around the church yard. Compliments are welcome and encouraged by the members of close communities. People share more in such communities; this contributes to their sense of belonging and their ability to navigate everyday life. The inability to relate to others in ways that are not institutionally regulated translates into difficulties in therapy. When they first arrive for a consultation, people often do not know how open they can be about their feelings and thoughts of the moment, whether it is acceptable to express affection for the therapist, disagreement with some of their views, or resentment of some of the values being flouted in therapy. Counselees sometimes find it difficult to determine which of the rules governing their interactions in the outside world they must continue to follow, and which ones they may leave behind when they enter the counseling room. The process of adapting to therapy is often one of a brief resocialization into what an organic community is.

Institutionality and procedurality are obstacles to intimacy, although intimacy is a key element of the community. Thus, we are faced with the paradox that the more institutions we have, the less of a community is left in our society. This is a traumatizing effect of modern society on most individuals, and at once the reason why establishing intimate relationships is so difficult when very strict and distant boundaries must be torn down. If the society forbids the giving of "unwanted compliments" or tapping another's child on the head in a shopping mall, this increases the traditional distance between officiality and intimacy. Assuming that intimacy involves the crossing of various boundaries (for example, an embrace is one level of breaking the rules of officiality in many contexts, a kiss is a further level and a sexual encounter yet another, more radical level), the more distant the rules of officiality are from those of intimacy, the more effort it will require and the fewer opportunities there will be for any intimacy. This applies to all kinds of intimacy as opposed to all kinds of officiality and procedurality and is the reason why in organic communities both institutions and procedures are held in check and kept to a minimum. Assuming that our need for intimacy is at least as crucial a human need as that for liberty or absence of unwanted intrusion by others, excessively institutionalized and procedurally regulated societies are a source of inherent frustration which, when accumulated over time, grows into latent trauma.

The healing effects of organicism on major trauma suggest that the absence of organicism might in itself generate ordinary trauma, and that, consequently, the preservation or introduction of additional organicism in social interactions might inoculate people against latent trauma induced by toxic social relationships. This effect is sometimes called "social support" or "community support"; it is used by social services when they assess the situation someone faces after a difficult divorce, or illness, or within a prospect of facing other major difficulties such as losing their job at an advanced age. The assessment of the person's needs in such cases often involves an elaboration of what kind of "social support" they have: friends, family, personal preoccupations and hobbies, in other words, organic relationships. There is a tacit understanding in such procedures that organicism can make a difference between someone's ability to live alone or need to move to a nursing home—indeed, between someone's ability to live in the first place or developing a propensity to commit suicide (Kleiman & Liu, 2014).

There is a sense in which we are systematically microtraumatized by an increasingly formalized, supervised, and overseen society, where organicism is regarded as subversive, and any closely knit communities between people who share key values are closely controlled by the state. Those forms of communality that are not mediated by, and do not directly rely on, institutions, are viewed with suspicion. The state increasingly regulates such communities, such as church-going groups, members of activist groups who share a social vision and ideals, even academic and artistic circles. Consider only the treatment those who academically or artistically oppose the war in Gaza, in the Middle East, receive as this book is being written in many countries that see themselves as old democracies. University professors and artists are held up at borders, their participation in intellectual and artistic gatherings and events is precluded, exhibitions and theater performances by such authors are cancelled, sometimes at the last moment, and some lose their jobs. An organic solidarity with the suffering of a fundamentally helpless population in another part of the world, which is an expression of elementary human empathy, is sanctioned by the state as subversive for official policy. The same is the case with various groups gathered around beliefs that are considered subversive for the dominant political or social culture. The election campaign in the US in 2024 was an example of how the state repressed beliefs and political views that it considered challenging to its values and interests. The American citizenry gathered around the Republican Party and then presidential candidate (now President) Donald Trump was described as dangerous, criminal, aggressive, even fascist. Legal proceedings were launched against the presidential candidate for a variety of offenses, ranging from offering "hush money" to a prostitute to refrain from revealing that he had had an encounter with her to tax evasion and various more serious crimes. Numerous people who protested after the previous presidential election, alleging electoral fraud, and who broke into Congress, were arrested and tried on grounds connected to national security, terrorism, and subversion of institutions. The same actions by pro-democracy activists in Kenya, the same year, and in many other countries, where the protesters broke into political institutions and demanded changes, clashed with the policy and blood was spilt, were described, by the very same American administration, as progressive and legitimate public expression of human rights and democratic values. There is an element of organicism in political ideology as far as its adherents sincerely embrace a common set of social values. The very foundations of liberal democracy rest on the principle that tolerance of an opposed political ideology and its activism is the cornerstone of civilized society, yet these principles have gradually been eroded to the point where a presidential candidate in a major democracy is criminalized and his voters described as dangerous, fascist, and intellectually inferior. There is, in principle, no difference between such policies of public castigation and exclusion at present, and the past practice of declaring political opponents mentally ill and keeping them by force in psychiatric hospitals (Buoli & Giannuli, 2017). The difference is mainly in the degree of repression and the ability of the state to implement the repressive policy. Where once the state was able to freely arrest and hospitalize political opponents, today the state uses public targeting, mass defamation, and pressures on institutions and businesses to reduce or cut out the sources of livelihood for their political opponents. The principle, however, is the same: it is the repression of what the state sees as uncontrolled joining of dissenting views who share important values and may thus present a cohesive challenge to the dominant view, regardless of how one might describe the dominant views. There is a sense of organicism in a political group that involves people who are willing to sacrifice their liberty or life engaging the state for a cause where they have no grounds to expect any personal benefit, in much the same way as there is an organic element in any kind of self-sacrifice for a value or ideal. On an intimate level, members of close communities are expected to make sacrifices and to transgress the ordinary rules of loyalty to the state. In criminal proceedings, for example, rules regulating the so-called aiding and abetting the offender tend to be far more lenient when they apply to family members, because socially, as members of the organic community, they are to a degree expected to "aid and abet" their members when they are in trouble. Such legal provisions reflect the collective awareness that loyalty to the organic community comes before and stands above loyalty to the political community, and the trends that militate against this recognition of organicism as the foundation of sociality overall are traumatising for individuals, families, and all other organic groups. If there is a sense in which modern repressively institutionalized society is "toxic", it is probably this sense (Mate & Mate, 2022).

De-traumatizing Everyday Life

How does MIP address the trauma-toxicity of non-organicism in institutionally and procedurally dominated human interactions that characterize our social structure?

The systemic trauma, described in the previous section, is the current modal world for most people. The circumstances which produce such a general crisis of quality of life cannot be changed on the level of ideology, by institutional intervention or by political activism, at least in the short term, because the existing institutional interests and way of life will fight back. Inertia is a powerful force in the operation of institutions and in official procedures, and in the consciousness of the subjects of both of these, who have become only too used to their subjecthood and lack of internal liberty. An individual cannot wait with the attainment of one's optimum quality of life for major, deep systemic changes in the institutional environment. However, simple changes such as the introduction of an organic relationship, or community, in one's social circle, may generate a massive difference internally and to some extent organizationally in one's "everydayness", as Heidegger calls it (Heidegger, 1992, p. 3E).

One of the most important influences of organicism on the person's overall social reality is the introduction of skills to change the nature of otherwise formal and institutionally mediated relationships. Someone who has an intimate and high-quality relationship with their counselor, or with the members of a therapeutic group that one is a part of, or with a church-going community, or with some other type of informal community will develop interpersonal skills which will allow them to use the institutionally mediated opportunities for contact with others in a way which will sow the seeds of organicism where otherwise there would be none. It is thus one of the key facets of MIP to *develop skills* that facilitate organic interpersonality even within the most detached and procedurally complex communities, thus breaking up the general spirit of such complex communities into the various mentalities that are cultivated in small subsections of society.

Attempts at a recreation of the community within the institutionalized society have been made for quite some time: the ideas in urban planning such as the creation of "15 minute cities" in China (the planning of cities so that each neighborhood contains everything a city dweller needs within 15 minutes of public transport voyage from one's place of residence) or the modular organization of neighborhoods in London, reflect the awareness by policy makers and architects of what has become known as the principle "small is beautiful" in urban planning. However, that is not the same as organicism that MIP envisions. Organicism involves the ability to communicate one's values and emotions in a way that will filter out those who can respond in the same way, and thus allow a person lost in the emotional and social wasteland of excessive procedurality in society to seek out others with whom connections could be fostered. An example of this type of skill can be found in teaching. When one considers the teaching styles of various university lecturers, it becomes obvious that some focus their efforts on establishing a particular culture in their classes where those students who can respond to the challenges of setting up a close learning community, rather than merely a study class within an institution, can find their intellectual home. Such a style typically leads to a division of any large class into two parts: one consists of students who join the lecturer to pursue interests and concerns that go beyond the minimum required by the course and by the institution, while the rest remain detached and pursue their studies in the same way as in any other class. Such lecturers have the skill of establishing organic interpersonality with their students and filtering in those students who have the same skill and the same type of sensibility. Often, such student groups thrive far more than the rest of the class: they become exposed to themes, discussions, ideas, and types of work that uniquely equip them to enter those areas of their future professions, or those organizations as potential employers, which they find the most exciting and promising. They gain a critical advantage. Not only are they more successful in their studies, and in their subsequent careers; they often achieve more in their private lives, establish life partnerships with others within the close communities that they join, develop value- and ideological alliances, and cultivate a level of personal enthusiasm that sets them notably aside from the other students.

MIP has a similar effect on interpersonal skills and the ability to filter through complex social interactions and reach those with a compatible sensibility, ideas, and values. A large part of gaining organicism in one's life is one's ability to find like-minded people, and this is often impossible without adopting a particular style of communication and mastering a way of thinking that reflects in one's interpersonal interactions that tease out those same skills and associated desires in others. MIP as a therapy process is focused, in part, on training clients to reinvent their way of thinking so that it is more productive of new organic relationships.

An example of the process where a new "sense" for intersubjectivity and a new set of communication skills are developed, or more precisely, cracked open from our subconscious knowledge of the sensibility of others, is a situation where one "contracts" an interaction by changing the slant and tone of it. This sometimes happens in official communications, in meetings, conferences, and the like, when a skillful speaker will twist the atmosphere and address the audience in surprisingly direct ways, yet ones so finely tuned that they would tease out otherwise strongly controlled reactions, repressed emotions, and humor. While a part of the audience will smirk at the breaking of the ordinary standards of communication, some will respond in a way that may change their way of thinking about the matter and will approach the speaker afterwards. We reach out to others not only by what we say and do within the format of our interaction; we also reach out by breaking or twisting the format. To do so requires considerable skill and focus, which cannot be faked or artificially produced: they arise from a particular attitude and way of thinking that one develops through self-examination and philosophical reflection in MIP. In such simple ways, communication skills can call into being alternative modal worlds, they can almost impose organicism onto an otherwise non-organic process, and, while perhaps antagonizing some participants, reach those with whom deeper organic interaction can be established. This type of technique can be applied in almost any group setting.

Whatever the technique or personal style that calls into reality different modalities, they arise from a particular modal way of thinking that, in addition to being versed in the basic principles of modal logic, is also trained in interpreting experience through the modal lens, rather than that of conventional propositional logic. Education, practical and applied, in modal logic is a key part of MIP.

The introduction of organicism changes our inner "knowledge of the world", namely a set of core beliefs about who we are and how we ought to relate to the others who constitute our sociality. Once these core beliefs are challenged, and then changed, our expectations of relationships with others change accordingly, even when the initial encounter with other individuals is generated through extremely institutionalized and procedurally highly regulated channels. One becomes more prone to cross barriers in communications, and more skilled at "skipping" rather than breaking the ordinary boundaries. This careful navigation of otherwise alienated relationships involves a degree of risk, but it also invites considerable rewards. The ability to turn a sterile and safe communication into one with potential to grow into genuine caring is sometimes considered a part of emotional intelligence; however, it is fundamentally a matter of good decision making which, like any type of decision making, depends on the sensibility of the decision maker.

Most commonly, the risks in skipping boundaries in psychotherapy are associated with mistaken expectations by the clients, or by onlookers. The closer and more intimate a therapist becomes with a client, the more room there is for accusations of impropriety and, perhaps more importantly, the more opportunity there is for the client to express potential misunderstandings. The crossing of boundaries is an introduction into organicism; it is a defining element of developing the capacity to transform inorganic relationships into organic ones; however, it requires a high level of skill and a sense of commonality that takes time to develop between the therapist and the client.

Our value systems are built in a largely heteronomous way: we learn our values from the society and from the important others in our immediate social circle (Fatic, 2009). In inorganic societies, the dominant values are potentially detrimental to the overall quality of life, because they focus the person's life goals and priorities in areas where close, informal human support and interchange are unlikely, even impossible. For example, pursuing an ambitious career goal in institutional social life typically means observing all the boundaries very strictly; such a life path often deprives the person of intimacy to such a degree that many professionally and financially successful people feel that they have fundamentally failed in their true priorities and life plans. At the same time, they enjoy social approval because of their attainment of socially desirable goals, such as effectiveness in business or in public service. In this way public culture encourages self-denial in the most intimate aspects of one's life path.

One of the roles of psychotherapy is to remind the client of the overall cost of giving in to heteronomy without serious checks, and to refocus the client's attention on the client's more authentic human needs and aspirations. Quality therapy tends to shift the client's ecology of values; it changes the client's "mindscape" or their life world in a hermeneutically comprehensive and at the same time profound way: it concerns a variety of aspects of the client's life; at the same time, it brings deep content to the surface. Gradually, the client starts to see different meanings in the goals and values that are externally imposed on them and develops a greater capacity to confront the heteronomy and say "no" to goals that might militate against the achievement of more authentic personal values. Such a situation both enlarges the person's personal space—allows one to become more confident in one's ability to make independent decisions—and raises the level of personal energy with which one is prepared to approach others on a more immediate level. A focus on various alternatives in setting up one's goals, which is common both to most schools of traditional psychotherapy and to MIP, and the development of communication skills and a new logical structure of thinking that brings in various modal worlds as real alternatives to one's context where problems articulate themselves, which is a particular feature of MIP, enlarges the person's sovereign dominion.

Individuals who are more independent of general norms are those who are more prepared to "go out on a limb" and risk changing or bending the procedural rules of intersubjective interchange. They tend to experiment more with the bounds of privacy and are thus generally more successful in creating personal commonalities with others than those individuals who rigidly respect all the boundaries. Someone who has personally benefited from shifting boundaries in modal therapy will be more prepared to try to shift their other boundaries with others, and will have developed, through MIP, more skills to do so in a way which is both non-threatening and productive of human warmth and a sense of solidarity.

The way in which alienation, not only in the toxic society, but also in largely depersonalized and professional psychotherapy, in many cases microtraumatizes us is like that of micro injuries occurring in sports. One of the reasons boxers, for example, suffer a far greater amount of neurological damage after their careers than fighters in Mixed Martial Arts relates to has to do with micro injuries. In MMA, the padding on the gloves is very thin. The force of the strikes is unmitigated by the gloves and, in an average bout, one or two powerful blows to the head typically "turn the light off" and end the fight. This is brutal, but the injuries are immediate and inflicted by a single blow or small number of blows. In boxing, on the other hand, the heavy padding on the gloves facilitates numerous blows to the head in each round that the person can absorb on their feet. As a result, a boxer may receive hundreds of blows to the head in each match, where every blow shakes the brain and causes microtrauma. The accumulation of such microtraumas generates a debilitating effect on the central nervous system as the boxer gets on in their career and in age (Forstl et al.,

2010). When the psychotherapeutic treatment of such equivalent psychological microtrauma is concerned—the microtrauma that is inflicted by society through the myriad of its toxic practices, ranging from administrative evil, which is reflected in the systematic frustration of even the simplest needs related to commonality and social living, to open repression and censorship, which are becoming increasingly common even in old and established democracies—a difference between traditional psychotherapy and MIP emerges clearly. The former, with its reliance on propositional logic, the assumption of external facts and situations as largely the "given" of one's life experience, and its efforts to empower the person to exist and, if possible, flourish in the "given" world, resemble the tactic of giving a shaken boxer more rest in the corner, better hydration and medical care, and psychological support to last to the end of the match. MIP, on the other hand, is like a tactic that would see the boxer leaving the ring. The latter strategy is radical, but dangerous for the sport, the establishment, the system, and potentially, the society. Our clients in MIP often decide to move away from the cities, to reduce their income voluntarily by reducing the amount of work they do and by switching to online formats, they address their trauma by developing routines that are subversive to capitalist society. They reduce their consumption, their ambitions, they change their conventional values. All of this is very rare in conventional therapy, which seeks to maintain the established values and make the person more functional and increase their agency within their given modal worlds.

In the case of the mass murder of primary school children in Belgrade in 2023, described earlier, the children spontaneously applied a modal approach. They largely ignored the therapists, the school authorities, and the recommendations issued to them, went out together without telling anyone, walked, spent time in nature, and emerged, after several months, seemingly unharmed. They share a deep empathy and a collective memory of what happened, which they have processed in a different setting, in their own way, and have turned it into deep friendships, much deeper than is ordinarily the case in late primary school. They have achieved closure of the experience in way that, to date, remains largely a mystery to the therapists, parents, and authorities involved in managing the crisis, and the children demonstrate this by the comment: "you can never understand what happened, and you have shown this by your reactions". The children have modally changed their experience, while integrating it into their chosen model of mutual relationships outside the school, outside the "natural resilience" model attempted by the authorities. The children chose to depart from what was offered to them as a set of interventions after trauma, and created their own privileged domain of healing and organicism to which access was granted to only very select adults, none of whom were therapists. In terms of the boxing example above, they simply chose to leave the ring and not tell anyone where they went to heal. It was their secret world, their hideout, where they shared psychological bread and wine with their peers in an alchemy of empathy, tears and hugs that none of us were allowed to witness or influence. This way in which a generation group weathered one of the most severe traumas in Europe this century is what, I believe, makes the "Ribnikar" school massacre a watershed moment in understanding modality in trauma healing, where children taught us just what the modal way ahead in the psychotherapy for trauma is: the organicism of intimacy (UNICEF, 2023).

A personal experience of benefiting from organicism is a form of emotional and social capital within the person. One who has experienced organicism as a cure for trauma—whether it is the cumulative microtrauma of living in a toxic society or a macrotrauma such as the one with children who witnessed the Ribnikar school massacre—is then able to invest those same moral emotions that make up one's intimate community in order to transform dissatisfying relationships into more intimate ones. Being healed by organicism crucially enables one to become an organic healer of others. MIP is a style of psychotherapy that both uncovers the organic cures and alternatives as modal worlds that compete with one's current reality, and helps individuals to develop communication skills and a modal logic-based way of thinking that works as powerful instruments in approaching personal crises, because it is only through such logic that one is able to identify the modal alternatives and decide to shift one's lifeworld in their direction.

References

Agamben, G. (2013). *Opus Dei: An archaeology of duty*. Stanford University Press.

Agassi, J., & Jarvie, C. (1987). *Rationality: The critical view*. Martinus Nijhoff.

Babich, B. (1996). On the order of the real: Nietzsche and Lacan. In Fordham University's *Articles and chapters in academic book collections*. 13. Retrieved November 14, 2024, from https://fordham.bepress.com/phil_babich/13blications.

Botton, A. (2004). *Status anxiety*. Pantheon Books.

Buoli, M., & Giannuli, A. S. (2017). The political use of psychiatry: A comparison between totalitarian regimes. *Internal Journal of Social Psychiatry, 63*, 2. https://doi.org/10.1177/0020764016688714

Burton, M. S., Cooper, A. A., Feeny, N. C., & Zoellner, L. A. (2015). The enhancement of natural resilience in trauma interventions. *Journal of Contemporary Psychotherapy, 45*(4), 193–204. https://doi.org/10.1007/s10879-015-9302-7

Catoira, P. D., & Bratton, V. K. (2018). El Chapo for Presidente: An examination of leadership through Mexico's drug culture. In K. M. S. Bezio & K. Yost (Eds.), *Leadership, popular culture and social change* (pp. 91–106). Elgar. https://doi.org/10.4337/9781785368974.00014

CNN. (2019). "Joaquin 'El Chapo' Guzman guilty on all counts". https://www.cnn.com/videos/us/2019/02/12/joaquin-el-chapo-guzman-trial-jury-verdict-ip-vpx.cnn. Accessed 15 January 2025.

Cocker, D. (2001). Crime control and feminist law reform in domestic violence law: A critical review. *Buffalo Criminal Law Review, 4*(2), 801–860. https://doi.org/10.1525/nclr.2001.4.2.801

Fatic, A. (1995). *Punishment and restorative crime handling: A social theory of trust*. Ashgate.

Fatic, A. (2009). *Freedom and heteronomy*. Institute for International Politics and Economics.

Fatic, A. (2016). *Virtue as identity: Emotions and the moral personality*. Rowman and Littlefield.

Fatic, A. (2017). Friendship with the company: Building corporate leadership through humanistic consultancy. In L. Amir (Ed.), *New frontiers in philosophical practice* (pp. 223–236). Cambridge Scholars.

Fatic, A. (2018). Introduction: Transitional justice as conflict-resolution. In A. Fatic, K. Bachmann, & I. Lyubashenko (Eds.), *Transitional justice in troubled societies* (pp. 1–58). Rowman and Littlefield.

Fatic, A. (2023). Joseph Agassi and the various guises of magic. *Philosophy of the Social Sciences, 53*(6), 483–490. https://doi.org/10.1177/00483931231200697

Forstl, H., Haas, Ç., Hemmer, B., Meyer, B., & Halle, M. (2010). Boxing: Acute complications and late sequalae. *Deutsches Arzteblatt International, 107*(47), 835–839. https://doi.org/10.3238/arztebl.2010.0835

Fukuyama, F. (1999, October 1). Social capital and civil society. International Monetary Fund. Retrieved January 18, 2024, from https://www.imf.org/external/pubs/ft/seminar/1999/reforms/fukuyama.htm.

Harari, Y. N. (2011). *Sapiens: A brief history of mankind*. Harper.

Heidegger, M. (1992). *The concept of time* (W. McNeal, Trans.). Wiley-Blackwell.

Hook, D. (2008). Absolute other: Lacan's 'Big Other' as adjunct to critical social psychological analysis. *Social and Personality Psychology Compass, 2*(1), 61–73. https://doi.org/10.1111/j.1751-9004.2007.00067.x

Kleiman, E. M., & Liu, R. T. (2014). Social support as a protective factor in suicide: Findings from two nationally representative samples. *Journal of Affective Disorders, 150*(2), 540–545.

Lacan, J. (2014). *Anxiety: The seminar of Jacques Lacan, book X* (J. A. Miller, Ed. and A. Rae Price, Trans.). Polity Press.

Ljotić, D. (2003). "Dva izlaza" ("Two exits"). In D. Ljotić (ed.), *Sabrana dela* (Collected works). Nova Iskra.

Marinoff, L. (2000). *Plato not Prozac.* HarperCollins.

Marx, K., & Engels, F. (1946–1947). *German ideology.* International Publishers.

Mate, G., & Mate, D. (2022). *The myth of normal: Trauma, illness and healing in a toxic culture.* Avery.

Nietzsche, F. (2006). *Thus spoke Zarathustra* (A. del Caro and R. Pippin, Eds., and A.del Caro, Trans.). Cambridge University Press.

Putnam, R. (1993). *Making democracy work: Civic traditions in modern Italy.* Princeton University Press.

Russell, A. (1976). Limitations of family therapy. *Clinical Social Work Journal, 4*, 83–92. https://doi.org/10.1007/BF02142610

Schopenhauer, A. (1966). *The world as will and representation* (Vol. 2. E. F. J. Payne, Trans.). Dover Publications.

Siisiainen, M. (2000). Two concepts of social capital: Bourdieu vs. Putnam. In Paper presented at ISTR Fourth International Conference "The Third Sector: For What and for Whom?". Dublin, Ireland: Trinity College. July 5–8.

Stuntz, W. J. (1993). Layers, deception and evidence-gathering. *Virginia Law Review, 79*(8), 1903–1956. https://doi.org/10.2307/1073476

UNICEF. (2023). Shooting in the Vladislav Ribnikar primary school in Belgrade. Retrieved November 20, 2024, from https://www.unicef.org/serbia/en/press-releases/shooting-vladislav-ribnikar-primary-school-belgrade.

Uslaner, E. (2010). *The moral foundations of trust.* Cambridge University Press.

Vinogradov, S., & Yalom, I. (1990). Self-disclosure in group psychotherapy. In G. Stricker & M. Fisher (Eds.), *Self-disclosure in the therapeutic relationship* (pp. 191–204). Springer. https://doi.org/10.1007/978-1-4899-3582-3_13

Walther, E., Nagengast, B., & Trasselli, C. (2005). Evaluative conditioning in social psychology: Facts and speculations. *Cognition and Emotion, 19*(2), 175–196. https://doi.org/10.1080/02699930441000274

Yalom, I., & Leszcz, M. (2005). *Theory and practice of group psychotherapy.* Basic Books.

Zimring, F. E. (1987). Legal perspectives on family violence. *California Law Review, 75*(1), 521–539.

CHAPTER 8

Conclusion

Abstract The conclusion summarizes the ways in which Modal Integrative Psychotherapy (MIP) may be seen as revolutionizing conventional psychotherapy by introducing the idea of "switching modal worlds", not just within the subjectivity of the client, but also "worlds", as sets of circumstances described in modal logic, within which subjective experience occurs. Such a shift of emphasis from an essentially subjectivist position to a fundamentally more ambitious conceptual approach to both lived experience and psychotherapy challenges certain conventional norms, including the blurring of the distinction between "reality" and "subjectivity" and the notion of how different experiential worlds might or might not be called into actual experience by the use of MIP technique.

Keywords Transformative thinking • Defining norms • Paradigms • Life strategy

In the Maasai Mara National Park in Kenya, the rules for trespassing are strict. Tourists who enter the park are given a specific time to drive through the park to their accommodation, depending on which camp they are staying in, and on the way out they must exit within a specified time frame. Nobody is allowed in the park without a reason. Movement is restricted to vehicles with rangers, as any solitary hiking would likely be fatal given the

A. Fatic, *Modal Integrative Psychotherapy*,
https://doi.org/10.1007/978-3-031-91934-3_8

nature of the ecosystem and the density of the population of predatory animals. One does not want to walk through the savannah in sight of a pride of lions, or to move next to a river that teems with crocodiles and hippos. Getting off the safari vehicle is forbidden, as according to the rangers, once a person is on foot, they are seen by the animals as food, and no longer as a group of visitors. Even the strong safari jeeps are occasionally attacked or chased, though fatalities among tourists never occur. Nobody is allowed in the national park to roam freely. Except the Maasai people, who herd cattle around the park. They can freely pass through the reserve with their cows: a perfect source of defenseless food for the predators. Attacks on the Maasai are almost unheard of, because, as rangers are quick to explain, they have a special "sense" for nature: they rarely use mobile phones, but they are able to judge, or feel, the presence of a jaguar or whether or not the lion they see walking in the grass is hungry and likely to attack. They move thousands of cattle through one of the most densely predator-populated ecosystems on the planet.

The Maasai live in a different modal world from the rest of us. I once spoke to one of them who explained to me why they carry sticks: it is partly because of the snakes. The snake species in the Maasai land include some of the most venomous and dangerous ones, but the explanation I got was that the stick is mainly for a single species of snake. My guide told me that the numerous and highly venomous forest cobras tend to hide in the trees and could easily attack but "they are shy" and do not usually present a problem, while the various vipers will only attack if they are provoked or stepped on. An exception is the Black Mamba: the longest venomous snake on the planet, and one that is affectionately called "the 20-minute snake" or "three steps snake" because after a bite, it takes up to 20 minutes or several steps for the person to die. This snake can be highly aggressive and is one of the fastest snakes in the world: it is able to move while holding its head a meter up in the air and give chase at the speed of a running human being. But the Maasai are not afraid of the mamba. They wait for it to raise up its head and open its mouth, which is black on the inside, and then hit it with a stick from the side, often killing it with a single blow.

The Maasai see and think about the savannah and the animals in a way that is incompatible with our way of thinking. The reality they move in is different from ours, because their senses, what they see in the bush, are not what we see. Where we see the glimpse of a group of cheetah or the shadow of a jaguar, they see danger or small risk or a passing animal friend who has just eaten. They see the reserve in different shapes, and interpret it in different categories than we do.

Modal Integrative Psychotherapy does the same in everyday reality. It does not think about ordinary experience in terms of propositional logic, facts, and "givens", but in terms of modal logic, in the categories of an actual world, possible (or irreal) worlds, and the paths and ways to jump from one possible world (the current reality) to a different one, where what is impossible in the current world will be possible, and conversely, some things that are possible in the current reality will, perhaps, become impossible. MIP resembles a process where a European tourist in the Maasai Mara is trained to see the ecosystem through the eyes of the Maasai, which would, then, enable him to move freely and do things in the Maasai Mara that no tourist can or is allowed to. MIP allows us to do things that we would otherwise be unable and disallowed to do.

This very principle makes MIP both exciting and controversial. It is a system of thinking and therapeutic intervention that tests the boundaries at every level as it is predicated on destabilizing the current equilibrium which, to our clients, is toxic, and reestablishing a different balance, in a different ambience that is articulated under different principles of reality. Just as the Maasai's world is not ontologically inferior or "less real" than that of the ordinary people (in fact it may well be more real), shaking the foundations of an accepted reality within which one is seen, or sees oneself, as troubled, disordered, or merely stuck sufficiently to seek psychotherapy might be the most productive approach.

There is also an element of rejection of the current reality in the MIP approach to therapy: it is a view motivated by the belief that what we describe as reality is often merely the toxic society and learned relationships that, while well established and generative of the boundaries that we all recognize, make true personal breakthroughs impossible. Perhaps the most important reason for this is the transformative as opposed to strategic thinking; the former characterizes MIP and modal logic in general, and the latter applies to most conventional forms of psychotherapy and is, needless to say, consistent with propositional, linear logic.

Strategic thinking is based on the idea of a goal that is articulated within the realistic circumstances of the life world one finds oneself in, and in developing various strategies, including those of self change, again within the defining parameters of the person's current life world, to achieve that goal. Such goals might involve the attainment of greater satisfaction, better relationships, and a variety of other desires that clients express in therapy.

Transformative thinking is very different from strategic thinking, because it examines the very foundations of the life world where one could set goals, seeking to "overthrow" the defining norms of that world and venture into a different reality. Most people arrive at the threshold of transformative thinking once their current life world, or modal world, is so exhausted that the goals they set themselves as a part of strategic thinking can no longer be attained in the current modal world. These are situations when the reality is rejected and another one sought out of desperation and disappointment, because the current reality has nothing more to offer. A good example of such an approach is when one is suddenly and comprehensively blocked in one's career: one is left without the means of subsistence, cannot get another job or source of income, one's field of expertise is no longer relevant or in demand, and one makes a decision to leave their country, culture, region of the world, personal circumstances, leaving one's family and friends behind, adopting new habits, new values, etc. Transformative thinking, in most cases, occurs as the result of a collapse of strategic thinking.

MIP focuses on transformative thinking not as a forced transition from strategic thinking, once it has failed, but as a principled alternative to it. This, of course, does not mean that we seek risky transformative decision where none are needed, but then, most people do not arrive for psychotherapy in such banal situations that most can sort out by themselves. Once a person is sufficiently stuck or suffers to undergo therapy systematically, this alone warrants the adoption of modal thinking, which looks at whether the foundations, or supporting beams, of one's current reality, which threaten to give way and appear to call for reinforcement, can be torn down and an alternative structure erected that will render one's life fundamentally different. Rather than waiting for strategic thinking to solidify the current life world in ways that may or may not be satisfactory, MIP looks to reorganize larger structures. To use the example mentioned above, when one's career shows systematic signs of failing, MIP moves before waiting for strategic objectives to be attained or missed (for example, trying to solidify one's position in one's career, or changing the career); it goes deeper than the strategic thinking and examines whether one can change the broader swaths of one's life, including the place one lives, one's skills, whether one can adopt completely different goals that can only be attained in a different life world, and whether one should leave the reality where the particular trouble seems to be only temporarily preventable.

One of Immanuel Kant's famous arguments is that the experience of reality cannot be separated from the experience of a dream, if the dream is vivid enough, except for two key criteria: constancy (one wakes up into the same reality that one appears to have departed when one fell asleep) and coherence (the overall perception of one's reality is more comprehensive and consistent through time compared one's recollection of one's the dream, which tends to be fragmented and brief) (Kant, 2001, Section 49). One interpretation of this argument is that for human beings, dreams, depending on the quality of the dreaming experience, could, theoretically, be as real as "proper" reality, if these dreams were able to envelop sufficient parts of the individuals' lives and preception and be as coherent as the experience of waking reality or more so. If this indeed is the case, then ontologically there is no difference that would be cognitively accessible to us between dreams and reality other than the epiphenomenal differences, such as the coherence, colorfulness, length and consistency of the experience. It is this point that modal logic can fully incorporate in its structure of thinking: both the reality and the dream are modal worlds, ontologically equal, or almost equal, to the observer. A dream, if it is very convincing and long, almost substitutes the reality, except that after the dream one wakes back into reality. However, should one be able to stay in a dreaming state permanently, there would be no difference between dream reality; the dream would become reality, and the reality would cease to be "real" to the person. If one can dream up a different reality, and this is common with great ideas, one can transform one's entire life experience, in the same way as Thomas Kuhn argues that science is transformed through shifts of paradigms that occur either when the current paradigm that organizes our perception of scientific reality is exhausted, or, very often, accidentally, by a quirk of imagination where one makes an unintended scientific discovery that changes the entire scientific world in various disciplines (Kuhn, 1962).

Similar to Kuhn's view of the shift of scientific paradigms, people seek psychotherapy and counseling when their current paradigm of solving their problems is exhausted. We develop mnemonic devices, shortcuts for elaborate life tactics in the form of experientially derived principles, which we use, consciously or unconsciously, when we face various situations. Our habits and patterns serve us well most of the time. However, at times of crisis, they become insufficient and one becomes stuck in their tracks. This is when counseling comes as a natural reaction to one's lack of resources to address life's challenges.

One of the problems with this view of counseling is that, while the counselor and the very counseling process can offer new tools and tactics, new strategic visions of one's way of life, and thus extend one's reach into one's difficulties, fundamentally people do everything they can rationally think of as potential solutions before they arrive for counseling. Once they enter the counseling room, they typically have a ready narrative that rationally articulates what they believe would be a socially acceptable formulation of their general difficulty. This is how we start therapeutic work: we work with the explicit narrative and seek to discover what other content is tied to that narrative, but remains unspoken, either because the person finds it unbearable or believes it unacceptable to others, or because one is not aware of the existence of the hidden narrative. Such processes are familiar from therapeutic practice and need no particular elaboration. However, once the hidden narrative is brought to light and all the options the person has at their disposal are examined, the changes and improvements of one's life strategy still remain fundamentally the same: one develops new skills and ways of thinking about particular situations, but one remains within one's general paradigm: no fundamental shift of the foundations of one's life strategy occurs.

Major shifts of life paradigms occur, typically, only after transformative events, including the death of close persons, serious illness, or other major life trials. After such events, people sometimes emerge profoundly transformed and prepared to change their lives comprehensively. MIP's strategy is located at the interface between these two types of situations. In the previously described, relatively regular, and ordinary situations in counseling, when people seek additional resources to address their difficulties because their own principles and tactics of dealing with such issues have become insufficient, rather than extending the reach of the existing tactics, MIP seeks a similar approach as that which naturally occurs after major transformative events. It attempts to shake the current modal world additionally so that a more fundamental change may emerge that will generate a completely new perspective, both on the issues that might be temporarily addressed by more conservative means, and on any future, major issues. MIP seeks transformative thinking even in situations that do not force such thinking through major, life-changing events that leave the person no other option but to change profoundly.

One example of this approach includes the need to develop an alternative to one's family in situations when the family betrays one of its members. This is a very frequent case in modern society, where to the dismay of us therapists, we often find out that people have severed all contact with their parents, because the parents are "toxic", and where family members have been isolated by the rest of the family "ganging up" against those individuals. The most frequent examples involve fathers, who after difficult divorces end up with sparse contact with their children, who live with their mothers. After some time, the fathers are often completely deprived of contact with their children because, once the children are able to legally make their own decisions, they come under such influence from the other parent that they refuse to see their targeted parent, typically the father. This often happens quite suddenly, overnight. In such situations, we see clients (fathers, but sometimes also mothers) who face major psychic difficulties, ranging from depression with suicidal ideation to major identity disturbance or affective difficulties.

Traditional psychotherapeutic approaches, by and large, would intervene in such cases by seeking to enhance the person's resilience and ability to wait out a potential reconnection with the child, to enrich their social life and try to prevent rumination over the trauma by introducing new preoccupations, potentially new relationships, etc.

MIP, on the other hand, would react early by seeking to develop an alternative modal world to that of one's family. It would try to render the person capable of mastering a different kind of reality before the family crisis would erupt to the extent where one is faced with major trauma. Early on, rather than trying to patch up the family, MIP would seek to position the person in an alternative modal world where one would develop different preoccupations and new emotions for other people, thus making sure that they build alternatives while the current options and living realities are still alive and well. Once the crisis is full blown, MIP would challenge the accepted patterns of therapy. Rather than working to merely increase the person's ability to withstand the stress caused by the savage family dissipation and the denial of access to one's child, MIP would suggest that the person might work against and around the typical norms: seek the child out, try to use the legal avenues to create opportunities to meet them, using friends and associates to break through the communication barrier, while at the same time cultivating an alternative modal world.

During the writing of this Conclusion, I started work with a client who fits the described scenario. All of the above elements of a family crisis apply to his situation. Now a man in his 60s, he married at the age of 45, helped his wife immigrate to Denmark, where he has lived for many years, and they became parents to a baby boy. Three years into the marriage,

George (let us call him that) decided that he had to end the marriage because he was the subject of constant abuse, both physical and psychological, by his wife, whom he only later discovered had been treated for years for a severe form of Borderline Personality Disorder. He felt that he had to leave the house to avoid a potential physical confrontation. Thus, he left his wife in their apartment and moved to a rented flat. The mother was granted custody of the child, despite many indications of her violent propensities; however, he was able to spend every other weekend with his son, and they cultivated a close and warm relationship. George was a carpenter and construction painter, and he taught his son how to use various tools and machines, which the boy enjoyed. The boy himself was gentle, gifted for the arts, and he played guitar and saxophone very skillfully. In time, George met another woman with whom he fell in love, and, while they lived in different countries, George introduced his son to the girlfriend. The two became good friends and the boy enjoyed his time travelling with George and meeting his girlfriend, especially going skiing together.

Some months into the relationship, George's ex-wife found out about the girlfriend, and that very evening everything changed for George. Although his son was 14, as of the next morning the boy stopped communicating with him. George was unable to reach him, as his mother forbade the boy to possess a mobile phone, and returned the one George had bought for him. The only way for George to contact his son was through his ex-wife's telephone, and after she had found out that he had another partner, this became impossible. At the time when I met George, he had not seen or heard from his son for 9.5 months. He had suffered a pulmonary spasm that nearly killed him, and only a speedy intervention of the hospital staff saved him. His health started to decline seriously, and he decided to seek a court injunction to continue to see his son. However, the city court decided to take a statement from the boy, who appeared in court with his mother, another woman from a women's rights non-governmental organization, and a psychologist from an agency for children. They were present while the boy was giving his statement, damning for his father. George subsequently sent me a transcript of that statement and reading it outside our session, I could hardly hold back my tears. The transcript was so transparently inconsistent and showed that the boy had been pressured to state things that contradicted each other, and I could only imagine how George felt.

George's view was that he needed to do what he had heard some of his friends had done: to hold steady and bear the absence of his son until he is old enough to reach out for him. He has been told that this was the best way for him to recover and try to build the rest of his life on more or less bearable emotional foundations.

He asked me what I thought and speculated about trying to find out his son's routine and meeting him. I encouraged him to do so. He mentioned the possibility of offering a mobile phone to his son when he meets him and asking him to take and keep it hidden so that they can communicate, which I also encouraged. I also suggested that he talk to social services and ask them to use their prerogatives to invite the boy for a meeting with George. George needed to be cautioned that he might face rejection from his son several times, and we conceptualized this as the boy reluctantly "taking a medicine of love". George and I developed a narrative together that, just like when a person takes a medicine, it does not work immediately, but after it gets into one's bloodstream and after several doses, the effects start to show; we stipulated that the same was the case with a father's show of affection and care for the estranged child. George seemed to be armed with a set of tactics to proceed and was looking forward to returning to Denmark to try them and report back. He felt that he was in a different reality now, where he had some options rather than merely trying to increase his tolerance level for the stress of being estranged from his child.

Many things can go wrong for George with this strategy. If he is unlucky, and the boy does not react well to his sudden appearance, he could be accused of stalking the child and face further consequences, potentially preventing him even more severely from approaching the boy. If the boy takes the phone from him, the mother might find it and engage in a revenge spree, lodging various complaints and using the system against George. It is possible that, by moving to this new way of proactive thinking and action that is contrary to all advice that George has received so far, and which has been safe for him legally, George might end up in a position where he is institutionally forbidden from approaching his son. I made sure that George was aware of the risks, but his response was that he was prepared to face them, because he was already in an almost desperate situation. He abandoned his strategy of waiting and engaged in planning how to find his son and try to work with him directly, against the prevailing climate of risk aversion that he encountered while facing the legal process.

All of the mentioned possibilities of hurtful developments for George, however, coexist with the equally, or more probable, possibilities that his son will talk to him, that his emotions for his father will awaken once he sees that his father seeks him out and is willing to be unconventional in doing so within an otherwise heavily regulated society that they live in. The boy may take the phone from George and, even if he manages to keep it hidden for a brief time, this will make a major difference for George, because he will at least temporarily be able to reach his son. In time, if he responds well to his father's attempts to reach him, the boy may find the strength to resist the overbearing mother, set his personal boundaries, and reconcile with his father after an abrupt and obviously forced break in communication.

The modal world of George's unconventional strategy may make (legally) impossible some options that, in the current modal world, are legally possible (but factually inaccessible) for George. However, it may make possible some outcomes that in the current world of risk aversion and acceptance of the break in communication are impossible. These possibilities mean life to George and they would change the very foundations of his emotional existence if he succeeded in reaching his son.

Another client I worked with turned out to be a drug dealer. He came for therapy because of anxiety, and at first I did not know what he did for a living. However, it soon became clear that he had a dissociated picture of reality and treated his business just like any legitimate business. His worry was that he had "too much merchandise" in his house (in fact, "a full house", in his words), and "the market was not so good", so he owed a large amount of money for the drugs that he could not sell quickly enough. He explained to me how the market worked and that his wife, whom he loved very much and had a three-year-old son with, had "kicked him out" of their apartment, so he went to live with his father. His wife was afraid that something might happen to the family because of his debt for drugs. Pedro (the client) often fought with his wife, but described her as someone who had always been there for him, and he loved her dearly. He was never violent to her, and their relationship was the brightest aspect of his entire life, against the backdrop of a difficult childhood after losing his mother at a young age.

Pedro was expecting that I would be fazed by his criminal career and would avoid working with him; however, I decided to venture into the process and we focused on an unexpected aspect of therapy: his relationship with his wife, rather than the acute problem with drugs. We worked through the problems in the marriage and the possibility that, if he lost his wife and his family, he would be left without the only part of his existence that "kept him sane" as he put it. We ignored the main problem with which Pedro arrived for the first session. By focusing on his family, Pedro started to perceive his criminal career as a danger to what he valued the most. He enlisted the support of his father, who was a real-estate contractor: the father found the capital to construct an apartment building in a rapidly developing area on the outskirts of the city, close to the airport, and the two of them arranged with the dealers whom Pedro owed money to take a part of the "merchandise" back and agree to be paid for the rest in installments. Pedro found a way to remove the drugs from his father's house and squeeze himself out of the drug business by shifting the drugs to another dealer, while he moved completely into the apartment rental business with his father. The relationship with his father was revived and his marriage started to flourish. Pedro found himself removed from his criminal career almost by default, by working on preserving his marriage. However, Pedro retained friends from the underworld and wasted no opportunity to explain to them how he "miraculously" refocused from what was bothering him the most onto what he valued the most, and how this "made the main problem resolve itself". While he did not understand that his "resolution" was a part of his shifting to a different, non-criminal modal world of his family, and abandoning the psychological and factual modality that involved the criminality of his everyday life, that is exactly what he did. A poorly educated young man, who could barely express himself in a basically comprehensible way in either of his two native languages (his mother and father were from different backgrounds and spoke different languages, both of which he had learned as a child before his mother died), Pedro was able to perform the classical modal shift: he called into reality a completely different set of circumstances, or modal world, simply by focusing on an alternative, while leaving the current modal world to "sort out its own problems", as he phrased it. A partly amusing consequence of my work with this client was that, given his social circle and his very simplified interpretation of what had happened, where he attributed his entire self-transformation to therapy, rather than to his natural ability to think modally (in fact, perhaps this was so accessible to him precisely because of his sparse education and thus a relative lack of the common habit of rational and analytic thinking), he described the experience to his friends in a way that, for a while, threatened to turn me into what my colleagues jokingly called "a Mafia therapist". For a while, I kept receiving requests for appointments by members of his circle, most of whom, in initial telephone conversations, mentioned his name and that they were from the same neighborhood, and, when I warily asked them about their occupation, the most frequent response was a hesitant "agriculture".

MIP is an adventure. It is very Nietzschean as a way of therapeutic thinking and can thus seem reckless at times; however, it involves informed risk taking and the introduction of the client, through the creation of a therapeutic narrative, into the basic principles of modal logic. Practical modal logic is an adventure compared to the everyday focus on propositional logic, which operates with truth conditions. It is a risky and potentially transformative way of thinking about reality compared to the safe and linear world of propositional logic that all traditional psychotherapy, and most of the traditional humanities more generally, accept and use automatically, and without much methodological reflection. Modal logic can be dangerous, but it is generally more promising of a new landscape of reality than propositional logic. So is Modal Integrative Psychotherapy. This book is about the promise, the risks and dangers, and the enticing vistas of transformation that the application of modal logic in psychotherapy can offer.

References

Kant, I. (2001). *Prolegomena to any future metaphysics* (J. W. Ellington, Trans., 2nd ed.). Hackett Publishing.

Kuhn, T. (1962). *The structure of scientific revolutions.* Chicago: University of Chicago Press.

Index[1]

[1] Note: Page numbers followed by 'n' refer to notes.

A. Fatic, *Modal Integrative Psychotherapy*,
https://doi.org/10.1007/978-3-031-91934-3_8

The manufacturer's authorised representative in the EU is Springer Nature Customer Service Centre GmbH, Europaplatz 3, 69115 Heidelberg, Germany. If you have any concerns regarding our products, please contact ProductSafety@springernature.com

Printed and bound by CPI Group (UK) Ltd, Croydon, CR0 4YY
30/09/2026
02225583-0007